The
Music
Teaching
Artist's Bible

The
Music
Teaching
Artist's Bible

Becoming a Virtuoso Educator

ERIC BOOTH

OXFORD
UNIVERSITY PRESS
2009

OXFORD
UNIVERSITY PRESS

Oxford University Press, Inc., publishes works that further
Oxford University's objective of excellence
in research, scholarship, and education.

Oxford   New York
Auckland   Cape Town   Dar es Salaam   Hong Kong   Karachi
Kuala Lumpur   Madrid   Melbourne   Mexico City   Nairobi
New Delhi   Shanghai   Taipei   Toronto

With offices in
Argentina   Austria   Brazil   Chile   Czech Republic   France   Greece
Guatemala   Hungary   Italy   Japan   Poland   Portugal   Singapore
South Korea   Switzerland   Thailand   Turkey   Ukraine   Vietnam

Copyright © 2009 by Oxford University Press, Inc.

Published by Oxford University Press, Inc.
198 Madison Avenue, New York, New York 10016

www.oup.com

Oxford is a registered trademark of Oxford University Press.

Library of Congress Cataloging-in-Publication Data
Booth, Eric.
The music teaching artist's bible : becoming a virtuoso educator / Eric Booth.
   p.   cm.
Includes index.
ISBN 978-0-19-536839-0; 978-0-19-536846-8 (pbk.)
1. Music—Instruction and study.   I. Title.
MT1.B6835 2009
781.071—dc22   2008025728

9 8 7 6 5 4 3 2 1
Printed in the United States of America
on acid-free paper

Overtures

"This is the most anticipated book in the performing arts world—by artists who want to teach as well as they play, by concert presenters and educators dying to engage artists who know how to communicate, and by audiences, young and old alike, ready to be transformed by artists who have the desire to teach, communicate, encourage, advocate, inspire, mentor…or, put more simply, to change lives. As a concert presenter eager to engage artists who know how to communicate effectively with their audience, I'm pleased—no, make that ecstatic—the 'bible' is finally here…and *the* master teacher artist wrote it!"

—Kenneth C. Fischer, President, University Musical Society, University of Michigan

"As ever, Eric combines his unique insights into the arts and education, his profound commitment to improving the teaching of the arts in this country, his intellect, his humor—and, in this case, his wonderful writing—to produce a book that stands a very good chance of, yes, becoming a bible for many in music education."

—Steven Seidel, Director of Harvard Project Zero, Director of Arts Education Program at Harvard Graduate School of Education

"Teaching artists have been too long overlooked and taken for granted as the crucial players they are in the American arts and arts education ecosystem. I know that the state arts agencies, most of whom already know and rely on Eric Booth, and all of whom rely on teaching artists to fulfill their mission of expanding arts engagement, welcome this foundation-building book. This is a book the field has needed, from an author we trust. Study these pages well."

—Jonathan Katz, CEO, National Assembly of State Arts Agencies

"The surge of interest in teaching artistry, along with the realization of its urgent need, has affected many of us deeply, and certainly myself as a performing and composing musician. Having had the good fortune to be energized and inspired by Eric Booth several times in and around Lincoln Center, I now welcome this elegant and informative distillation of his ideas and experiences in *The Music Teaching Artist's Bible*. Like a bible, it is a compilation of helpful hints to be carried around with one as one goes through the important work of one's life. However, Mr. Booth's work does not present itself as The Given Word, but rather as an opening and a welcoming to our calling. I can easily imagine 'converting' some of my more self-involved colleagues to a wider and vastly more vibrant and exciting artistic life by using the ideas in this book. We look forward to a time when all artists are, at least in part, teaching artists."

—Jon Deak, composer, Associate Principal Bass, New York Philharmonic

"Like Gray's *Anatomy of the Human Body* for doctors, Eric Booth's *Music Teaching Artist's Bible* is the foundational resource for not just music teaching artists but those of any art form. Eric brings years of hard-earned learning and experience as a teaching artist working across multiples sectors, together with condensed observation, potent insights, and immediately accessible, practical skills, and drops it on your doorstep. I see dog-eared copies on every great teacher's bookshelf only moments from printing."

—Lisa Fitzhugh, Founder and Executive Director, Arts Corps

"*The Music Teaching Artist's Bible* fills a gap in the arts learning field, providing the first foundation book for the burgeoning field of teaching artists. Both the arts and education need more and better teaching artists, and teaching artists need this book. Eric Booth is the nation's leading authority on the subject, and his writing is as lively as a teaching artist's workshop."

—Robert Lynch, President and CEO, Americans for the Arts

"This book is a must-read for any musician who wants to be a teaching artist, or who is curious about how to be more effective in this growing field. Eric Booth, with decades of experience as a teaching artist himself and as a pioneer in teaching artist professional development, is the only person who could have written this pivotal work. It belongs in every musician's, every conservatory's, every teaching artist's library."

—Barbara Shepherd, Director of National Partnerships,
The Kennedy Center, Education Department

"In *The Music Teaching Artist's Bible* Eric Booth has given us a humane, inspirational, and practical handbook for artists who teach; more important, his insights provide a pathway to revitalized, fully engaged, twenty-first-century musicianship."

—Bill Ivey, Director of the Curb Center for Art, Enterprise, and Public Policy at Vanderbilt University, and former Chairman of the National Endowment for the Arts

"This is an engaging, provocative, and practical book: engaging in its style, provocative in its ideas, practical in its guidance to teachers, whatever their art form or discipline. Just what those of us who have experienced the teaching artistry of Eric Booth expect and admire. He's taught us all."

—Richard Deasy, Director, Arts Education Partnership

"Even for those who don't set out to be a teacher, the fact is that every artist is, in fact, a teacher. So go ahead and embrace your inner teacher and read this practical, yet oh-so-inspirational book. There is no question that the ideas Eric Booth has to share will make you a more effective teacher and a better artist!"

—Ann Meier Baker, President and CEO, Chorus America

"In a world where the teaching and learning of music have all too often been parsed into lifelessness by competing camps—classical versus contemporary, arts for art's sake versus arts for learning, certified music teachers versus visiting artists—this book is about reclaiming and synthesizing our authentic connections to music and musicians in the contexts of community and public education. This document is a much-needed breath of fresh air, 'expanding the sense of the possible' in concerts halls and classrooms gone stale from a lack of the revitalizing oxygen of music as lived in lives."

—Arnold Aprill, Founding and Creative Director, Chicago Arts Partnerships in Education (CAPE)

"Like the Bible itself, this book tells the genesis of a new kind of artist. Eric Booth is a prophet who has lived that history and can see clearly how teaching transforms artists' lives and how the arts and learning will be transformed by teaching artists."

—Nick Rabkin, Executive Director, Center for Arts Policy, Columbia College Chicago

"Musicians and other performing artists have always been involved in teaching from the stage and in the studio. But the modern realities of schools and concert halls require a more sophisticated approach to long-standing practices. Today's musicians need techniques for engaging listeners, rules for working with schoolteachers who provide sequential skill building, and methods for generally building the public's love of music. *The Music Teaching Artist's Bible* provides an insightful set of answers to questions on how teaching artists can best work with teachers in schools, colleagues in the community, audiences, and others to best serve the overall goal of delivering artistic and educational experiences to children and adults."

—Michael Blakeslee, Senior Deputy Executive Director,
MENC: The National Association for Music Education

"Like Bach's *Well-Tempered Clavier*, Booth's 'bible' is both the ultimate summation of technique and a pathway to a new era. By codifying the emerging practices of teaching artistry, he equips musicians and educators with the essential tools for embracing the coming age of deepening participation in music and the expanding roles of musicians."

—Jesse Rosen, President and CEO,
League of American Orchestras

"Eric Booth's wisdom and practical advice for teaching artists will have resonance for every instructor. *The Music Teaching Artist's Bible* offers a comprehensive definition of the role of an artist in connecting listeners to music of all types. Going even further, Booth inspires reflection on what it means to be an audience member and, more broadly, a learner in a world filled with artistic experiences waiting to be discovered."

—Marc Scorca, President and CEO, Opera America

"The master teaching artist Eric Booth generously shares his enthusiasm, creativity, and expertise not only in documenting this important endeavor but in offering insight and inspiration to others. If you are an aspiring young artist who loves sharing what you do with others, get this book!"

—James Undercofler, President and CEO, The Philadelphia Orchestra,
former Dean, Eastman School of Music

"It's about time Eric Booth collected his thoughts for our benefit! If you ever had the privilege to work with Eric, you'll recognize his voice on every page and rejoice at the opportunity to bring it home so you can reflect on the guidance and wisdom within! And, if this is your introduction to him and the field of teaching artistry, you are in for a treat."

—Leni Boorstin, Director of Community Affairs,
Los Angeles Philharmonic

"Eric Booth has long been in front of the movement to transform education through the arts. No one can seriously dispute that we need a more creative, generative education system. In this book he once again articulates a force for change, the teaching artist, and the practices and values that are driving this important force for education transformation. He generously provides his special insight into the work of the musician as educator and artist. The giant reform efforts of the recent past yielded less change than was hoped. Yet profound change is under way. Eric is one of the very best we have at identifying and articulating the positive forces for change in the arts and learning. Anyone involved in music and education will benefit greatly from the insights, values, and practices in this timely book."

—David O'Fallon, President, MacPhail Center for Music, Minneapolis

"You *must* run and get this book! If I had to name a single person who has revealed to me the secrets of effective teaching, that person is Eric Booth. As a passionately dedicated mentor, Booth has led me by hand every step of the way in developing my teaching artistry. Now, the world has the opportunity to experience the same personal and hands-on guidance through his book. It has everything you need to know about getting started, discovering opportunities, and making the process a meaningful and rewarding journey. It will bring teaching artistry to the foreground of our education consciousness and undoubtedly become our bible."

—Airi Yoshioka, teaching artist, member of Damocles Trio, faculty at the University of Maryland, Baltimore County

"One could not ask for a better guide to the world of a music teaching artist than Eric Booth. With an unmatched professional résumé, Booth is simultaneously a cartographer, mapping out the high points and low points of the terrain; a field guide, sharing time-proven strategies for big challenges and little problems; and a guru, providing inspiration for novices and veterans alike. *The Music Teaching Artist's Bible* is destined to become an essential resource for music teaching artists and anyone who works with them."

—Phillip Alexander, Senior Program Officer, Office of Partnership Support and Research for Empire State Partnership

"This book could not have come at a better time: musicians of all genres are searching for ways to connect to audience and culture, and to survive without compromise; our schools and society are desperately in need of the skills and ethos that musicians can teach. What better person to bridge the gap than Eric Booth, a true leader and inspirer of the field of teaching artistry. In this book Eric not only supplies great stores of the profoundly practical, but also eloquently articulates the purpose: to make all culture the province and joy of all people."

—Nick Jaffe, Editor, *Teaching Artist Journal*

"Teaching artists are the heart and soul of any successful arts education program, and Eric's experience and knowledge of the field are one of a kind. His book is virtually a 'how-to' for the entire arts world—administrators, artists, teachers, donors, grant givers and receivers. To not read it is to do a disservice to the entire education system."

—Chris Silva, Executive Director, Bardavon 1869 Opera House,
Poughkeepsie, N.Y.

"Eric Booth is *the* master teacher artist himself. His visionary, provocative, and truly useful book explores the profound connections between art and learning. For any reader, music teaching artist or not, this is an always engaging, often surprising, and ever-challenging read. My father, Leonard Bernstein, would have been ecstatic about Eric Booth's brilliant book and the astonishing power in the work of teaching artists."

—Alexander Bernstein, Vice President of the
Leonard Bernstein Office, Inc.

"In *The Music Teaching Artist's Bible*, Eric Booth has followed his long-espoused and sage advice to teaching artists and educators, 'Engagement before information!' and created a groundbreaking 'text' that will revolutionize our notion of 'instructional texts.' As a facilitator Eric has always been a master at modeling what he is 'teaching,' while gently but firmly moving us along with stories, humor, and our own new knowledge. He has accomplished that same magic with *The Music Teaching Artist's Bible*: before we know it, we're hooked, we're learning, and we're thinking in new ways. While the book focuses on music teaching artists, most of the lessons in this text will be inspiring and instructive to all teaching artists and those engaged in supporting those artists. This will become one of the A+ Schools Program's primary resources for training teaching artists."

—Gerry Howell, Executive Director, A+ Schools Program

"Eric Booth's teachings will change your life. The wisdom Eric shares in *The Teaching Artist's Bible* has already helped countless musicians and ensembles to passionately share their love of music with the world. Whether teaching a private lesson, planning an artist's residency, or struggling to launch your musical career, you will find answers to your deepest questions in *The Music Teaching Artist's Bible*. This book should be required reading for every twenty-first-century musician!"

—David Wallace, faculty at the Juilliard School, senior teaching artist,
New York Philharmonic, author of *Reaching Out: A Musician's
Guide to Interactive Performance*

"Eric Booth is a preeminent teaching artist who has chosen a career as an intrepid boundary-crosser. He has fashioned an astonishingly rich compendium of music education practices in *The Music Teaching Artist's Bible*, drawn from his keen eye in witnessing music's evolving role in education and from his vantage point of advising the preeminent musical arts learning organizations, orchestras, and conservatories in the United States and Europe. Through his yearning to envision music's success beyond the barriers of cultural elitism and the parameters of jargon and hearsay, he offers generative taxonomies, staunch parables, brilliantly illustrated principles, and down-to-earth advice that will be of vast importance for all teachers whose mission is to education in, about, and through the arts. Timeless gems are found throughout this book, a vastly informative and eminently useful operating manual for those who teach music anywhere and under any circumstance in the twenty-first century. In the final chapters, Booth provides a miraculous vision of an international movement where networks of teaching artists contribute to arts learning for the sake of community and the spirit of our youth. All in all, *The Music Teaching Artist's Bible* takes on special importance for the far-reaching enterprise of music learning as a medium and model for creativity, imagination, aesthetic sensibility, and community service in education."

—Larry Scripp, Director of Music-in-Education and the Research Center for Learning through Music, New England Conservatory

"It is always a distinct pleasure to be engaged in writing and in person by Eric Booth's thoughtful ideas and seasoned experience. Mr. Booth's seminal treatise in *The Music Teaching Artist's Bible* once again demonstrates how deep, integrated, intentional, and purposeful thinking reaches across all boundaries—with practicality, humor, and sage wisdom. There is always more work to do in public education in the arts than any one category of professionals can provide. This publication points out that with all of our unique capacities, every individual at play in the teaching and learning of the arts for young people has an important role. Eric Booth provides a 'chapter and verse' of advice for music teaching artists, which perfectly situates them to be successful within school settings. If music is a window to our soul, then *The Music Teaching Artist's Bible* flings the window wide open."

—Richard Burrows, Director of Arts Education, Los Angeles Unified School District

"Eric Booth has been a guiding light for us. His friendly insistence that virtually any listener can be given the keys to unlock great works of art has had a profound influence on how we approach performance and outreach, and on our increasing belief that the two are never separate."

—Johan Sirota and the Chiara Quartet

This book is dedicated to the musicians I have taught and worked beside for so many years, who have, perhaps unwittingly and always generously, been my teachers. Many more might be identified, in ensembles and orchestras, in workshops, classes, and meetings, but I must name those who have had such a direct hand in bringing out the understandings that fill these pages. Thus, I dedicate this to Denise Dillenbeck, Sarah Johnson, Richard Mannoia, Paola Prestini, Rachel Shapiro, Misty Tolle, David Wallace, Tanya Witek, and Airi Yoshioka. Your commitment and skills make it easy to leave the future in your hands. I am as grateful as I am proud.

Acknowledgments

The chapters in this book are mostly essays that appeared as articles entitled "Edifications" in issues of *Chamber Music* magazine since 2003. During these years, the positive response has been gratifying. A regular reader dropped me a note suggesting that a collection of "Edifications" essays would provide a solid foundation of what a music teaching artist needs to know and be able to do. She was right, and thanks to the good people at Oxford University Press, here it is. I have tweaked and embellished the essays to give this book more cohesion, and I have written new overview and concluding material to enhance its biblical proportions.

I would especially like to thank Margaret Lioi (Executive Director of Chamber Music America) for her commitment to teaching artistry in giving the topic such prominence in the organization's flagship magazine, and to the two editors I have worked with at *Chamber Music*—Karissa Krenz and Ellen Goldensohn—for improving each essay, issue by issue.

And I must acknowledge a few essential colleagues who have taught me most of my lessons about teaching artistry that inform these pages: Arnold Aprill, Edward Bilous, Deb Brzoska, Tom Cabaniss, Madeline Cohen, Hilary Easton, Ann Gregg, Judith Hill, Polly Kahn, John Knowles, Andrew Krichels, Carol Ponder, and David Shookhoff.

Contents

Part I   Context

1

What Is a Teaching Artist?

There is no consensus definition of *teaching artist* in the evolving field of arts education. Five years ago, even the term would spark arguments from those who preferred the traditional labels of *visiting artist*, *resident artist*, or even *artist educator*. Part of me hopes there will never be a consensus definition for a practice so varied and dynamic. There are no consensus definitions of the words *creativity* or *art* either. For very good reason—sometimes there is no single term to capture a deep truth. (Leonard Bernstein said his definition of art was that it had three attributes: it holds a complex and profound truth; it cannot be expressed in any other way; and the world would be worse without it.) Perhaps a term like *teaching artist* must be sounded, gestured, drawn, or performed in a room with engaged learners to capture its genuine connotation. And the world would be worse without teaching artists.

We still live in a time when you are a teaching artist if you say you are. That, incidentally, is the original meaning of the term *profession*—when you professed a vocation rather than earned a degree or certification. Whether the profession of your vocation brought you a living depended on the quality of your work, not on your credentials. This is still true of the field of teaching artistry—with no official credentialing, you work if you are good, and you mostly get better through experience.

One clunky definition of the term I use is *an artist who chooses to include artfully educating others, beyond teaching the technique of the art form, as an active part of a career.* Yes, this could and should include just about all artists, all musicians, because we all find ourselves teaching in bits and pieces throughout our lives. We teach when we talk to family, friends, strangers, and colleagues about music. We teach by example. As you will read in these essays, I believe that 80% of what we teach is who we are, and like it or not, our example in the world teaches people what it means to be a musician. And for the sake of our art form, I hope you teach as artfully as you perform.

This book is dedicated to helping you teach artfully and effectively—in performances, in schools and after school, in dialogue with colleagues, friends, family, and strangers. This book aspires to change the way you define what teaching and art can be to one another, to your life, to music, and to our culture.

Most of this book is specifically focused on music teaching artistry, but some sections, like this chapter, include our teaching artist colleagues in dance, theater, and the visual and literary arts to address the concerns of teaching artistry as a field. These broader sections present the context of an emerging profession, of which music teaching artists are an essential, leading part. Certainly there are differences among the various disciplines, but in this first-ever book for our field, I feel the need to present a foundation for all teaching artists, truths across the disciplines, so we can work together to advance the field, not just succeed within the discipline-specific piece we represent. Just as someone with a passion to become an elementary school teacher must study the history and psychology of learning, the developmental stages before and after the elementary school years, and various philosophical approaches, so we should learn a little about the history and practices of teaching artistry to deepen our practice in music. I would be doing music teaching artists a disservice if I did not present a context for our work that illuminates the big picture and the shared vision, before we delve into our beloved part.

Here are two additional definitions of a teaching artist that resonate for me:

- A teaching artist is the model of the twenty-first-century artist and, simultaneously, a model for high-engagement learning in education.
- A teaching artist is the future of art in America.

I believe these statements to be true, and when you finish this book, I hope you will too.

By the way, that statistic cited earlier—80% of what you teach is who you are—is a made-up number. That invented percentage captures the actual truth that whatever the teaching techniques, whatever the words or activities, it is the understandings and the spirit of the individual teacher that spark the potential to transform others. If you doubt that number, just recall the great teachers in your own life. It was not the quality of their handouts or presentations, or the cleverness of their curriculum, that inspired you to change the direction of your life. It was the quality of who they were as people, their teaching artistry as humans, that had such an impact on you. If you adopt some of the messages in this book, you will be on the path to having more of that kind of impact on others. You will become an active contributor to revitalizing the art of music in a culture that predominantly promotes it as entertainment. You will become part of the solution rather than a frustrated part of the problematic status quo.

Let me clarify the difference between art and entertainment. Entertainment is not the opposite of art—please, Lord, don't let entertainment be the enemy of art, be opposed to art in any way, or we are goners. What distinguishes entertainment is that it happens within what we already know. Whatever your response to the entertainment presentation—laughing, crying, getting excited—underneath the surface, it confirms. Entertainment says, "Yes, the world is the way you think it is." It feels great to have your worldview confirmed in the many dynamic, imaginative, exciting ways our entertainment industries provide.

Art, on the other hand, happens outside of what you already know. Inherent in the artistic experience is the capacity to expand your sense of the way the world is or might be. The art lives in an individual's capacity to engage in that fundamental act of creativity—expanding the sense of the possible—every bit as much as the art resides in what's being observed.

For example, imagine three people sitting next to one another listening to a late Beethoven string quartet. One is having a life-transforming artistic experience as she enters that musical world, expanding her grasp of what the human heart and spirit can contain and the depths to which such knowing can be expressed. The man next to her is having a very entertaining evening, enjoying the beauty of the music, admiring the way the ensemble works together, drifting off to think about some problems at work, thinking how cute the violist is, but coming back to relax in the beauty of the occasion. The next guy over was dragged there by his wife, hates the event, and is getting nothing out of the music. The same musical offering becomes a work of art, a piece of entertainment, or an ordeal based on the individual's capacity to create personally relevant connections inside the music.

Those internal skills determine the difference between art and entertainment every bit as much as the music being played. We can't label something art just because the experts say it is. I have heard audience members describe an evening at a pops concerts in a way that demonstrates that it clearly was a powerful artistic experience for them. Conversely, I have heard far too many symphony attendees describe their experiences at a classical concert of officially certified "art music" as barely entertaining. I have heard teenagers describe their experience of dreadful-to-me rock music in ways that make it clear they are having arts experiences. Art resides in the participatory experiences as much as in the objects that ignite them. Art lives in the verbs every bit as much as in the nouns.

Teaching artists are the designated experts in the verbs of art. Their skills can support, guide, educate, and illuminate people's capacity to individually succeed in creating artistic meaning in our best artistic offerings. What teaching artists know and can do is essential to engaging new audiences for classical music, and for leading the entire field toward a culturally relevant future. Artists create in the artistic media that produce marvelous nouns; teaching artists create in the medium of the verbs of art.

For centuries we have defined art by its nouns—the performances we pay to go see, the objects that grace our homes and museums. We live in a time when a majority of the public does not know how to engage well with those nouns to create personal meaning, to grasp the art they contain. Many Americans are rudimentary in their skills with the verbs of art with which we create artistic experiences; they feel incapable, unsuccessful, and so, too often, disinterested or averse. Today, the verbs of art are as important as those nouns. Good teaching artists know how to work with the verbs together with the nouns. That is their hybrid gift, and that is what makes them invaluable in bringing new audiences into the richness of works of art.

For most Americans, art events seem expensive, and if they are only going to have entertaining experiences (at best) at an ensemble's performance because of their limited inner capabilities with the verbs of art, there are many more stimulating entertainment events available for a lot less money. Our future lives in the experience economy, wherein people get valuable, rewarding personal artistic experiences inside the music, experiences worth the substantial investment of time, attention, and money—and risk—in buying a ticket. Teaching artists possess the skills to help individuals, groups, and artistic organizations accomplish that goal upon which our future depends.

Teaching artists are also artists, very often *superb* artists—this is what makes them models of the twenty-first-century artist. Teaching artists recognize and take active responsibility for the fact that it is no longer enough just to be able to play the hell out of an early Mozart piano program. Musicians now need additional skills to engage audiences, to help them tap the richness inside that world made by Mozart. I know that condescending attitudes still exist that assume any artist who chooses to also educate can't be a first-rate artist. Well, it just isn't true.

People are welcome to cling to their outmoded prejudices, but in the meantime many of the finest young artists want to develop educational skills; they don't want to perpetuate the nineteenth- and twentieth-century prejudices about teaching. I encounter hundreds of artists in the top orchestras and arts organizations who work hard to learn education skills way too late, angry that they didn't have a chance or a conservatory climate that encouraged them to learn teaching artistry during their schooling. The fine young artists who want to expand their kit bag of essential skills will be grabbing the jobs and redefining what the arts can be in our new century.

You may have noticed that my definition of the artistic experience— the capacity to expand the sense of the way the world is or might be—is very like a definition of learning. You might say the core activity of both art and learning is making personally relevant connections between yourself and new things. I think "arts education" is a redundant phrase—we are talking about the same fundamental human act. Teaching artistry is the artful, effective, engaging, successful, joyful, transformative, proven way to guide humans into and through those experiences.

I hear many musicians agree with such ideas in principle, and then immediately exempt themselves. They say they are not good at speaking; they hate teaching; kids give them the creeps; they don't want to learn new skills because it is hard enough just to make the music well and scramble to make ends meet. They respect musicians who are good talkers and are willing to let them carry the responsibility in their ensembles. I watch them sit, benignly smiling, through the audience interactive stuff, waiting to get to playing the music, which is all they really care about. Two comments to such musicians: (1) With that attitude, you and your ensemble are going down—smaller and smaller audiences, less income, less excitement—and taking the rest of us with you. (2) There is a role for every musician in the teaching artist's world, even if you are not a good talker and get hives around eight-year-olds. We all need to join this work of supporting audiences' capacity to succeed in the crucial act upon which the future of classical music depends—making personally relevant connections inside the music. This is not the responsibility of a designated charming few; it belongs to all of us. There is a role for everyone, a way every musician can contribute without being embarrassed, or being forced to do things that are not personal strengths. If you take in the perspectives and suggestions in these pages, you will find many ways to contribute well, happily, comfortably, creatively, importantly.

I hoped the preceding paragraphs would provide some reasons for thinking seriously about developing your music teaching artist skills. In chapter 4 you will find an even better reason: teaching artist skills make you a better artist. An improving music teaching artist is an improving musician. I will save the arguments for that chapter, but I find that the rewards of music teaching artistry are altruistic (it can revitalize our culture's embrace of the art form), financial (it is one of the few sure ways of increasing income in a musician's life), personal (it is directly rewarding on a regular basis), and even artistic (it provides new kinds of creative satisfaction).

As you adopt and adapt the skills described in these pages, you join the history, burgeoning present, and promising future of teaching artistry. Artists have been going into schools since there were American schools. Music programs constructed for educational purposes have been going into classrooms and auditoriums for fifty years or more—Young Audiences (YA), the first major national arts education network, began with a home living room performance for children by Yehudi Menuhin, and YA started sending classical music performances into schools in 1952. YA now has thirty-three active chapters around the nation and 5,200 teaching artists in its network.

In those early years, there were fine programs developed by many individuals and organizations, and some heroic experiments around the country. Teaching artistry as a field really began in the 1980s. In response to the arts education cutbacks in schools during the Reagan administration, arts organizations began to provide services directly to schools, and artists became key deliverers of those services. Arts education organizations like Lincoln Center Institute (where I started learning how to be a teaching artist), Urban Gateways in Chicago, and others began to train and send teaching artists into schools in growing numbers.

Story has it that the term was officially coined by June Dunbar at Lincoln Center Institute in the early 1970s. She told me:

> I guess I was the originator of the term "teaching artist." I came
> up with the words as a reaction to the dreadful one used by
> my predecessors at what was then known as the Education
> Department at Lincoln Center. The words they used to describe
> the activities of artists in schools sounded to me like a description
> for a typewriter repairman, plumber, or an irritating educationalese
> term: "resource professional." Anyway, my term seemed more
> direct and specific, and it stuck. ["Resource professional" was
> actually inherited from language in the federal government grant
> that established the Lincoln Center education program.]

So, at its origin, the new term shifted the identity of this "resource professional" away from the needs of the institutions and funding authority involved toward the unique hybrid practice we still struggle to define. The neologism teaching artist puts artist in focus, where it belongs.

In the early years, teaching artists encountered some tension with music and arts teachers. I recall many music teachers expressing fears that having musicians come into schools was a cheap way to replace their jobs. They proclaimed, rightly, that a teaching artist coming into their school as a visitor cannot provide the consistent skill development and embedded presence that builds a lifelong love of music. Sadly, some TAs in those earlier years didn't ease those tensions: they arrived with a self-important attitude that put off teachers; they didn't adequately learn about and accommodate the realities of schools; they didn't respect school music teachers as artists in their own right, and as their best allies in enriching the creative lives of students. I have seen such tensions all but disappear in recent years, as history has shown that TAs do not become replacements for music teachers when the school budget ax falls on music programs (indeed, they often become advocates for rehiring music teachers); and the professionalization of teaching artistry inculcates respect, more preparation and inclination to build good partnerships with school music teachers, and a greater range of ways to succeed within school culture.

Having seen hundreds of programs around the country, I can state that the best music learning for students springs from the collaborative efforts of three kinds of professionals working in coordination—a teaching artist, an in-school arts teacher, and an informed classroom teacher. The teaching artist brings in that spark of energy and outsiderness that can serve as a catalyst and inspiration for the in-school work. The TA is an emissary from a strange and different culture, wherein people dedicate their lives to creating in an art form. The commitment they carry and the risks they take to live an artist's life resonate in their 80%, in the feel of the person who enters the room. Music teachers can provide the sequential skill building and consistent improvement that enable a young musician to learn to find success and satisfaction within the discipline—that is, if schools allow them the time and support to do what they can do. The informed classroom teacher can integrate the work of the other two into the many other kinds of learning that matter to young people and schools; they can provide context and connections.

Recently, I have noticed the field agreeing that the music teacher actually belongs at the top angle of this equilateral triangle of contributors. The triad is optimum, but the teaching artist and classroom teacher add resources to that essential spine of learning provided by a passionate music teacher. Teaching artists are increasingly becoming outspoken advocates for stronger school music programs.

The number of TAs in the United States grew through the 1980s, and so did their expertise. During that time, most programs hired artists who seemed to have the teaching gene, and they shed those who "didn't get it." The notion of teaching artistry as a trainable practice, as an artistic discipline of its own, emerged slowly. In the early years, programs and schools hired artists who happened to be good with kids, and basically asked them to work some creative magic in classrooms. If the teacher and kids were happy, that was a great TA. There were training programs that focused on readying teaching artists to contribute to the particular needs of the program that was hiring them. Such training tended to be speedy and strategic, often only a day or two, with the hopes that new teaching artists would learn through experience. Some training programs were deeper, but very few lasted more than four or five days. Ongoing professional development, once a TA was hired, was inconsistent and problem-focused—for example, a two-hour, onetime workshop on multiple intelligences (MI) or learning disabilities was (and frequently still is) typical. A dedicated educator could take years adjusting his or her teaching to include MI or greater inclusivity, but the quick one-shot workshop, with no follow-up, was all the TAs got.

In the 1990s, new challenges appeared for TAs. The national standards (voluntary) for the arts were cobbled together, prompting almost all states to create their own arts learning standards (mandatory). Creating national standards for arts learning was a challenging and healthy process for a field that previously had never been required to come to agreement. State standards were different because laws required that work in schools align with the newly adopted standards; so starting in the late 1990s, what teaching artists actually did in classrooms was actively impacted. Quite a few TAs participated in the development of those standards, state by state; then TAs faced the transition in our work from "creating magic in the classroom" to "guiding learning that aligns with state learning standards." Along with many, I initially bristled at the implication that I needed to change my delicate work to accommodate legislated norms. I balked at the very word "standards." However, in working with the standards in practice, I, like many TAs, discovered the following: they were rather benign; they aligned readily with what I wanted to teach; they prompted better conversations with teacher-partners; and they reminded me that artists themselves carry the highest standards and live by them—so the whole notion of applying standards was artistically authentic.

This taught me a lesson you will find in these pages—teaching artists are at their best when they stay grounded in authentic artistic practice rather than overaccommodating the needs and demands of schools or other institutions with which we partner. I believe arts practice is so deep and flexible that we can almost always find ways to stay artistically true and also effectively guide learning in many settings.

Other challenges also entered the work of many teaching artists in the 1990s. They were asked to create professional development workshops for teachers and other professionals. They were asked to become effective partners, trying to actively plan with teachers to deepen and expand the impact their in-school time can have. They were often thrust into the role of facilitator to enhance the quality of work in their partner institutions. They became involved in many of the arts learning experiments that cropped up around the country, sometimes working as program designers, data gatherers, or researchers, in projects such as the Empire State Partnerships, A+ Schools, Bernstein Center Schools, the Annenberg Initiative, and Chicago Arts Partnerships in Education (CAPE), as well as programs led by the Getty Education Institute and the Galef Foundation.

Teaching artists were asked to take on assessment challenges—to develop ways to document and illuminate some of the learning that happens with their students. This was a difficult, even distasteful, step for many because it was too much like testing and felt to many like a violation of teaching artists' most basic goals. However, artists are marvelous assessors of the quality of work, and so TAs found authentic and practical ways to bring the best of what we know as artists to respond to the institutional necessity of illuminating the learning within arts engagement. TAs were asked to become advocates, too, learning how to present a case for arts learning that can change the way funders support and understand our work.

As TAs grow into the twenty-first century, the greatest challenge is the largest arts learning experiment happening in the country today—arts integration. Arts learning is infused into the study of other subjects—for example, bringing music learning into a social studies curriculum—with the hope that learning in *both* subject areas will be boosted by bringing them together. It's a gamble. If we lose, then the arts become a handmaiden to other subjects, actually diminishing their impact on young lives. If we win, and we have to be smart and rigorous to win, then the arts have a much larger contribution to make in American schooling. It is too early to say how the adventure is playing out (see chapter 20); I have seen examples of failure on both extremes, of using the arts merely to pep up a boring curriculum and, conversely, overemphasizing the arts component of an arts-integrated project. I also have seen extraordinary work in which music provides access to deep inquiries from which the study of both history and music bloom. I recall a music and American history unit built around the theme of how music has been used to keep people alive. The class investigated songs of the Civil War–era Underground Railroad, work songs, protest songs, and also the songs the students themselves treasure so strongly they feel they are a lifeline. The musical exploration catalytically launched students into much more invested learning about history—because they were artistically involved, because they felt the relevance of the history in their hearts and guts.

All these new challenges teaching artists took on added up to a dramatic increase in what was expected of them, and what they had to know to be successful. TAs couldn't be expected to know how to address state standards, facilitate, assess, advocate for funding, build strong partnerships, and integrate their artistry with social studies just by having a knack. They needed training. And the training had to connect well with their artistic aspirations, or we strangle the artist in the teaching artist.

Such professional development programs have started to arise, and teaching artists have taken on the commitment to expand the scope of their practice. The teaching artist lineage welcomes you to this growing profession. There are many signs of growth. We have a flourishing peer-reviewed professional journal (the *Teaching Artist Journal*, now based at Columbia College Chicago, published by Taylor and Francis: http://tajournal.com). When I started this journal in 2002, I had to confess in my sales pitch that no one had any idea of how many teaching artists there were in America. I made a few guesstimates that around 15,000 individuals were making a significant percentage of their living through TA work. But the true number might well have been lower or four times as high. I had to admit there was no national association, no annual conference, not much evidence to the public eye. The publisher Lawrence Erlbaum finally shook my hand, saying, "OK, we will publish it, but let me tell you, of the eighty-two journals we publish, this will be the first put out for an audience that has no visible evidence it exists." Within four years, it was in the company's top 10% of best-selling journals.

There are more than thirty regional efforts by teaching artists to build local professional communities—groups like the New England Consortium of Artist-Educator Professionals (NECAP), Teaching Artists Organized in the San Francisco Bay Area (TAO), and Artist to Artist (in Minneapolis and St. Paul). Courses in teaching artistry are offered at Manhattan School of Music, Juilliard, Columbia College Chicago, and many other schools of music, and a new program has just been launched at the Meadows School at Southern Methodist University. Every month I learn of another arts organization offering a new program to develop and support TAs. The Association of Teaching Artists is an online site based in New York State (http://www.teachingartists.com). The first major national research study of teaching artists is under way, and several states have launched research on their own teaching artist population's identity and needs. We are increasingly working in nonschool settings: in senior centers (as a part of the creative aging movement, which was founded by dance teaching artist Susan Perlstein), in businesses (to provide professional development and creativity training), in health care and higher education settings. I was asked to give the closing keynote address at the first-ever United Nations Education, Scientific, Cultural Organization (UNESCO) worldwide arts education conference—how significant that UNESCO turned to a teaching artist to bring this unprecedented event together!

Welcome to a flourishing, if still somewhat disorganized, field. We need your participation. So do the arts. So does music. So does American education. So does your own checkbook.

Permit me a little autobiography. Since there is no established pathway into teaching artistry, it may be helpful to give some sense of how I found my way to the understandings in these pages. I was a hardworking, conservatory-trained New York actor who hated doing eight performances a week. As a side gig, out of curiosity more than commitment, I began working at Lincoln Center Institute in the late 1970s as a theater teaching artist. I learned its approach, called aesthetic education. I got fascinated and immersed myself in the work. I studied, took every kind of gig, started projects, worked with many organizations, wrote, talked, experimented. I began training teaching artists in the early 1980s and have continued to expand my practice. Work led to work, as it often does when it is filled with passion. Even though much of my teaching artistry has been played out at national conferences and in work with large organizations, and includes making speeches in recent years, I make sure I spend time in classrooms, time with teaching artists, and time thinking about teaching artist practice every year. I also make sure I continue to make art, all the time—the philosopher's stone in the alchemy of teaching artistry. It is tough to rehearse and perform in plays when you are on the road so many weeks a year. So, every week I complete a poem—to walk my talk of primary creation. Every event I lead is always grounded in the principles you find in these pages; while the examples here are all about music, the principles apply to all teaching artistry.

For example, not long ago I led a half-day workshop on "creativity, but not art" for the board of directors of a Fortune 500 company. It is a sad truth that mainstream America sees a huge gap between the importance of creativity and the gooey irrelevance of art. That is the most common workshop/speech I am asked to do in the corporate world. My task is to close that gap, without hitting the art-alarm until the participants themselves discover the innate connection between creativity and artistry. I use my teaching artist skills to come in under the radar of their prejudice that art is a fluffy waste of serious business hours, and make sure they get enough learning about creativity to validate their investment of half a day of their valuable time. That day, we began with a fun, fast competitive word game. The workshop participants reworked their word list several times following steps I outlined. In the last step, I sent them back to their word collection with one final assignment to revise according to an important personal experience they had once had. Halfway through this step, they realized they were composing something that looked suspiciously like a poem. But it was too late! They were already creatively engaged. They insisted on completing their poems, sharing them, comparing them, and having me judge the best—so we had to create a rubric for assessing the quality of such a poem. This was all beautiful artistic work, exactly what they wanted in their workshop—all from my teaching artist skills.

With my longtime colleague Edward Bilous (composer and chairman of the Literature and Materials Department at Juilliard), I started Juilliard's Art and Education program, connected with the Morse Fellowship, in 1994–1995. It included a full year's classroom preparation for the students (described in chapter 12) and a subsequent year or more placed in two New York City classrooms as a Morse Fellow, inventing and delivering a year of classes for the same students. I have little musical background, can't read music, never studied it. Juilliard was the first time I delved deeply into training music teaching artists—until then I had trained artists only in my art form of theater or in mixed-discipline groups. The years that I led and developed that program provided a profound opportunity to explore the ways to bring musicians into their teaching artistry—and the ways not to!

I have now worked with thousands of musicians, in hundreds of trainings, with many hundreds of ensemble musicians, with players at many of the largest orchestras in the country, and with teams from many orchestras through the Knight Foundation's Magic of Music Program and the Mellon Foundation's Orchestra Forum. I have taught the professional development of the New York Philharmonic's teaching artist faculty for ten years now, with many of those teaching artists coming out of the program I led at Juilliard, making great careers as musicians and teaching artists—I have worked with some of them for a dozen years in a row. Do you have any idea how challenging (and terrifying) it is to teach the same gifted people for twelve consecutive years? The opportunity has pushed me to keep going deeper in the work we care about. They have taught their teacher well, which is why I have dedicated this volume to them, those named and the many others. (One of them, David Wallace, cowrote chapter 26, titled "Interactive Performances," with me. I highly recommend his book *Reaching Out: A Musician's Guide to Interactive Performance* [2007]). Three decades of work in this field have taught me what works and what doesn't, and those understandings fill these pages.

Having worked with teaching artists of all disciplines for many years, I have heard endless debates about which discipline is the hardest, easiest, most accessible, most fun. Judiciously, I never offer an opinion on the subject, but this seems like a good place to fess up. Music teaching artists are the most in demand and the hardest to find.

I have had the same conversation in five cities in the last few months—local arts educators want to expand a program but can't find music teaching artists strong enough to do the work, so they give up or downscale the ambition. Music is the hardest art form to talk about. Teaching artistry is the most challenging to develop in music, partly because it is so opposed to the predominant ways the artists have been trained for so long and partly because it confronts traditions of the discipline. As you will discover in several chapters, becoming a good music teaching artist challenges some traditional ways of thinking, preferred habits of mind, and unquestioned professional norms. I believe the confrontation is not only healthy but essential. However, it does make things more difficult for the musician than for the actor or dancer. Painters and writers and media artists have their own challenges. But musicians, with their enormous potential, with significant demand for good practitioners, and with their art form struggling, are the focus of this book.

I began this introduction with the admission that we can't precisely define what a teaching artist is. Let's return to that unanswerable question. Teaching artistry is an improvisation in the verbs of art, as is the kind of reflection that tries to identify what a teaching artist does. Here are the improvisations from eight smart colleagues of mine, all current or former teaching artists, who responded to my inquiry in 2003 to create a definition of a teaching artist:

> A teaching artist is a practicing artist whose teaching is part of that practice. Teaching artists don't necessarily have education degrees, but they might. Teaching artists are role models for lifestyle, discipline, and skill. They pass on an oral and experiential tradition in ways of thinking, seeing, and being. They are educators; in the truest sense of the word (the root of the word *educate* is to "draw out"), they "draw out" rather than "put in." They are guides/facilitators/bridges to creativity. Teaching artists are social activists.
>
> Tina LaPadula, Arts Corps, Seattle

> Teaching artists are arts translators, whose primary responsibility is to use their own art form's language, precepts, concepts, strategies, and processes to translate the personal and collective arts events of other individuals into a meaningful experience.
>
> Richard Burrows, Los Angeles Unified
> School District

A teaching artist is a practicing artist who is steeped in (lives in, thinks in) an art form—and who has made a substantial commitment to share her artistry with students and teachers in schools.

Judith Hill, music teaching artist

A teaching artist is one whose proficiency in one or more arts disciplines is complemented by knowledge and experience in facilitating the acquisition skills and knowledge in and through the arts among students, teachers, and other practitioners.

Richard Bell, National Young Audiences

A teaching artist is a practicing professional artist who extends the definition of practicing professional artist to include collaboration with classroom teachers with the goal of advancing teaching and learning. This goal is achieved through the design and presentation of activities that aim at illuminating the curriculum by engaging students in the medium of their craft, its skills, procedures, and social/historical contexts.

Daniel Windham, The Wallace Foundation

A teaching artist is an artist who actively engages learners in consciously developing the aesthetics of their own processes for learning.

Arnold Aprill, Chicago Arts Partnerships in Education (CAPE)

When an artist "teaches" through his/her work (and by teaching I do not mean giving information as much as opening possibilities), art is produced. When a practicing artist agrees to break down the components of art-making to fit some more linear model, then I suggest that art is being taught about rather than taught. When a practicing artist, on the other hand, is able to tap those more aesthetic and original ways of communicating that have made his/her art production deeply satisfying, then I think the real potential of the teaching artist is achieved. He/she is not teaching about art; he/she is teaching aesthetically, is being an artist in the way he/she relates to learners and situations.

Linda Duke, Krannert Art Museum

A teaching artist is an artist who has both extensively engaged in and reflected deeply on the creative, perceptive, and reflective processes inherent in making and viewing works of art and who has made a commitment to turn this reflection into action by guiding others to make works of art, perceive works of art, and reflect on the connections between art and the rest of life. . . . A teaching artist does not want to shape those they teach in their own image, but support learners to become more of who they are.

Christine Goodheart, arts learning consultant

To conclude, let's return to the beginning. Etymologically, the word *art* comes from an Indo-European root meaning "to put things together," and the word *teach* comes from the Greek meaning "to show." So, the term *teaching artist* is born of two verbs (appropriately, since the work of a teaching artist is more about creation than information) and might be said to mean "one who shows how to put things together." Let's put together a new future for music.

2

Teaching Artists in the Arts Learning Ecosystem

The arts appeared on day two in human history, beating the wheel by an aeon or more. In all those millennia, the original four disciplines—music, dance, visual arts, and theater—have each evolved in their own ways, and the only new kid on the artistic block since then is the literary arts. I sometimes refer to teaching artistry as the sixth artistic discipline, or as the in-between artistic discipline that closes the gaps.

The arts evolved within the oral and guild traditions until their professional expressions in recent centuries. Professionalism brought about more formal and institutionalized training, although much "amateur" and "folk" art and music still thrives in the oral tradition. In its shorter history, teaching artistry has been passed down from practitioner to practitioner. The increase in numbers of teaching artists in the 1980s and 1990s brought about more opportunities for training and hiring. This new century has launched a trend called "the professionalization of teaching artistry." The label is something of an overstatement, more vision than current reality. The field is still pretty disorganized, disparate, undefined—there aren't even clear paths into or within it as a field. There are gatekeepers of quality, but those tend to be employees at organizations that do the hiring, and state and local arts councils that publish an official roster. There is little agreement among these organizations or agencies regarding determinations of quality. There is usually a catch-22 for new TAs: they need experience to get hired, and they can't get experience without being hired by one of those organizations that insists on prior experience.

By the standard definitions of a field, it is only now becoming one. There is now a peer-reviewed professional journal, more and more conservatories and universities are offering courses that develop teaching artist skills, and there are a few places where a committed student can sort of major in it as an emphasis within an arts or education department, but it isn't yet really an academic field. Its first library of basic documents is being gathered at Columbia College Chicago. We are beginning to see the first appearances of written tradition in our field—articles and Web resources appear more frequently. There are now blogs, workbooks, DVDs, and books about aspects of the field. The term *teaching artist* got its entry in Wikipedia in 2007. Independent organizations are springing up to support and bring together TAs, and this is beginning to open up the pathways into the field. There was even a hit Off Broadway show by a theater TA about being a TA (*No Child*, by Nilaja Sun). There is one national award program, a paid residency (the Teaching Artist Fellowship) at Montalvo Arts Center in Saratoga, California; a national competition picked the most qualified TAs, with many top leaders in the field serving as judges. As fields go, teaching artistry is still in its adolescence but growing up fast—within the next five years, I am certain many more features of an established field will emerge.

This is the first book on music teaching artistry, but I do not aspire to present a complete "how-to." Rather, I hope to set a solid foundation and an inspiring vision for a field that still struggles to coalesce around either. Much as any "bible" cannot tell its readers and fellow believers how to handle every occasion, this book seeks to set down the essentials to invite ongoing rediscovery and development.

Six Strands of Arts Learning

In this and the next chapter, I offer two overviews of the distinctive elements of teaching artistry. In this chapter, I offer an analytic view of how TAs fit into the arts learning ecosystem as a whole; in chapter 3, I propose the fundamental elements of TA practice.

I use the term *arts learning ecosystem* rather than the more common *arts education* because the field is larger than the school connotations of the word *education*. While most of their work does happen in schools, TAs increasingly work in a variety of settings—from arts institutions to nursing homes to hospitals to corporate boardrooms. We will take the wider view in this book because I hope music TAs will be leaders in the expansion of the field.

Also, linking the words *art* and *learning* reminds us of their fundamental connectedness. The great twentieth-century physicist David Bohm gave an instruction that I try to live by: when one is faced with seeming opposites, look for the larger truth that contains them both. Americans in general, and many people within the arts in particular, see art and learning as two separate endeavors, two different fields. When I look for the greater truth that contains them both, I find they are basically the same endeavor. The experiences of making connections, of artistic engagement, of learning, tap the same skills, aspire to the same goals, and produce the same creative satisfactions and bursts of aliveness. When I seek the greater truth that contains both art and learning, I find teaching artists.

I propose there are six basic strands to the arts learning field. Arts education professionals, as well as those with only a vague sense of the field, tend to blur the distinctions, viewing them as one giant undertaking rather than interdependent and overlapping elements. These six do not function in discrete, exclusive ways, in reality or in good practice. However, there is a value in clarifying the distinctions, pointing out the differences in their goals, beliefs, locations, and delivery systems. Teaching artists have different roles in each strand.

The Six Strands of the Arts Learning Ecosystem
Arts appreciation
Skill building within an art form
Aesthetic development
Arts integration
Community arts
Extensions

Arts Appreciation

Its purpose: Teach *about* art.

This kind of traditional arts education relies heavily, almost entirely, on giving information as the path to greater appreciation. We associate this thread with academia (college survey courses, general music in primary and secondary schools), but it appears in lecture series, preconcert events, in parents telling children about the arts. Its strength can lie in the profundity of the arts and in the knowledge of most presenters; its weaknesses are its reliance on telling and the belief that information is a powerful way to open up the power of the arts.

Today, fewer and fewer Americans can take that kind of information presentation and turn it into a powerful personal experience in listening to the music. This is the thread of connoisseurship, with the taint of elitism and higher education. It tends to ignore or assume the learner's motivation. Its effectiveness is most often assessed by testing the retention and mastery of the information given. This strand produces effective results for those who already feel they belong inside an art form, derived from experience in their background, those who are excited by the lecture format, and those with academic aspirations in their listening.

Teaching artistry doesn't have much of a place in this thread. Some individuals with teaching artist skills do participate in this strand, but there is limited play for their teaching artistry within its historical goals. Teaching artistry does not happily limit itself to the goal of teaching *about* art; a good TA giving a lecture would instinctively expand the goal of the occasion to include elements of the other strands described here.

Skill Building within an Art Form

Its purpose: Teach you how.

This is the artist training strand, containing the many ways in which motivated people gain the skills, knowledge, lore, and savvy of the art form. Dedicated individuals from preschool music teachers through the top violin professors at the top conservatories all belong to this same strand.

Some say this purpose is exactly what distinguishes teaching artists from other artists who teach—TAs do not train young artists for the professional track. It is said that the stern advanced ballet instructor at the School of American Ballet is *not* a TA. In truth, it's not so simple—if she is exclusively focused on technique, perhaps she is not; but if, as is likely, she teaches about musical elements, opens up connections between ballet and life... who are we to say she isn't a teaching artist? And what does it matter anyway? What do we gain by rejecting her as a likeminded colleague? Let's err on the side of inclusion.

This thread is doing very well in music. It is fair to say that the technical training of musicians in conservatories and university programs is at the highest level ever, as discussed in chapter 9. The weakness is that the students, the world, and the professional field are changing faster than the training programs. This creates a tension between the skills being prioritized and those needed to live a full, rewarding life in music. I believe this strand is in the slow process of redefining the essential skills of the twenty-first-century musician.

Many music teaching artists also teach in private lesson settings and in schools of music. They tend to be excellent music teachers, as they use their expanded education skills to personalize, deepen, and intensify their students' learning journeys.

Aesthetic Development

Its purpose: Invite you in.

Although the word *aesthetic* sounds elitist, this thread is the antidote to elitism. This is the learning that opens up the power of the arts to the widest number of people. The need for this thread has grown steadily as the culture changes. I argue that the gap between the sense of having a rightful, meaningful place in the arts and the average citizen's sense of self has never been greater for any culture in human history.

Teaching artists are the masters of this strand of arts learning. If magic is the experience of a result without an awareness of the process, then teaching artists are the shamans of the magic of the arts. They understand and are able to open up the processes, and enable a wide variety of people to discover the power of meaningful, personally relevant arts experiences.

This strand of arts learning develops audience skills—the cognitive, emotional, and spiritual tools to set aside caution and prejudices to be able to enter artworks and make meaningful connections. This strand taps innate aesthetic competences, so that people can enter the arts without having to build up skills or formal knowledge in a discipline. It can involve the development of critical capacity too, but these analytic skills are quite different from audience skills. The skills of the critic incorporate prior knowledge to make judgments of quality, to place artworks in contexts and illuminate aspects of them; audience skills are about willing suspension of disbelief, wholehearted entry into the world of an artwork, and discovery inside it. Of course the two work well together, but we tend to train neither and live with sloppy examples of both.

As the importance of this thread expands with the necessity and difficulty of attracting new audiences to traditional arts offerings, the demand for teaching artists rises. I believe it will rise so high that teaching artistry will come to be seen as an essential tool of the twenty-first-century artist.

Cognitive psychologists and educators are discovering that the aesthetic component is fundamental to all learning and is a crucial element of great schooling. I will often start a speech to nonarts audiences with a pop quiz: "How many have made an important business or personal decision recently based on your high school algebra or trigonometry? [Few hands are raised.] How many have made an important business or personal decision recently based on aesthetics—and let me add, that includes not only the appearance of things, but also a choice based on a gut feeling, applying a lesson from a previous experience, using intuition? [All hands go up.] Well, now that we have redefined aesthetics and established its importance to our lives, let's talk about art."

And about that word *aesthetic*. Its etymological meaning has nothing to do with esoteric or intellectual processes; it means "to perceive." The philosopher John Dewey once remarked that he was unable to define the word *aesthetic*, but that he did know its opposite was *anesthetic*. That is the aesthetic development teaching artists most value—waking people up from the somnolence propagated by our aggressively anesthetizing commercial culture, to see the beauty, meaning, humanity, courage, and joy around us.

Arts Integration

Its purpose: Catalyze learning.

This is the biggest experiment in arts learning in America, probably the world, today (see chapter 20). It is a crucial experiment because so many programs are placing their chips on its essential gamble: by bringing arts learning together with learning other subject matters, *both* can go further as a result.

Teaching artists stand out front in this experiment. They are asked to collaborate with other educators in designing and often in leading such projects. The stakes are high—the arts are easily used as window dressing to pep up a boring curriculum.

The key to the arts-integrated curriculum is artistic engagement of the learning on the front end of the project, and then guiding that creative energy, that investment and curiosity, into serious play in the subject area. Arts learning practitioners are learning their way into this strand. Teaching artists are usually determined champions for this arts engagement component, while other practitioners who are less steeped in the subtlety and ineffability of arts engagement can let its primacy get lost in the competing, louder, more readily assessed aspects of the arts integrated project.

Community Arts

Its purpose: Enrich community life.

This strand may appear as a play dealing with a community issue, a mural, a chorus—and there are hundreds of arts organizations, usually small and extraordinarily dedicated, that live for this work.

There is uncertainty in the arts learning field about the difference between teaching artists and community artists. I feel the debate is mostly a waste-of-energy red herring—the same individuals participate in both kinds of work, and there is an intermixing of practices. The only useful distinction to draw regards ultimate goals: teaching artists aspire to have their learners engage in meaningful art-making, and community artists seek to enhance the lives of communities through meaningful art-making. In their negative prejudice toward the other, community artists (CAs) assume TAs want art for art's sake and promote the agendas and beliefs of arts institutions; conversely, TAs assume CA projects place artistic quality in a secondary position and produce less than the best possible art. There is a grain of truth in those prejudices, but reality and a growing arts field do much better if we build on the much larger common ground—TAs create healthier communities wherever they are allowed to work at any length, and CAs produce excellent artworks with their participants. Community artists are the lead figures in this strand, and they are often the same people that practice teaching artistry.

In 2004, I helped design and lead a rare joint conference of Americans for the Arts and the National Assembly of State Arts Agencies, the two largest arts advocacy groups in the country. This was an enormous gathering of the suits of the arts. The conference theme was *making communities more livable through the arts*. Throughout the conference I had to keep reminding the participants that the goal was not to get communities to support the arts, or to find ways to bring communities into the arts, but for the arts to serve the needs of communities. The arts people kept defaulting to more self-serving views of deeper relationships with communities, probably because survival thinking is so prevalent in arts organizations. By the end of the conference the shifted priority had settled in, and I was able to announce to the field, "The era of art for art's sake is now officially over. It was a fifty-year experiment, in a time of affluence, and it didn't work to expand the impact of the arts. We close that experiment and return to a time of art for many purposes, as had existed for the previous ten or twenty thousand years, and it doesn't mean the art produced is of lower quality." The sage of the community arts field is Arlene Goldbard, and I highly recommend her book *New Creative Community* (2006).

Extensions

Its purpose: Use the power.

The huge power of artistic engagement is increasingly being tapped to accomplish other goals. The creative arts therapies are used to ease psychological distress and make people's lives work better. The arts are finding a place in health care, as medical scientists discover the benefits: patients leave hospitals sooner, depression can be alleviated, pain is less debilitating, children heal faster, wellness requires creative expression, and so on. Medical schools are using teaching artists to enhance the observational, empathetic, and communication skills of doctors in training.

The arts are appearing in businesses to develop teamwork skills, boost creativity, and build leadership. This is serious money—Second City, the improvisational theater company in Chicago, now makes well over a million dollars a year in its corporate work. In his best seller *A Whole New Mind*, Daniel Pink proclaims that the M.F.A. is the new M.B.A.

Teaching artists stand at the entrepreneurial forefront of this strand. It is just beginning. People in the arts are discovering they have skills the world wants to acquire, and effective teachers who know the arts (that's right, TAs) are positioned to lead the advance.

I mentioned earlier that the most common gig I am asked to do with businesses is teach "creativity but no art." They want the business-certified goodies of creativity—competitive advantage, profitable innovations—their future depends on it, but they don't want to gunk it up with all the gooey irrelevancy and emotionality of the arts. I can deliver it, staying under the "art" radar with activities that tap art skills without naming them. How glorious it will be when we need not apologize for the word, and Americans think of art as powerful, relevant, and fun.

The strength of this strand is its unlimited potential and effectiveness in achieving many kinds of results. The weakness is that few TAs have experience making the transition from achieving arts learning results to achieving the other results nonschool clients want. There is not yet a body of practice or a communications mechanism for the pioneers of this field. But it will grow into a major new opportunity as we learn how to deliver this power, with teaching artists doing the laboratory work that moves the strand forward. An example is the May 2008 launch of the Memphis Symphony Orchestra's new partnership in leadership training for FedEx executives—designed and led by teaching artists in the orchestra. The team of musicians, led by oboe player Joey Salvalaggio, spent most of a year planning with FedEx management to develop a profoundly original and effective program—one they expect will spread within FedEx and to other companies in Memphis and beyond.

3

Guidelines for Teaching Artistry

Pedagogy. It's a terrible word, isn't it? Sounds vaguely illegal, probably immoral. Etymologically, it comes from the name for the slave in
ancient Rome who led the citizens' children (only the males, of course)
to and from school and kept an eye on their learning in general. I wasn't
thrilled to learn our beloved teaching practice derived from slavery, but
I have come to think of our lineage as the nameless thousands who have
served to lead people to and from learning encounters, and kept a general
eye on their learning welfare. We must always remember that *they*, the
learners, do the learning; we are the guides, and we watch over their learning health and progress.

The science (what pedagogy means) of teaching artistry not only *seems*
unformed and indefinite, it is. Teaching artists don't agree on an irreducible
set of core beliefs or practices; perhaps they never will or should.

In this chapter, I presume to propose twenty-five guidelines that apply
to all artistic disciplines. This list does not purport to be a compendium of
recommended teaching artist pedagogy. Certainly TAs will not, could not,
adhere to every guideline in every situation; rather, think of these as the
foundation ideas upon which to improvise and build. Remember that this
list applies to all artistic disciplines; it is the first offering of its kind to our
burgeoning field. Music teaching artists will find that some of the guidelines
are less applicable in their work—we will study how these guidelines apply
in music in greater detail throughout the following chapters in the book.

Let's acknowledge that teaching artistry doesn't own these practices;
most are guidelines of *any* good teaching. Most would appear in the artistry
of a strong classroom teacher and a creative trainer in a business setting.

I propose these as the elements of the art form of teaching artistry,
just as rhythm, melody, harmony, and so forth, are the essential elements
of music. These guidelines underlie the discussions and examples of the
following chapters that explore how they work in music. I try to live by these

guidelines in every opportunity I am given—from an hour with inner-city third graders to a daylong retreat with a corporate board of directors. Not all TAs will agree with all these guidelines, but most of the best naturally apply the following in their own ways without feeling any need for label or list.

This collection derives from asking myself the question: What advice would I give to a new teaching artist in any artistic discipline? Some of the guidelines may seem obvious, some may seem difficult—they are all worth your serious consideration in the long-term process of developing your skills.

1. Placing a High Priority on Personal Relevance

While information about the art form or particular work of art is valuable and important, a higher priority shapes our lesson design and instruction. The number one goal is to support people's capacity to make personally relevant connections within the artwork or art form. This is what distinguishes a music teaching artist from a great music history teacher—the latter wants to teach information and build skills in the discipline, the TA wants to artistically engage each participant so she can enter the artwork and explore it in ways that matter to her. We support people to help them make connections. Notice that idiom—make connections; it is the world's smallest creative act. They must engage creatively to accomplish this; you can't compel someone to create.

2. Using Engagement before Information

Not everyone agrees with me about this, but I place engaging learners, getting them to participate actively in your work, as a higher priority than the actual information you deliver. This prioritization respects learners as people, reminding us that they have to be involved participants in the work you present rather than merely acquiescent recipients of your information. After they are engaged, your information will have a far greater impact and relevance, will be desired, retained, and used. It can be argued that the key question TAs ask themselves in every challenge is: How can I best engage this particular individual or group, for this particular learning goal, in this specific situation? Once that entry point is discovered, and pursued as the priority, the pertinent and valuable information begins to become clear.

3. Tapping Competence

Most Americans over age nine think of themselves as artistically incompetent. Up to about nine years, kids feel omnicompetent, but developmental stages kick in around that time that make them say they suck at drawing, and one innate expression after another falls from their plate of owned abilities. I theorize the change has to do with self-consciousness, peer awareness, and increasing discernment about issues of quality. Sadly, as we try to bring people into the arts, too often we inadvertently confirm their sense of incompetence by making the arts seem difficult, or implying that you have to know a lot to do them right; we make the artistic event more formal than fun. Our task is to avoid the trip wire of caution and sense of incapacity, to engage people, to hook them with what they *can* do rather than emphasizing what they can't do. Certainly many educated and arts-experienced individuals feel competent and thrive in the current arts traditions; but teaching artists can bring in new audiences, who don't feel competent, who don't find a concert hall a safe or inviting place. It is no surprise that the most reliable demographic characteristic of an orchestral subscriber is a person who played an instrument when young. With music program cutbacks over decades, these people will dwindle in number, so we must get better at tapping other kinds of musical competence to bring in new subscribers.

4. Knowing the Learners

Have a sense of what students (or other participants) are able to do at the grade level (or particular group level) you are teaching, what is interesting to them, what kinds of challenges will catch their attention. Don't make assumptions if you don't know that group because you will not be accurate. And when you miss—say you assume they know less than they do, or that they will find an activity fascinating, but they find it too hard or just weird—then you have damaged your potential with them. Working with students, if you don't personally know people that age or have a feel for the group you are working with, do your homework. Spend some time visiting a class at that grade level, talk to students of that age to get a feel for them, talk with the teacher about the students' capacities. We don't teach in general, we teach specifically. Certainly activities can be adapted and adjusted for different groups, but you have to know the groups to make the adjustment really work.

5. Planning Backward

Good TAs are good at creating excitement in a room, making things fun. We are not so good at identifying a learning goal and shaping every element of the occasion to reach it. It is a sign of our field's growth that merely being able to work some magic in a classroom is no longer enough;

we have to be more strategic, more intentional, as educators. Some have resisted this growing demand to aim for and achieve learning goals, fearing it smothers the spark we bring. I think that's nostalgia, passive resistance, or just plain laziness. It is entirely possible to identify an arts learning goal with the other individuals responsible for the group (like the classroom teaching partner or program manager) and align a group's process to meet it without killing the art. Other educators don't take us seriously as colleagues, rightly, if we cannot agree on learning goals and meet them. We must be as intentional and responsible about the "teaching" component of our hybrid profession as its "arts" component.

6. Planning Thoroughly

It is wise to overplan a little, knowing you will probably not get to every part of the plan. Organize your lessons in blocks of material, to give yourself flexibility during the session—you can use or skip over blocks and have plenty to choose from as the teaching-and-learning improvisation unfolds. Also, be prepared to ditch parts of your plan and improvise within the subject area in response to exciting moments (or disasters) that crop up in class. However, don't count on improvising in place of lesson planning or the flow will get sloppy, and the goal will not be reached. Our busy lives can lead us to justify the occasional underplanned lesson; however, high-quality planning sets the stage for high-quality teaching. Without thorough planning, the learning and the resulting satisfaction will be less full. Even great improvisers in the arts have years of experience within the material to allow improvisation that delivers first-rate results.

7. Never Forgetting Fun

We do not use fun just for its own sake, but fun as an integral part of the activities we present to the students. (Chapter 10 is all about play.) Embedding fun as a design component of your work, you devise activities that students jump into, rather than comply with, because of the appealing nature of the challenge. Play is an essential aspect of artistic experience, so make sure to include serious play centrally in your teaching. Every time. Play is more than just a peppy warm-up, more than a clever artistic challenge—play is an attitude you bring, an atmosphere you create, a freedom you lead participants into, because it is so alive with learning and results. The TA himself must find the class or workshop fun to spark a fun atmosphere for the learners.

8. Controlling the Classroom

This is a big topic, and one that brings the most anxiety to new teaching artists. In my experience, problems with control are as much the result of weaknesses in the lesson, problems of what is being asked of the students, or unclear expectations as they are weak classroom management skills. In the early going, you will probably do well to put a few clear "control practices" in place, such as raising hands, a signal for silence and group focus, ground rules of respect. Set them out simply and clearly, carefully articulate your expectations of the students, and adhere to them, with particular attention at the beginning. If the students sense your contract with them is fair and well-intentioned, they will almost always buy into your structures and practices. Be sure to enlist the classroom teacher as an ally and partner (and most will give you excellent specific suggestions if you ask). To ensure that an activity is developmentally appropriate and exciting for students, do your homework—ask some young people, try it out with a young person, if you are in doubt. The classroom may be a little more unfocused than you are comfortable with, or the level of chaos that erupts when you are working with students may be more than the teacher's comfort permits—these are issues to be discussed between you and the teacher. An angry or disciplinarian approach to the students rarely works for more than a moment, and it undermines your longer-term relationship with them. Never shout. Never beg. Never bribe. Always make fair agreements and adhere to them. Always love the opportunity and the participants and manage the occasion for their benefit.

9. Clarifying Instructions

I cannot overemphasize how much you will help yourself if you carefully prepare the instructions you will give—get them down to the absolutely lucid minimum number of words and steps. Any ambiguity or vagueness will detract from the students' full involvement. They will start asking for clarifications; their anxiety will rise, and the energy and focus will dissipate. I even suggest that you write out your instructions and practice them aloud with a willing friend or spouse, then polish them until they are just right. Also, always ask yourself if you can give the instructions partially or completely without any words; there is theatrical power and fun in wordless instruction. For example, start immediately with a call-and-response clapping pattern that grows in complexity and ends up with variations on syncopation, which gets the class dancing as they clap, and you have begun your lesson on syncopation well. You can easily do all of this without a spoken word.

10. Setting the Work Environment

Students take their cues from you. You need to engage their interests and set a working tone that builds up their courage and confidence to try new things. They need to feel safe enough to be sure they will not be embarrassed or look stupid, and they must be respected for the many competences they bring. The way you relate to them and the overt classroom management practices you use indicate how you want them to work with you. It is said that you have ten minutes to establish the work atmosphere with a group; I have also heard the harsher truth that you really have only about two minutes. Be aware that participants drink in everything you do to determine the degree to which they will pour themselves in or try to undermine. Good teaching artists are brilliant at very quickly establishing a safe and charged, welcoming and irresistible atmosphere. That is the paradoxical but true goal—a safe and charged working atmosphere. We ask our learners to take a leap of faith with us, to engage in the risky act of creativity; we must make sure the safety is there so the risk always pays off.

11. Turning the Responsibility for the Learning Over to the Learner

The deepest learning is accomplished as the learner grapples with new information/ideas/challenges and finds satisfying solutions through her own endeavors. Of course, your guidance, feedback, and information are part of the process, but try to create opportunities for the students to do their own learning within the activities you propose. Set up and shut up, as often as possible. The best teaching artist practice can be simply setting a good challenge and then staying out of the way as students learn through it. As I got better over the years, I said less, guided less, and trusted the activities to provide the learning on their own—as works of art do.

12. Practicing the Activities You Propose

I hold it as a rule for myself that I always do the activity I am going to ask learners to do. This enables me to get a clear sense of the kinds of experiences and challenges they will have in my exercise, and it enables me to sharpen the instructions for the activity. It also helps me lead a much better reflection with students about the activity because I have personal experience to speak from. Every time I have skipped this bit of professional preparation, the work has been worse as a result.

13. Scaffolding: Step by Step

In designing activities, make sure that you set challenges that start at an interesting but accomplishable level, and then offer further steps within which students can succeed at each stage. Each step must be slightly more challenging than the last, in a freshly intriguing way, or they lose interest.

The psychologist Mihaly Csikszentmihalyi theorizes that "flow experience," also called "optimal engagement," happens exactly halfway between boredom and anxiety, so each step must seek that balance in its challenge to keep students fully engaged. You will be able to guide learners into surprisingly complex work if you provide steps that enable them to build on their competences and enjoy the progressively more difficult steps.

Succinctly give learners enough of a framework for the lesson to prevent their wondering why they are doing things or where it is going. If learners are disoriented, many feel concerns that constrain their participation. At the beginning of the class, and sometimes during it, let them know, with just a single sentence perhaps, the general shape of the time together and the "why" of activities. This explanation should be very brief, and you need not divulge any secrets you have in store, but it helps learners feel safe enough to invest themselves in the activities.

14. Remembering Reflection

This part of arts learning is the most frequently overlooked and the most often jettisoned when time gets short. However, adding opportunities for participants to get a grip on what they have just experienced, including a variety of ways for them to perceive what they have just accomplished, and how, is essential to a rich learning experience. Teaching artists often use discussions and journal writing to engage students in reflection; however, there are many ways to reflect, and many of them are so active and lively that they become activities in themselves (see chapters 21 and 22).

15. Balancing the Focus on Process and Product

American culture, including its schooling, focuses on products. We go for the gold, the grade, the answer, the test result, the bottom line. Certainly, the arts and artists love products—we are not creative in general, our productivity explodes when we imagine the thing we want to create and pour ourselves into making it. However, creative processes are juicy with learning. We need to balance the learners' focus. Because we live in a belligerently antireflective culture, teaching artists provide remedial reflective work through the arts. We must develop a taste for the reflective habit of mind in our learners by making it simple, rewarding, productive, and frequent. John Dewey told us that we do not learn from our experiences unless we reflect on them. Artistic processes are so fast and packed that we must pause and guide participants to attend to how they did things, how peers did things, and what their choices were based on, or the learning gold is lost.

16. Separating Observation from Interpretation

We tend to blur these practices. Try to maintain a clear, consistent pattern of guiding participants to notice what is there before following the natural impulse to judge, interpret, like, dislike, or have an opinion about it. Most people jump to judgments before they see; indeed, most tend to see through the selective filters of what they already believe. Institute an observational practice and adhere to it: "When we listen to music, our first comments afterward always identify things we heard in the music before we move on to discussions of how we felt or how good the music is." This is hard for people; we jump right to "I hate it" or "That was scary." Use each judging comment to bring people back to observation: "What was it you heard in the music that created that feeling of being scared?" The regularity of the practice can, over time, build the internal habit of mind. Interpretations become deeper and more informed if they emerge from an awareness of what is really there, and it is up to us to embed the habit, through repetition, as a consistent priority.

17. Witnessing

The artistic work teaching artists invite learners into is atypical for school life and unfamiliar for most people, so we must "mirror back" to learners what they are accomplishing. Witnessing may be our most important and subtle role—only we can affirm for a learner that the strange feeling of power she just had is important and repeatable, or that the weird idea he just stated is creatively excellent, or that one part of their small group composition demonstrated an important musical idea that Beethoven also used. The *outsiderness* of the TA, being an authentic representative of the arts world, gives such identification and affirmation extra power. Even if students have completed a challenge that seems simple, note the things they had to do, the artistically significant problems they solved, and the authentic musical value of these actions. Choices and discoveries that may seem small to us who are familiar with an art form may be momentous to people encountering an art for the first time. Listen extremely carefully to what students say, and mirror back their answers when they contain a useful germ of insight that the student didn't quite have the words to express clearly. When you mirror back, be sure to be rigorously faithful to what the student did say; don't embellish or distort.

18. Making Choices and Noting Their Impact

Choice making is not only a crucial act of art (and life), it is also an essential focus for participants' attention. Identify choices and consistently encourage participants to notice the choices they are making. I recommend explicit use of this four-step sequence on a regular basis once the goal of a project is embraced: (1) a brainstorming period that generates a number of choices to broaden possible options and results, (2) an awareness of key moments of choice among those options, (3) a reflective opportunity to grasp why that seemed like the best choice, and (4) a reflection later on the consequences of the choice. This sequence is so profound it can be used productively with beginners or the most advanced masters. This focus on choices can also reduce the harshness of judgmental critiques that often pop up around creative work (e.g., "Michael's clapping pattern was stupid" gets deflected with "What choices did Michael make in his clapping pattern?"). Focus on choices creates a level inquiry field for looking at any artwork; for example, you can look at the choices a student made in a classroom musical assignment and at the related choices made by Brahms.

19. Using High-Quality Questions

Good questions are not only open questions (don't have a single correct answer); they also grab people with their inherent interest, invite the discovery of personal relevance, and launch an interesting answering journey. The quality of your questions, those that are clever, subtle, elegant in some way, will make a major difference in the quality of the answering by the students. One great question can make a great class or a great project. Imagine the difference in two projects studying songs of the Underground Railroad. One begins with the question, "What navigational information did escaping slaves glean from these songs?" The other one, referred to previously, kicked off with, "Where in life do people use art to stay alive?" Also, attend to the quality of student questions, push them toward asking the best possible questions, and always celebrate a great question from a student. It may be drastic, but in training teaching artists, I *never* allow them to ask a closed question (one with a single correct answer). While closed questions can be useful and efficient, they are too associated with the suffocating school pattern, expected by those in control, of demanding that learners produce the right answer. This mental stance is so profoundly opposed to the artistic way of thinking, I urge TAs to avoid its taint at all costs, in order to nurture artistic ways of thinking.

20. Working with Classroom Teachers

When you enter a classroom, you enter that teacher's domain, as a welcome guest. You must be a guest who is sensitive to and respectful of the patterns and practices set up by that teacher, even if you don't like them. You may ask for help from teachers, and most will fully support you. Some teachers will not participate in the ways you would like; you may ask for specific things, but do not try to force the teacher to participate more fully. Always support the teacher in front of the students. Always try to engage the teacher to the maximum of his or her comfort level, and gently expand that participation just a little bit more with each visit. Try to tap into other things that are happening in that classroom (this can be casual or more intentional): other subject matter being studied, objects hanging on the walls, and so forth. If there is something you definitely need, ask directly.

21. Using Warm-up Activities

Because so much goes on in the students' day, they need a little adjustment to get their minds and bodies ready to do good work with you. Your warm-up may be brief or more involved; it may be easy or hard. But use those few minutes to get the group focused and eager, and use this time to experientially introduce something central to the lesson that follows. A good warm-up activity is inherently playful and fast, includes everyone, is active, and experientially introduces the key artistic skills that are emphasized and developed in the rest of the class. I recommend you use a cool-down activity at the end, perhaps a reflective exercise, to settle the energy that has been stirred up. It is responsible partnering to hand a calm and focused group back to the teacher, rather than a hyper group the teacher then has to calm down after you leave. This kind of group management makes for good collaboration.

22. Connections to the Curriculum

There are many ways to make authentic links between the art work and the other kinds of work that occur in any classroom. The connections can be quite literal (dealing with the same subject matter), or they can be quite subtle (dealing with a metaphor that applies to both music and history, for example). Making such connections is valuable for the learning and is most valuable when the students themselves make the connections rather than being fed them. For example, if you were working on rondo form, you might ask the class for suggestions of other places they know about, in schools studies and life, that use cycles and have forms like rondos. Students spot very obvious connections quickly and are not particularly excited by them—they are studying Germany, and Bach was German. Their discovery of a deeper connection is a good indicator of personal investment—for example, a colleague of mine had a student point out that the rondo form can be like school, when you come back in the fall to the same building and class structure but take on slightly more advanced content (see chapter 20).

23. Planning Meetings with Teachers

Try to get every participating teacher to be present and to speak. Use an introductory question that everyone is to answer, perhaps. For example, "What learning, related to our work, have you seen in your students in the last week?" Whenever possible, engage the teachers in an activity related to the work you wish to share with students—the subsequent conversation is much richer. Make sure that everyone present has expressed support for any plans that involve everyone; if someone is laying low, ask directly for that support. Reconfirm or set the meeting's agenda at the beginning, to assure everyone that their concerns will be addressed, and at the end restate the conclusions and agreements for what each must do. Don't begin the meeting with scheduling or logistical issues—although important, they tend to hijack the meeting and flatten the quality of the thinking that follows. Announce at the top that the last ten minutes will be dedicated to scheduling and logistical matters to allay fears that their practical concerns won't get addressed. Every planning meeting is an opportunity to draw teacher partners further into the arts, so plan simple but real ways to accomplish this goal in every meeting, along with the issues that will be addressed.

24. Staying Fresh

Staying fresh in your work, keeping the same edge of excitement and enthusiasm, is not likely to become a problem for quite a while in your work. At the beginning it feels as if one is scrambling to keep up. However, it does arise for many hardworking teaching artists over time. You must love this work and be actively in touch with your natural enthusiasm when you are with students. Though the following may seem harsh or naive, the rule of thumb I use is this: being a teaching artist is always something more than just a money gig. If ever you find you are doing it only for the money, something is wrong. When I feel a touch of staleness creeping in, I always delve more deeply into the artworks involved, and their complexity and value usually revive my interest in the unique opportunity of the work at hand, and in the distinct voices of these particular artist-learners.

25. The Law of 80%

You will see this law referred to often in these pages. While all that good planning and group management you must do makes a huge difference, 80% of what you teach is who you are. Of all the teaching you do around the arts, the participants' deepest learning comes from seeing how you, the emissary from the arts, think, listen, speak, dress, make meaning, respond, discover, handle trouble, play, joke, improvise, and so on. An artist coming into a classroom or workshop is different, interesting, and learners tune into who you are more deeply than you know. Your authenticity as an artist is one of your greatest strengths. Don't feel you must hide your artistic enthusiasm, your personality, your abilities, or your personal passion behind a "teacher" mask. This law brings with it a great responsibility. We must bring a high-quality 80% to every opportunity, even to the groups we don't much like and on the days when we are tired, have a cold, or would just rather be elsewhere. As an artist, it is a spiritual responsibility to bring the best of ourselves to each opportunity, and not just pretend. Because they can tell.

A Few Odd Guideline Tips
- Learn students' names fast; it makes a real difference to them (and to you). Use name tags or seating charts, whatever it takes. And do not mispronounce students' names; if you aren't sure of a pronunciation, ask. Don't just butcher it.
- Arrive early so that you are settled, focused, and ready. Be prepared for the possibility that you may start late or be interrupted. Do not run long (even if you started late), especially in schools; this creates a real problem for the teacher.
- Try to communicate with teacher partners between classes, to see if plans are unfolding as expected, to find out about other class events you might tap into, to make sure some conflict has not arisen. Doing this builds a sense of partnership.
- Never promise things to the students that may not happen.
- Do not offer candy as a reward for classroom work.
- Giving homework assignments may or may not be effective— because you are not an everyday visitor, an assignment may

detract rather than add to your impact. It may annoy your teacher partner if not cleared ahead of time. If class work requires students to do something at home, get approval from the teachers, plan it carefully with them, and have the teacher reinforce it and remind students so it does not get lost in the flurry of school activity.

- Use yourself as a performer or demonstrator if possible; live performance has a powerful impact on students if used strategically. Also, try to devise activities in which you can perform the students' musical work; this provides a stunning, but authentic, enhancement to their accomplishments.

4

The Best Reason for Being
a Teaching Artist

M any musicians have told me that they have no interest in acquiring educational skills: "Hey, I spent enough years learning how to play this instrument. I don't need to start learning new skills." Or "Why do you think I went into music? Precisely because I wanted to speak the language of music and not education-ese." Fair enough. So why bother?

Before we begin to answer that fundamental question, let's clarify our terms. By *education skills* I don't mean Mr. Rogers-y vocal tones, high-energy comic charm in the auditorium, or kiddie musical games. Education is not limited to particular buildings like schools or performance spaces (although these chapters will address those common places for learning encounters); nor are education skills acquired only in courses you took or might have taken in a preservice teacher training program (although great classroom teaching brims with the kind of teaching artistry we will explore in these pages). By *education skills* I mean a range of capacities to draw anyone into exploratory experiences. Do you remember my definition of art in chapter 1?—the capacity to expand our sense of how the world is or might be. The education skills of a music teaching artist are the ways we can guide others into such artistic experiences in music.

Our culture (and our vivid, perhaps scarring, personal histories) associates *education* with formal schooling and *education skills* with dynamic instruction. The typical instruction game is played by one who knows and others who don't know, and its goal is to get as much from the knower into the not-knower as possible. The instruction game is played for high or low stakes and certainly has its value in classroom and preconcert occasions, and anywhere information transfer is the goal. Instructional skills are a part of the good educator's kit bag, but they are not the power tools in a teaching artist's kit bag. They are not the reason musicians are brought into schools, nor the skills hoped for when musicians speak to audiences. Yes, it is powerful to define rondo form succinctly and interestingly at just the right moment, the moment when the learners are hungry for just that info-nugget you can provide. To clarify this point, let's invert it: certainly we want scientists to be able to use metaphors effectively in their writing and teaching, but that is not the key power tool of scientific teaching and learning.

The more essential power tools of teaching artistry are the ways to draw people into personally relevant, exploratory experiences in music so they become genuinely curious about how and why rondo form has an impact on them, so they can notice other places in life where experiences appear in rondo form. The music TA is a guide of the verbs of art more than an expert and purveyor of its nouns. The nouns of art (the paintings, scores, recordings, information) are tombstones that mark locations where significant acts of aliveness once took place; they await fresh verbs (attention, personal connection, response, discovery) to bring them back to life.

The practice of a music TA answers questions more like, "How can I lead learners to discover what they find thrilling about this piece of music?" than "How can I teach learners what is important about this piece?" More "What musical choices might the composer have made right at this point?" than "Here is what you need to notice next." The guideline is engagement before information. The education skill is drawing people in rather than putting information out. The markers of success are curiosity and the discovery of relevance more than the retention and regurgitation of information.

As a teaching artist, I sometimes lead an activity in theater, to illuminate a point in music. I perform a small poem four times, with a different preparation each time. The participants do each preparation with me and then pay close attention to the impact of the preparation on the quality of their experience within the live performance of the poem. The four preparation strategies are (1) no preparation, (2) a biography of the poet, (3) a mini-lecture on the poem, and (4) a story about the circumstances that prompted the creation of the poem. Although responses vary, there is wide agreement on the following:

1. No preparation left them flailing to orient to the poem while it was unfolding and missing the point because they never figured out how to be with it, how to pour their attention in effectively.
2. The poet's bio put them up in their heads and made the listening experience more comfortable but cerebral and dull.
3. The mini-lecture gave them things to look for, which they did; but it also irritated them and made them attend through the lecturer's perspective, making them "successful" at identifying elements of the poem and caring less about it.

4. The story, if shaped and shared just right, invited them to discover their sense of the heart of the poem and have a strong emotional response as they listened, and made them want to hear it again.

Strategy 1 is the way the music world mostly works—we believe works of music stand on their own, we trust that everyone arrives skilled and prepared enough to make satisfying connections on their own, and we provide written information for the noninitiates who might have found their way into the hall. Those newbies are not so likely to come back—the sheer power of the music may work for them, but the occasion is challenging, the formality distancing, and the personal challenge difficult for most Americans. We must never forget that the vast majority of Americans don't believe they are able to "get" classical music, and many don't find a concert setting a safe or welcoming place.

Strategy 2 appears in our written program materials and in the information offered by most musicians who speak before or after they play, which is fine but doesn't effectively open up audience readiness to find a personally relevant connection.

Strategy 3 is associated with academic mind-sets and can be helpful to some, while diminishing the personal edge for many. Most people find the helpful-academic approach makes them feel less competent to really find a place inside the piece, and they feel they are probably not getting the most important point if they do discover things.

Strategy 4 is just one of the teaching artist's many ways to bring people inside the world of a piece of music so they can discover aspects of it and find why they value being inside it.

In chapter 11 we will take up exactly this skill: How do teaching artists select the way to bring people into a musical world? The answer is specific to each piece of music. Choosing an entry point is as creative as the performer's experience of playing the piece. The challenge is compounded by the fact that we often have both sophisticated and naive listeners in the same audience—so we can't aim our intervention at one group without distancing the other. If we use strategies 1, 2, or 3, we may enrich the encounter of the sophisticated listener, but we risk alienating the naïf. And if we use strategy 4 ineffectively, we diminish the experience of the dedicated fan. Opposite ends of the musical experience spectrum in the same hall at the same time—what do we do? Remember David Bohm: when we see seeming polarities, look for the larger truth that contains them both. That search is the future of classical music, and the commitment and skills to lead that search are what teaching artists provide.

There are no easy paths to mastering teaching artist skills. My favorite arguments for developing these skills are making money (ensembles and individuals with good education programs get more gigs), building future audiences, sustaining your own artistic curiosity as a musical artist, deepening your satisfaction in connecting with audiences—reasons enough to explain why professional development programs for teaching artists are increasing around the country, even in conservatories, whose job it is to be conservative.

But perhaps the most mysterious and powerful reason of all is the one I didn't dare mention for my first decade of work with musicians. I sensed its truth from my own teaching artist background in theater, but I waited, observed critically, asked, and listened for many years. It makes a claim radical enough to spark doubt, to challenge traditional thinking, and (if we get lucky) to further the growing interest in the field. Here it is in a nutshell: being a teaching artist makes you a better artist.

I don't mean that education skills necessarily improve musical technique, although I know a number of musicians who would assert as much. I argue instead that the capacities you develop with a serious embrace of music's educational side advance your growth as a musician.

A few years ago, I asked fifteen musicians with well-developed teaching artist skills to tell me whether those skills have influenced their music-making—and if so, how. (I don't claim to have surveyed a statistically balanced sample of musicians, just to have investigated an identifiable minority with a demonstrated commitment to education.) To the question of whether they thought teaching made them better musicians, all but two replied with an emphatic yes. And the two who weren't so sure that teaching had improved their musicianship detailed several ways that teaching had improved their musical and artistic lives. One respondent—violist Phillip Ying of the Ying String Quartet—went so far as to claim that the "potential benefits of learning teaching artist skills are so great that I believe exploration of and training in these skills should be a part of every musician's education."

In analyzing my "data," I found that my respondents cited more than thirty different, specific benefits—suggesting the personal, idiosyncratic nature of the relationship between teaching and artistry. Let me shmush (to use a technical term in data analysis) all the feedback into four categories. (I won't dwell on the powerful practical benefits the respondents named, such as changing the way ensembles or soloists plan programs, composers revise compositions, commissions are developed, and artists learn to tap into other art forms. I also won't mention how large a majority said their teaching artist skills funded their chance to live a life in music, providing enough money that they didn't have to take temp work or any job they didn't like. Almost all who work in ensembles mentioned that their education programs keep their ensemble alive.)

Following is a summary of the respondents' points. In presenting them, I hope I can also convey their tone of forceful certainty. That, as much as the content of their answers, spoke to the importance of acquiring such skills.

Expand the Act of Performing

Teaching, most of the respondents stated, changes you as a performer. The change mentioned most frequently was becoming freer in performance, looser and braver at improvisation. Greg Beaver, cellist of the Chiara Quartet, wrote that the ability to "respond to an audience and adapt the performance energy to the needs of the crowd, or completely switch direction, is very important in structuring a teaching presentation as an ensemble. Inside the ensemble, this ability to improvise without stepping on others' toes is the essence of great chamber music."

Others found that teaching sharpened their ability to hear nuances of sound. Through the ears of learners, they discovered weaknesses and new possibilities in their own playing. Several described how teaching brings them back to basics in fresh, deeper ways. Freelance violinist Denise Dillenbeck explained:

> The connection of teaching and performing makes it impossible for me to stay arrogant, about the violin or about music, and drives me further inside my art form to understand it better. Because I have to clearly and convincingly articulate how to shift, why to use vibrato here, what we should think about phrasing, to my students, I find it drives me back into the violin to really investigate these things. How does shifting really work? And instead of mindlessly using this bag of tools, I take apart the puzzle and look at each piece like it's a gemstone, absorbing its colors and qualities—and then when I put the puzzle pieces back together, the whole picture is much more vibrant, because I've been involved with each part of it so intimately.

Three more perspectives, from three different musicians, capture how education has illuminated their artistry:

> There may be some things that I have forgotten as a performing artist, but when teaching I am always devising new techniques

to fit that particular student's need, and then I apply them to my own style and become better as a true artist. You can only teach what you truly are as an artist!

Imani Gonzales, freelance vocalist,
Kennedy Center teaching artist

Through my teaching artist work I become increasingly aware of my artistic choices, my intentions as an artist, and what skills or techniques best serve in each piece of music. This happens because I have helped others to explore similar choices for themselves.

Carol Ponder, vocalist, freelance teaching artist

Spending time with second graders or second-grade teachers demands of you a clarity of thought which is not always on your mind as a composer. You must distill everything and make sure that your thoughts and your music are connecting in a "primary" way, so suddenly you realize that your thinking as an artist has been cloudy, vague, unformed. You seek to clarify and distill things to their essential expressiveness and this bleeds into your next piece of music.

Thomas Cabaniss, composer, former animateur
at the Philadelphia Orchestra, faculty at the
Juilliard School

Change the Rehearsal Process

A surprising number of ensemble players noted that they ask different kinds of questions about music during dialogues with learners, and that these interesting questions prompt them to bring different, richer questions into rehearsal. (Indeed, I find the quality of the questions an artist asks tends to grow as his or her teaching capacity grows. I notice that the capacity to ask, and to engage in answering, great questions is the single clearest indicator of the depth of a musician's education skills.) Notice how Phillip Ying describes this kind of inquiry-based thinking: "The success of a teaching artist is often related to an ability to zero in on the essence of a piece of music, to define it clearly and to communicate it effectively. What exactly do I want others to know about this? What do I want them to hear in the performance of it?"

Some musicians noted that teaching expands the dialogue within the ensemble. Edward Bilous writes, "I have a greater repertoire of images and metaphors to use when conveying my ideas about music. In rehearsals I am able to speak about my work with greater ease and directness." Others note that learners' questions bring fresh perspectives, which if taken seriously, deepen the dialogue in rehearsal. According to Thomas Cabaniss:

> You hear what kids have to say about what's important to them, and you are reminded of why you began to "do" music in the first place. This, in turn, changes the way you go about the music making. I don't mean to suggest that second graders transform your artwork into some lowest common denominator of artistic expression—far from it. You watch how second graders are transfixed by mystery, and you wonder, "Have I made it all too transparent?" You talk to high school students about their perceptions of art, and you think, "Is what I'm doing relevant to the world today, or am I secluded in an ivory tower?" You work with teachers, and you ponder whether your work as an artist is moving society forward.

Sometimes the feel of rehearsal is enriched by education experience. Judith Hill, vocalist and education director of Cappella Clausura (and formerly Lincoln Center Institute's first full-time teaching artist), remarked: "My teaching artist work is so strongly based in process and in play (trying things out), it has definitely seeped into my own rehearsal process. I approach a new score with a different mental attitude (much more playful and discovery-oriented), and I tend to try out a wider range of possibilities 'just to see' what would happen."

Several respondents noted that, through their guidance of others, they become more aware of the profound nature of the creative process. The result is more creativity in their rehearsals—in addition to solving technical and musical challenges of a new piece, they do more brainstorming and experimentation, looking for deeper answers and relating the music to other art forms and aspects of life. The creative play of the rehearsal process itself is refreshed in a sustainable, musically deepening, lifelong way.

Deepen the Relationship to the Audience

It is hard to be jaded, cynical, or bored by audiences if you are really involved with them. Almost all the responding musicians said their educator's instincts sparked a refreshed openness and eagerness about audiences. Several said audiences (and not just youth audiences, but all audiences) become more personal to them, and they care more about making a good connection. Denise Dillenbeck describes her experience of this attitudinal adjustment:

> It changes the personal desire to connect with people in the audience. They become less a blank group of people, and I have a greater sense of the individuality of each person, a sharpened awareness of what each is going through, trying to do while listening, and I want it to work for each. This makes me pull apart the piece more, take greater care with each part—why did the composer do that?—and push through the awkward and frustrating stages of not completely getting a given section, to get to a realization of why that part is there and what meaning it contains—and then having much more richness when I put all the pieces back together. Teaching totally changes me this way—it would be too easy to overlook this discovery process and just take stuff about playing the violin for granted if there weren't other human beings in front of me that I actually care about, and they are there looking me in the eye and asking me to help them grow.

Teaching artist mind-sets expand the range of connection with audiences. As described by Phillip Ying:

> It is a given that everyone experiences music uniquely. Being a teaching artist enables one to understand the broadest range of audience experience. An audience in a famous concert hall that sits quietly and knows every note is far different than an audience that is hearing that music for the first time in a setting that allows for spontaneous reaction. A teaching artist learns to approach music from many perspectives, understanding that not everyone will learn or be engaged in the same way....Having the opportunity to be a teaching artist in a wide variety of settings, for groups large and small, in different physical spaces, at different times of day, all adds to a better understanding of what makes an effective performance.

Balance the Suffocating Aspects of a Musical Career

Nietzsche wrote: "Don't die of reality." The realities of most musicians' lives make it hard to keep a full connection to the aspects of the art that give a life in music its emotional and spiritual resonance. But some find extraordinary ways to sustain their musical passion within the challenges of a real-world career. Being the guide for others' learning in music is a powerful, proven-effective way to keep the essentials alive and growing. The following comments capture a sense of the responses from the wider group of their colleagues:

> Being a TA has made me a much more appreciative audience member. I am open to a wide range of compositional styles, and I have become the type of listener I encourage my students to be. I am concerned less with the initial, often superficial reaction of whether or not I "like" a piece of music. Rather, I listen for what is interesting about a work. I approach visual art and dance in a similar way because of my experience as a TA, and my ability to have a deep aesthetic response has been profoundly influenced by my work as a TA.
>
> Tanya Dusevic Witek, freelance flutist; faculty,
> New York Philharmonic and Carnegie Hall/Weill
> Music Institute education departments

> As an artist living in a society that truly undervalues the role of the creative, I feel proud to work in different teaching roles that allow me to bring music to new art-makers and appreciators, listeners and future art advocates, who will find ways to make art part of their everyday life.
>
> Paola Prestini, composer; director of
> VisionIntoArt, teaching artist

> The critics can evaluate my success or failure as a composer, as is their right; I can only testify that TA work makes my music mean more to me, and that is all due to the interactions I have with teachers and with kids.
>
> Thomas Cabaniss

> I strongly feel and see around me that our musical artists have been deceived in general that they need not deeply experience teaching artistry. Granted, not everyone will be able to encompass both. But unless more of us do, the art will have to resurrect itself at a later age, and we will be responsible as the generation that let the edifice crumble. (Yes, I obsessively think in terms of the symphony orchestra, for starters.) But this is not the point, either. The point is more that when one teaches, one learns. When one learns, one can let others observe and benefit. What have I learned through teaching "artistry"? Among a

thousand things I could say,...I'll say that the most effective way to help creativity blossom is not to teach it but to merely keep the "student" focused and encouraged to find it within.

Jon Deak, composer, associate principal bass,
New York Philharmonic

I take my work as a musician much more seriously and respect it for its potential to move people. Witnessing the gravity of how music can affect children made me realize its power. So often I have asked, "What right do I have to keep playing music when the world is falling apart? I should be doing something else, to help people more directly." Once I began this work, I realized that there is a place for this in our society. My conviction for music is stronger than ever.

Airi Yoshioka, violin, Damocles Trio; faculty,
University of Maryland, Baltimore County

Let me close with an etymological note about the word *connoisseur*. A classic word of learning in the arts, *connoisseur* implies that there is one who knows and who tells those who know less, which includes most of us. That definition is the old understanding of learning in the arts, and it implies that the exchange is about information, far from the act of creating. In the emerging world of teaching artists—those who thrive on the active interplay of skills of music-making and meaning-making with others in and around music—engagement becomes far more important than information. A careful reading of the word *connoisseur* reveals a secret at its heart. It does not mean one who knows a lot; rather, it is one who is adept at coming to know. A connoisseur is a master learner. Teaching artists are the connoisseurs of the twenty-first century, the artists who can engage themselves and others in the joyful experiences of lifelong learning in music.

5

Balancing the Two Economies of Today's Musician

"It's the economy, stupid."

Monofocused America seems to live and die by its economic ups and downs. People in the arts suffer because we seem peripheral to this economic monomania; we feel battered and reactive—dependent on its good-times largesse, fearful of the economic crunches, powerless to make much of an impact on either. We read of advocacy research that argues the enormous economic impact of the arts in this country, but it sadly seems to trickle down to few of us. In recent years I have noticed people who run arts education organizations following the ups and downs of the stock market closely. It certainly isn't because they have large personal investment portfolios. They know that when the market slides, their support from wealthy individuals is going to dry up. A recession means deep cuts in their services to children, including arts experiences. It breaks our hearts—the Dow Jones Industrial average drops too much, and young lives get even more desiccated.

The etymology of the word *economy* reminds us of something essential that we often forget. Coming from ancient Greek roots, *oikos* meaning "house" and *nemein* meaning "manage," the term originally addressed resources within an individual's daily reach. The sense of economy meaning management of a nation's resources arose only in the seventeenth century, and the study of economics (often called "the dismal science") began in the nineteenth century. What has this got to do with a life in music—other than the impact economics has on the many decisions that influence our creative lives and underfunded organizations? What has economics got to do with education and art? Other than the welcome bank deposits that derive from our teaching artist skills, how do economics provide an essential reason for being a teaching artist?

I believe all musicians, all artists, function in two equally important economies at the same time: the market economy that runs America, and also the overlooked "gift economy" that runs healthy communities. This term derives from Lewis Hyde's important book *The Gift: Imagination and the Erotic Life of Property*. (Doesn't that subtitle make you want to read it?) Artists function concurrently in both the commercial economy and the gift economy. Even though we tend to contort ourselves to the dictates of the former, and take for granted the importance of the latter, a satisfying and sustainable life in the arts requires success in both economies.

Let's highlight a few features of the two economies. The market economy deals with numbers of people buying and selling experiences and "things" within "contracts" with clear beginnings, deliverables, and ends. The gift economy is far older, primitive even, and it deals with person-to-person gift exchange. Several crucial features distinguish the gift exchange from commerce: the gift binds people to one another personally, beyond the moment of exchange; the gift must be passed along in some way to sustain its worth; and the giving preserves the spirit of the gift. These three features create extraordinarily valuable benefits that the market economy cannot: they create communities of various kinds, they bind people together over time, and they revitalize the spirit.

The arts trade in both economies. Certainly, works of art, and the experiences of them, are bought and sold, and their commercial values drive the institutional thinking around the arts. Good luck to any music organization, large or small, that does not attend to the realities of the market economy. Art is also a gift, and we overlook the personal component, the generosity, and the spirit of art at our peril. I would argue that an arts organization has a "product" of any distinctive value to sell only when the gift aspect of its art is alive and well.

Artists know this truth experientially, and they live by it. People describe good musicians as gifted, and we feel gratitude for that gift whenever we are fully expressive in our art. When the art part of our lives is flowing, we are functioning well in the gift economy—we are making personal connections, we are revitalizing the spirit of the gift we have, and we are generously passing along the gifts we were given. Is this economy a real thing or just some woo-woo New Age notion? It is absolutely real—we feel it, and we poignantly feel its absence. The currency of the gift economy sustains us to at least the same degree that cash does. And we suffer at least as much in the poverty of the gift economy as in commercial scarcity.

In my work with musicians across the country, I see the pressures and frustrations of the commercial economy. The financial demands may or may not be greater than in the past; few artists of any era have enjoyed an easy financial ride. However, musicians' participation in the gift economy is the internal Wall Street I focus on—if these stock holdings are not doing well, I see personal recession or depression. I must confess, I see gift-economy poverty in the lives of many orchestral musicians. While not in the majority, too many have almost given up on their active participation in the gift economy, to accommodate the needs of the market—and I see the results in too many unhappy, even ungenerous artists creating a mean-spirited, tense artistic community. No gift exchange.

Musicians in chamber ensembles are often unsung heroes of this balance, in my experience. They know they must thrive in both economies, and they refuse to compromise one for the other. Among all artists, chamber (and choral) musicians are among the clearest and most successful in shaping careers that respect and unite both economies. It is no fluke that increasingly I see orchestras trying to revive the creative vitality of their musicians through chamber programs in their outreach and education work. I have worked with players in twelve orchestras in the last few years, trying to reenergize their personal investment in the gift economy. Frequently, I discover that the players who seem the most alive and joyful are the ones with the most active nonorchestral music lives on the side.

The "education" or "community connection" component of an ensemble, however it is expressed, is the place where the gift economy is most prominently conveyed. Certainly, musicians give and connect through performance when doing their best work. However, the personal expression of giving in education efforts invites individuals to give more and to develop new, imaginative ways of giving—the hallmarks of success in the gift economy. The musician who takes time to think about how she can be more effective with each subsequent fifth-grade class she meets; how she can transform a preconcert "talk" into a fuller, more dynamic engagement than the last time; how she can change this school concert into an arts-inspiring exploration in ways she never did before; how she can assess the success in a private lesson to include awareness of the student's greater passion for music—this is the musician getting rich in the gift economy and investing in the future of both economies.

Certainly education efforts can generate money (they are often described as "cash cows" in the orchestra world), but they must never be driven exclusively by cash concerns or they join the market economy and deplete rather than rejuvenate the individuals involved. The preconcert workshops and talks, the school and community engagements, the moments of speaking during a performance, the conversations with audiences before and after a performance and even in the grocery store line invite us to grow in the ancient ways of being successful in the arts, not only in the fatter checks they produce for our accounts.

Success in music requires our ongoing growth as educators, as much as it requires our development as musicians. Our impulse to give must motivate a never-ending inquiry into more and more effective ways to pass along the many gifts of music. The additional responsibility of our era is to become more and more adept at helping people feel successful in receiving the gifts we offer.

I would go so far as to suggest that commercial success in music is at least as dependent on skills in the gift economy as in the market economy. Humans come to life in the gift economy offered by musicians, even though the usual expression of that enthusiasm comes through the market. Indeed, audiences come back a second time only if they have been rewarded experientially for their money and time investment in a ticket. Commerce (and its expression in good marketing) brings them in; experientially receiving the gift brings them back. The music group, large or small, whose members dedicate considerable attention and energy to their effectiveness as educators, as agents of musical experience for everyone they encounter, is the group that is going to thrive. Such a group or organization will thrive in both the professional and personal ways that make a life in music worthwhile.

Deep inside, artists know that the heart of their work does not originate with the self. Rather, it is an offering, a blessing. Lewis Hyde reminds us that a gift perishes unless it is moved along. We continue to receive that gift of art only when we pass it on as often, and in as many ways, as we can.

May it never get to the imbalance point in your artist's life that Marshall Sahlins describes in *Stone Age Economies*: "Hunter gatherer societies have affluent economies, their absolute poverty notwithstanding." May you live in gift abundance.

Part II The Overlooked Essentials

6

Role Play

The Four Angles of Arts Learning

If you ran the world, what would you include in the "full musical learning" of every child?

How did you organize your answer to that delicious question? Did you start thinking about the genres of music you would like a young person to know about and enjoy? Perhaps you thought about a series of instruments you would like every kid to learn to play. Maybe you even thought about taking that child to live performances of many kinds of music. Whatever your answer, it was based on your experience of coming into music—including what worked for you and compensating for what was missing.

Howard Gardner considered that question many years ago. Some readers may know of Gardner as the psychologist–education researcher who proposed the theory of multiple intelligences (MI). MI has gained widespread acceptance throughout the education world; to win agreement from the many fiefdoms of education is a rare accomplishment that affirms the importance of the theory. (MI theory proposes that intelligence is more than a binary quality you either have or don't have; it is more than the math and language skills the SAT test addresses; it identifies at least eight distinct kinds of intelligence, each of which every individual has to a greater or lesser degree in his or her personal mix. Musical intelligence is a distinct kind, and I'll bet readers of this book tend to be way above average in that regard.)

Before Gardner gained fame for his MI theory, he wrote about artistic learning, dividing it into four essential roles within which every student should have experiences and develop skills, in whatever discipline the student is engaged. He feels that each of these roles is distinct and complementary, and that fully rounded learning includes a series of activities that challenge students in all four roles to develop the abilities inherent in each: creator, performer, audience and critic. Let's look at each.

Creator.   In music, this is the composer. Although there is plenty of creativity in music performance, composing focuses the choices we make, the kinds of cognitive tasks we engage in, as primary creators. These are different than the interpretative choices and cognitive tasks of performance (which are also creative but sometimes are called secondary creating, meaning creating interpretively within a primary creation). Sure, there are situations in which the boundaries blur, like improvisation, like virtuosic cadenzas—but cut me some slack here, I am trying to make a point.

Performer.   Musicians know a lot about this role. Certainly, it includes the interpretative work mentioned earlier, but also the personal courage, the technical skills, the inner communicative capacity, the effective use of rehearsal, the stamina and focus that make for successful performance.

Audience.   We tend to think that audience skills are knowing when to clap and being pointed in the right direction with your eyes open—preferably including nodding enthusiastically and cheering in a standing ovation. There are more. Audience skills include skills of the heart, such as the capacity to set aside preconceptions and prejudices and encounter something new with openness—a healthy curiosity about differentness. They include the skills to make personal meaning during the improvisation between musicians and audiences in performance. There are skills of the spirit and of emotional memory and attention that are needed to effectively engage in the audience challenge of entering the musical world, exploring and making personally relevant connections.

Critic.   Although you may have been burned by some nasty or dumb critic, this is not the moment for critic bashing. (I have seen local papers where music criticism is the extra-income job of the regular sports writer. At one small-town paper, the music reviewer also wrote the obituaries!) The skills of the critic are important and powerful, even if we have suffered when those skills were misused. While audience skills set aside preconceptions to allow open encounter, critical skills apply previous knowledge to shed light on the musical world. Critical skills put the work under focus in relation to history and knowledge of the art form. The critic is sharply observant of detail and can remember and compare with accuracy. The critic does not tear down but illuminates the work through a variety of analytic processes.

I hope you can appreciate the value of each role and the benefits of each kind of learning in the different situations where they are emphasized. We have to recognize that musical education in this country is not organized to support Gardner's point of view. School music programs or those out-side school, including private lessons, are wildly imbalanced in favor of performance skills. Compositional skills are rarely tapped in general music learning; with only scattered exceptions, this fundamental aspect of musi-cal learning is almost completely ignored. And critical skills? Everyone is critical around music, but the skills that develop critical capacity are rarely addressed. Critics are usually poor models of good critical skills! Music theory classes help, and they do succeed to some degree—but these are hardly mainstream. And audience skills? We don't even think of them as skills, and we certainly don't push these skills of heart and spirit beyond decorum and attention.

The skill-building track of each of the art forms is imbalanced in its own way. While dance tends to balance the creator and performer in a healthy way, there is little attention to the critic or audience. Theater seems imbalanced in the same way music is, but with even less emphasis on creating, and slightly more opportunity to develop the critic thanks to the toehold of plays in high school English class assignments.

American culture is skewed against the development of any kind of balance among those four skill sets. *Audiences* are often arrogant, feeling more entitled and quickly judgmental than respectful and eagerly adaptive to the world being offered. Americans place great demands on the new— they are cautious and insecure—and are generally unwilling to bring an open readiness to encounter new work on its own terms. We do not think of ourselves as *creators*, and we often let atrophy, or at least limit to small expression, the skills of making stuff we care about that delighted us as kids. Apart from the celebrity few, creators in the arts are not much respected in America. In 2003, Princeton Survey Research Associates undertook the 2002 American Perception of Artists Survey for the Urban Institute. Their study found that 77% of the adults in the nine major cities surveyed know a professional or serious amateur artist (57% know a professional or serious amateur musician), and 95% are active in the arts through doing art, know-ing an artist, or attending arts events. Almost all of those surveyed—97%— are moved or inspired by art. However, only 27% believe artists contribute a lot to the general good of society—compare that with 82% for teachers, 66% for scientists, and 63% for construction workers.

In America, *performance* is done by specialists—except for amateurs who keep the arts alive in the general public. (Incidentally, choral singing is by far the largest amateur arts participation in this country—one-sixth of American households have a chorus member in them.)

Anti-intellectual America has dumbed down the role of *critic* to review-ers whose job is to help audiences decide what to spend their money and time on, balkanizing the true critic's skill set largely to connoisseurship and academics. We believe as a culture that everyone should have an opinion, but there is no need to base it on anything more solid than preferences.

How did those four roles play out in your life? How balanced was your musical education? I would guess that until you reached more advanced levels, it was very imbalanced, and it may have remained very imbalanced unless you went out of your way to delve into these different kinds of learning.

Total focus on performance may help produce excellent performers, and many members of conservatory faculties would argue that total focus is required, since there is so much to learn. In one conservatory, I heard a teacher say there are hardly enough hours in the day to practice as much as excellence requires. At another, I heard a faculty member tell a student he hoped those liberal arts courses wouldn't waste too much of his time that would be better spent in the practice room. I don't think an imbalance is essential; indeed, I think it is artistically stultifying. Sure, there must be periods of complete focus on one role, but tunnel focus on any single role does not lead to a healthy destination. I regularly encounter the opposite of the traditional view—widely curious, experimental, playful musicians who can play difficult material as well as anyone and still mess around with composing and improvising and love to hear new music. Breadth of artistic curiosity and interest does not necessarily reduce quality or commitment, any more than tunnel vision guarantees quality.

And here is the point—there is a cost to imbalance. Part of the cost is limited perspective and limited joy among musicians. The happiest musicians I know are those who fluidly use the range of roles in themselves. This may not mean they are actually composing concerti and writing reviews; however, they are so familiar with the skills involved in composing that they naturally, playfully use those skills in rehearsal, or at home, or in writing, or in a dozen little ways. They apply positive critical skills toward their own work, toward their peers and colleagues. And they delight in those audience skills of openheartedness, readiness to set aside prejudices and preconceptions.

My Juilliard students tell me that the most terrifying group they perform for is their peers. They know what is going on in their minds, as they look for mistakes, compare technique and musicianship. As they described the way their peers pay attention at a concert, I hear: all critic, no audience skills. Well-rounded musical artists drink in and find personal meaning in the good work that others provide and that other art forms and daily life provide. They apply their full artistic selves, and they resonate with the benefits of a life in music. These skills developed in the four complementary roles help create the fullness of a life in the arts.

Many musicians I meet are unhappy in their musical lives, even those with good careers—many orchestra musicians, for example. Almost invariably, they are not using their full complement of skills. Too many feel like technicians in their work, not creators. They rarely bring a full open heart to opportunities in music and in life. They are critical all right, but they do not take part in the athletic, constructive workout in the critical gym. Imbalance leads to unhappiness.

There are two teaching artist implications to Gardner's truth: (1) Since 80% of what you teach is who you are, take care to develop the four kinds of skills in your own life. If you are not working out as a creator, get cracking. It need not be only in music—write poems, paint landscapes—experience primary creating on a regular basis. If you do it in music, it may feel weird to do some composing if those skills have been long out of use. Play with those skills gently, practice, keep it an ongoing part of your musical life—even if you never share what you compose. Work on your audience skills consciously, so you have ready access to and pleasure in all the goodies our rich musical world offers. Keep your intellect developing with what you see, so you can bring ever-more-informed frameworks to the music you encounter. Gardner's views offer more than an abstract theory; they suggest a map to sustainable satisfaction within a consistently stressful life in music—not only for you, but also for your students. (2) Include all four kinds of learning in your teaching—whatever kinds of teaching you do. Whether it is private lessons, group instruction, or helping out your dopey cousin Ralph, give some assignments that exercise the composing muscles. Listen to music together and model those best audience skills. Demonstrate how to use the critical mind to discover more in the music you hear. Use improvisation and outright composition as a part of your lessons. Take responsibility for giving all students the feel for all four essential roles, finding the pleasures in them. And model all four roles for every student.

And even if you don't have occasions that look like "teaching," we are all teachers all the time. We teach by how we behave with one another, within rehearsals, with friends and family. Be an active user of all your musical skills, and you live a life with fuller musical engagement; you show others the power of music to create greater harmony in life.

7

Inside the Liminal Zone

What do you do when you don't know what to do? That in-between place, between what you know and what you don't know, is an overlooked but crucial area in the arts and arts learning. It is sometimes called the *liminal zone.* You know this zone—you perform in it when you improvise, and you listen from inside it, moment by moment, as you make personal connections to music you have not heard before.

The word *liminal* comes from the Latin for "threshold," a transitional space between two places, and is sometimes used today to describe various kinds of experiential thresholds. It has sister words like *subliminal* ("underneath the threshold of awareness"), *preliminary* ("before the threshold is crossed"), and *eliminate* ("take away from the threshold"). Liminal spaces are rich with possibility. We encounter the new in the liminal zone, which is also where we turn those opportunities into the satisfying or disappointing experiences that determine the quality of our lives. Our creative selves come out to play in the liminal zone. It can be the threshold of discovery, surprise, learning, and delight—if we can function well there. It can also be a place we push past quickly to enter familiar and comfortable mindsets—our preconceptions, quick judgments, and need to be seen in ways our egos demand sometimes snap to instantly close the uncertainty of the open threshold.

Most people are a little wary of the liminal zone, even anxious within it; humans naturally resist change and feel a little cautious of the new. This may be a hardwired species-protective trait, giving us a limited tolerance for the unfamiliar, especially in the arts, which can impact us in deep and subconscious ways. It is a habit of mind to be able to adjust that tendency and choose another natural attitude that flourishes when we feel safe and engaged—receptivity and curiosity to make personal connections to the art. In the moment of encountering unfamiliar works of art, our attitude and skills enable us to either create a personal connection (experiencing the sense of delight and satisfaction that makes us hungry for more), or tolerate the uncertainty and keep trying, or bail out—speeding through the liminal zone by snapping to a quick negative judgment (making it less likely that we'll be fully open to connect the next time).

The liminal zone is the inner place where we create the connections that make our experiences of art, where we come to love new music, becoming active participants, or we choose to direct our scarce free time, attention, and discretionary dollars in other ways.

I believe our culture has failed miserably in nurturing a healthy curiosity about differentness in our children. We have brought them up in fear (partly for good reasons), but we have not balanced this with a boldness of curiosity, a responsible management of their willing suspension of disbelief, a sense of capability in encountering the unfamiliar, an irrepressible imagination, a yearning to enter and play in the liminal zone.

As educators—and remember, we are all educators in music, even those of us who hate doing children's concerts and don't give lessons—we must become more skillful in slowing down our audiences' passage through the liminal zone, helping them expand their repertoire of things to do when they don't know what to do.

Years ago, I led a weeklong workshop for twenty classroom teachers, none of whom had any musical background. The subject was "How We Pay Attention to Art." The first day, we listened to a section of a recording of a twentieth-century string quartet, "modern"-sounding classical music. The teachers tried valiantly to like the piece, but listening for melody or a sense of a story in the music (neither was part of the composition) didn't produce any satisfaction for them, and they didn't know what else to do while listening. They concluded that they were not sophisticated enough to "get" the piece and felt dumb, or they decided that they just didn't like it and felt a little angry that I had chosen to play something like that. End of story—they just wanted to move on.

Over the next days, we focused on our work within the liminal zone. Because we were exploring all artistic disciplines, not just music, I chose not to do what music educators traditionally do—give people more listening tools, particularly telling them about the piece or giving them suggestions for how they should listen. Instead, I chose to focus on attitude. We talked about the discomfort of not-knowing, the tension that turns into frustration and rejection if it lasts more than a few moments. The concert setting is particularly challenging for this discomfort because you can't simply walk away when you aren't making good connections (as you can in the art gallery); on the other hand, being stuck in your seat provides opportunities to reengage and move past first judgments. We developed a kit bag of things to do when we don't know what to do—whether we're standing in front of an abstract painting, watching a modern dance, or listening to a piece by Webern.

At the end of the week, I played another recording for the group—a segment of Samuel Barber's woodwind quintet. All were instructed to make careful note of their inner responses. On the first listening, they used an average of six, and as many as nine, different listening strategies. And I hadn't taught them anything about music or Barber all week. But in the course of relaxing, letting go of the discomfort of not knowing, they discovered a different, exploratory attitude and many more connective tools to try. They listened for a melody ("Okay, no melody"); they listened for repeated patterns ("Hmmm, no periods, just commas"); they kicked back to see if they had an emotional response ("Nope, nothing there"); they noticed the fantastic virtuosity of two instruments ("Maybe I should just admire the playing"); and so forth. No, there is nothing particularly unusual in the appearance of these strategies; what was unusual was that they came up with all the strategies themselves, and the discomfort of uncertainty was gone. Gone with it was the quick-judgment impulse, replaced by a playful, eager, open curiosity to discover what Barber had made for them.

Best of all, the teachers asked to hear the two-minute selection again. They made more connections in that next listening ("It *does* have a kind of structure," and "It includes a lot of sound extremes") and felt even more satisfied and interested at what they discovered. They began to swap listening strategies and asked to try out one another's to see what they got. The liminal zone became a playground—ultimately they asked to hear the segment seven times. Far beyond the issue of liking or disliking the Barber quintet in particular, they developed courage and curiosity to encounter unfamiliar worlds and ask questions. After the seventh listening, they still had more questions ("Do musicians love or hate to play this piece?" "Are the instrument pairings in the piece unusual, and why did he do that?"), and they were ripe for some instruction to satisfy their curiosity.

The teachers tapped a vein of their innate musical competence and were able to apply it excitedly to connect to the music they previously would have rejected out of hand. It didn't take a music theory course—such a course would probably have dampened the lively interest that built and built. It didn't take a lecture full of musical information, the way we usually try to help willing people succeed in the liminal zone—which kills more interest than it awakens in the classical-music-uninitiated. It took different habits of mind.

If we can adjust listeners' mind-sets when they're in the liminal zone, we accomplish two things for the hearers: (1) the realization that they can use what they already know (even if they don't have any musical training) to connect with the piece in a satisfying way; and (2) the desire to meet the piece on its own terms rather than waiting for it to come across the threshold to them and dazzle them with its charm.

In addressing the issue of audience habits of mind, we teaching artists must first focus on them in ourselves. Are you yourself curious and open in the encounter with new music in the liminal zone? Remember the law of 80%, which states that 80% of what you teach is who you are. Do you stay open, curious, receptive (the way you would want an audience with little musical background to do?), or do you quickly snap to opinions and judgment? Musicians themselves can be cursory in the liminal zone, feeling they know so much and have such confidence in their skillful listening that they don't bother to open wide and enter the world of the piece to see what it holds on its own terms.

This difference highlights a distinction between audience skills and critic's skills that plays out in the liminal zone. Critical skills (which are not necessarily well used by critics) apply accumulated knowledge of the art form, with the goal of determining quality to contribute to the growth of the art form and artists. (Contrast this with the now more prevalent reviewer, whose job is to help consumers determine the best places to invest their spare money and time.) The listener's skills certainly include the use of personal knowledge to create satisfying connections, but audience skills set aside preconceptions and preferences; they include capacities of the mind and spirit to encounter and explore the world of that piece of music in open and wholehearted ways. I find that many musicians let the critic's skills colonize the liminal zone. Musicians tell me that many peers listen hypercritically by habit, focusing on technique with a hard competitive edge, looking for everything they do imperfectly. This habit is bad news when you serve as an educator. Just a whiff of these habits of mind scare off naive listeners or make them feel inadequate. When you snap, "Barber was getting back at wind players he hated," or "Barber is so egotistical," you narrow the space in the liminal zone for others (and yourself), and you make them less courageous to tap what they know and aspire to connect.

I cannot count the number of times I have had this experience with a colleague at a performance: we both listened, and right after, the friend began to critique the work, pointing out things that my naive ears had not even noticed. I was busy discovering much more rudimentary and rewarding things about the work. It damages my experience (not to mention my friendship) to get a whack of critical opinion while I am still reflecting on the ephemeral experiences I had.

In the next chapter, we will dig into the habits of mind we need to sustain a creative vitality in the liminal zone—healthy habits for ourselves and those habits we need to nurture in others. Let's preview a few.

Notice what is present.   Develop the habit of giving full attention to what is in the music. This may sound obvious, but we are usually sloppy in our noticing—our listening is a jumble of impressions including reactions, opinions, irrelevancies, and judgments more than a humble willingness to discover what is there. As we perceive more about what is actually in the piece, we develop a richer relationship to it. The mental habit is full, open attention. My students began a real relationship with Barber in the liminal moments when they noticed "the horn playing high and the oboe playing low, both really quietly—I never heard that before." The teaching artist guideline (guideline 16, as described in chapter 3) that builds this capacity is to *always* embed practices that invite observation before interpretation.

Pose questions and experiment with answering.   One of the ways we naturally try to make connections within music is by posing questions and then seeing how the answering goes as we listen on. Listening to the Barber, my students became more engaged in the piece when these questions popped: "I wonder if the composer has something in mind with that instrument pairing?" "Will the bassoon get a star turn later?" One student even asked herself a very sophisticated question—"Where in life do I feel controlled chaos like that?"—that makes her poised to find deep relevance in the listening. Teaching artist guideline 19, about always asking rich questions (and never asking closed, single-answer questions), builds a culture in which people start asking better questions themselves—and this guides them to deeper listening. Even though we are rarely aware of this organic process, our listening is guided by the questions we pose to ourselves. The quality of our questions determines the quality of the experiences that follow.

Be playful.   The nature of the liminal experience is experimenting, playing around, improvising, seeing how you can explore this new world (remember guideline 7). The stakes are low, and the rewards are potentially great. Audiences usually feel playful as listeners only if the content of the music is playful; however, that feeling of serious play can bloom inside the open discovery of a requiem or an angry, bleak movement. If we can offset the usual discomfort of uncertainty with the many pleasures of play, listening to classical music begins to become fun—which is exactly what we must accomplish in the bidding war for people's discretionary time.

Liminal habits of mind make a real difference in the real world. Many years ago, a visual arts teaching artist and I co-led a three-week workshop for twenty people focusing on the connection between art and learning. After three weeks of exploration together, we had become a brave posse of inner adventurers. On the final day of the workshop, we had the treat of meeting not in our usual neutral New York City workshop room but in a SoHo gallery where our visual arts teaching artist had a one-woman show on display. She hadn't told anyone about her paintings, so the location and the discovery were going to be a surprise and a closing-day celebration. The plan was to work at the gallery all day, ending with a little party.

I got there early to set up with the artist, and I saw her paintings. Every one of the fifteen or so pieces was a giant (six feet tall, hung vertically) oil painting of a vagina. Different colors and shapes, but huge and unmistakable. I watched as each of our participants (including three men) arrived at the gallery. I sat by the glass window so I could see their expectant faces as they came down the block. Then they stepped into the gallery, saw the paintings, and stopped dead. I could hear their inner voices screaming, "Run!" but they stood. I could see them begin to practice what they had learned to do in our weeks together when encountering something new. I watched them, one by one, take a breath, relax, and—in highly individual ways, and even as the inner alarm bells were clanging—overcome the reactive instinct, center themselves, and engage as explorers. Within half an hour, the group was noticing color choices in the paintings and jumping up to point out places where they found something the artist had done that really worked. We had a great party at the end, pretty loose, even looser with the cheap wine, as we celebrated our heroic accomplishment as learners in the gallery of taboo, as colleagues in the liminal playground.

8

The Habits of Mind of Musical Learning

In the last chapter we entered the liminal zone—that mysterious internal space of not-knowing, in which we encounter the new. This in-between state is the overlooked epicenter of audience experience, where people come to love, like, hate, feel stupid or confused, be drawn in or repelled, find or not find satisfying personal connections to music. I argued that the ways listeners react when in this zone are largely a function of how many inner tools they have for connecting to the music as it unfolds. Teaching artists can—must— help people develop those tools. Expert tour guides in the liminal zone, teaching artists can teach people what to do when they don't know what to do—and teach what *else* to do if what they already know ain't working.

Traditional arts teaching provides information that helps listeners follow a piece—to recognize, categorize, and appreciate. While this approach helps in some ways, it also limits many listeners, especially the new ones we are trying to engage. It steers them to recognize elements *we* find important—and away from discovering their *own* connections during an uncertain encounter. Good teaching artistry provides a variety of tools and strategies to help listeners make their own connections to the new music, including its formal elements. Great teaching artistry develops *habits of mind* for encountering new works of art. Such habits create connections not just between music and the mind but with the heart and spirit, where music really makes a difference in people's lives.

What happens when we shift away from the traditional approach? What if instead of guiding listeners to strive to identify features in the piece (rondo form, the interesting cello and violin dialogue), we focus on the kinds of questions they ask themselves during the piece, or how to focus on expectations the composer raises? The difference is deep: the word *identify* is derived from the Latin for "sameness," whereas the word *discover* derives from the words for "open up." Identification is a cognitive exercise, the kind of "getting it right" that school testing demanded of us for so many years.

(I even question orchestra education's near-universal reliance on instrument identification as the place to begin the welcome to this strange thing called an orchestra. It seems such a small and binary way to introduce a whole new world—"yes, I got it right, that was the bassoon." I am reminded of a Polynesian maxim, "We stand on the back of a whale fishing for minnows.") Discovery goes deeper; it is a creative act, and it gives us the same blip of excitement composers or performers get when they create. The distinction between teaching people how to identify and encouraging them to discover evokes the adage educators often use: *Give a man a fish, and he eats that day. Teach a man how to fish, and he eats for a lifetime.*

In the traditional approach, the clarinet player tells me (an audience member) to keep an ear out for the way the melodic line changes in its third appearance. The music plays; I spot it—great! While this is a way to help me find my way inside a new piece, it doesn't go anywhere inside me, and it may confirm the pervasive view that "classical" music is not really exciting or relevant. It gives me the satisfaction of doing what the teacher asked. However, if I *discover* something myself—an interesting change in the melody when the clarinet picks it up for the third time, a different feeling inside when the clarinet comes in—the moment has much more excitement, resonance, and impact. Say I don't find that significant feature; if I am curious and ready, I will find something else that matters to me. At least that is the gamble. And the gamble is important for all of us to take. The traditional approaches may be comfortable and familiar, but they are not working to bring in the new audiences we need. They are not working to excite people about new music.

Let me introduce you to a notion of "habits of mind" put forward by educators Arthur Costa and Bena Kallick. Their ideas apply directly to learning in the liminal zone. As defined by Costa and Kallick, a habit of mind is "a disposition toward behaving intelligently when confronted with problems, the answers to which are not immediately known: dichotomies, dilemmas, enigmas and uncertainties." Their books Habits of Mind: A Developmental Series (2000), published by the Association for Supervision and Curriculum Development, along with practices developed in a network of schools built around the habits of mind concept, are having a strong impact in the education field. Some say Costa and Kallick's contribution is as important as Howard Gardner's multiple intelligences theory of the 1980s. Their research, theory, and practice have identified sixteen habits of mind that they use as the basis of their teaching-and-learning system:

Persisting
Thinking and communicating with clarity and precision
Managing impulsivity
Gathering data through all senses

Listening with understanding and empathy
Creating, imagining, innovating
Thinking flexibly
Wonderment and awe
Thinking about thinking (metacognition)
Taking responsible risks
Striving for accuracy
Finding humor
Questioning and posing problems
Thinking interdependently
Applying past knowledge to new situations
Remaining open to continuous learning

Costa and Kallick propose that a good learner has this full repertoire of mental habits at the ready to apply in the encounter with the new. The list of sixteen habits has not been derived from or explicitly applied to learning in the arts. In my view, that opens a big opportunity for teaching artists to do so. What other subject so naturally evokes a learner's innate creativity and capacity for wonderment and awe? Other education trailblazers have grabbed the notion of habits of mind.

Ted Sizer and Debbie Meier from the Coalition of Essential Schools developed this set through their work at the Central Park East Secondary School, the CPESS Habits of Mind:

- *The habit of perspective:* Organizing an argument, read or heard or seen, into its various parts, and sorting out the major from the minor matter within it. Separating opinion from fact and appreciating the value of each.
- *The habit of analysis:* Pondering each of these arguments in a reflective way, using such logical, mathematical, and artistic tools as may be required to render evidence. Knowing the limits as well as the importance of such analysis.
- *The habit of imagination:* Being disposed to evolve one's own view of a matter, searching for both new and old patterns that serve well one's own and other's current and future purposes.
- *The habit of empathy:* Sensing other reasonable views of a common predicament, respecting all, and honoring the most persuasive among them.
- *The habit of communication:* Accepting the duty to explain the necessary in ways that are clear and respectful both to those hearing or seeing and to the ideas being communicated. Being a good listener.
- *The habit of commitment:* Recognizing the need to act when action is called for; stepping forward in response. Persisting, patiently, as the situation may require.

- *The habit of humility:* Knowing one's right, one's debts, and one's limitations, and those of others. Knowing what one knows and what one does not know. Being disposed and able to gain the needed knowledge, and having the confidence to do so.
- *The habit of joy:* Sensing the wonder and proportion in worthy things and responding to these delights.

*For more information: http://www.essentialschools.org/pub/
ces_docs/about/phil/habits.html*

The first habits of mind offering in the arts came from researchers at Harvard Project Zero, one of the nation's foremost arts education research centers. Based in the visual arts, the Studio Habits of Mind grew from work in the VALUES Project, a network of schools and educators led by the Center for Art and Public Life, the Alameda County Office of Education, and Project Zero at the Harvard Graduate School of Education. Here are the Studio Habits of Mind:

- *Develop Craft.* Technique: Learning to use tools (e.g., viewfinders, brushes), materials (e.g., charcoal, paint), and artistic conventions (e.g., perspective, color mixing). Studio Practice: Learning to care for tools, materials, and space.
- *Engage & Persist.* Learning to embrace problems of relevance within the art world and/or of personal importance, to develop focus and other mental states conducive to working and persevering at art tasks.
- *Envision.* Learning to picture mentally what cannot be directly observed and imagine possible next steps in making a piece.
- *Express.* Learning to create works that convey an idea, a feeling, or a personal meaning.
- *Observe.* Learning to attend to visual contexts more closely than ordinary "looking" requires, and thereby to see things that otherwise might not be seen.
- *Reflect.* Question & Explain: Learning to think and talk with others about an aspect of one's work or working process.
- *Evaluate.* Learning to judge one's own work and working process and the work of others in relation to standards of the field.
- *Stretch & Explore.* Learning to reach beyond one's capacities, to explore playfully without a preconceived plan, and to embrace the opportunity to learn from mistakes and accidents.
- *Understand Art World Domain.* Learning about art history and current practice. Communities: Learning to interact as an artist with other artists (i.e., in classrooms, in local arts organizations, and across the art field) and within the broader society.

For more information: http://center.cca.edu/about/news/6

In recent years, I have been developing my own offering to the exploration of those inner capacities that constitute intelligent functioning. I am developing a set of habits of mind that great teaching artists should aim to develop in listeners. My work seeks to answer this question: What are people doing inside when they engage creatively? Not just engage in the arts, but when they are able to invest themselves creatively in any rich world? I didn't limit my theorizing to the arts because the skills of full attention do not belong just to our field; they are a birthright—but they happen to be developed more fully and rewarded more deeply in the arts than in any other field.

Imagine: What if your teaching goal were to develop habits of mind in your students, and you used music as the subject matter in which to practice and improve? How would your teaching be different? I have been exploring that question with teaching artists and teachers around the country—arts and nonarts teachers—and the answers are that the pedagogy can look very different.

Following are five specific habits of mind I recommend you consider raising to a high priority in your teaching, followed by suggestions for practical ways you can go about developing those habits. We want listeners to make personally relevant connections while listening because, as research affirms, that is what provides a strong enough reward to bring them back on their own—to make them become as passionate as we are about the arts. I propose that these five will help accomplish that goal.

Attention—full, open, active. It is a skill to be able to set aside preconceptions, reactive impulses, and the jumpy mind and to fully open one's attention to listening—and one also needs to *persist*. Full attention is a habit we develop, one that serves us well throughout life. It is a state of open noticing, much like the effortless receptivity to new sights, sounds, and smells that one adopts when traveling in a new land. This quality of attention may be the scarcest commodity in America today, and among the most valuable. The arts invite, celebrate, and reward it well.

Inquiry. We all self-navigate as we listen, and the questions we pose to ourselves determine which way we go and how far we get. If the only question you know how to ask is "Where is the melody?" you're going to be disappointed by many new pieces. Those who notice hints from the composer in the way a melodic line or fragment of a phrase raises expectations of the direction of the piece, those who are curious and experimental, will delight in proposing questions for themselves while listening and in following the answering processes. For example, in George Crumb's *Black Angels*, the Dies Irae theme is suggested and introduced in various small ways until it appears fully in surprising and satisfying fullness later in the piece. Great musical inquirers have a kind of inner Geiger counter that finds the "hot" aspects of a piece. Listening becomes an inquiry, spurring a mental interchange with the composer and musicians.

Playful attitude.   Listening is a real-time improvisatory dialogue between the performers and each audience member. Audience members bring their history and capacities to the unfolding moment. We must learn to hold each moment lightly because the music moves so fast. To make this sort of listening work, we apply the number one rule of improvisation: Whether in acting or in music, an improviser always says "Yes" to the partner's offered comedic or musical line—and goes with that affirmation to find what comes next. Saying "No" breaks the interplay. An actor who starts an improv scene with "I haven't been able to find you since you stole my nectarine" can build on a response like "After ten years of living with you, I know how to save you from yourself." But she can't go anywhere with "I don't know what you're talking about." Encourage trying things out, experiment with hunches, have fun with the game of listening.

Flexible empathy.   We all have many selves inside us—intellectual and emotional, childlike and wise, sensual and cerebral. Rich music invites us to connect with these many capacities, often fluidly and quickly. The willingness, even eagerness, to switch the ways in which we connect to a piece, instead of demanding that the piece meet us in the ways we prefer, expands our human repertoire and the range of music we love. In hearing audiences talk about classical music, too often I am reminded of the psychologist Abraham Maslow's quip, "If the only tool you have is a hammer, everything begins to resemble a nail." If the only tool you have is an appreciation of classical structures, Debussy and Ravel are going to be judged as lousy nails. But if you make contact with the part of you that has a feel for through-composition, tone color, and elegant orchestration, you may create the experience of a lifetime.

Reflection.   We live in an aggressively antireflective culture, yet music is an inherently reflective medium. As teachers, we need to gently guide people into the quiet studio of their own meaning-making, affirm the importance of that inner view and of the aesthetic and personal satisfaction of making something to keep. Research by the Wallace Foundation, the John S. and James L. Knight Foundation, and others affirms that listeners' having a significant emotional or spiritual experience is what brings them back to classical music. Reflection is what gives those moments their impact. We will delve into reflection later in the book (see chapters 21 and 22).

All five of these habits of mind will take any listener—you or a first-timer—deeper into the joy of musical encounter, and all five will spill out of the encounter with music to inform a richer, more holistic, more authentic everyday life.

Much as I might dream of a Costa-Kallick-like school to teach the artistic habits of mind (conservatories or schools of music don't prioritize such skills), daily life provides us only occasional opportunities to develop these capacities in others. To take advantage of those occasions, I recommend a handful of practices for teaching artists to use every time they teach to prioritize and build these habits of the music-listening mind.

Work small.   Dedicate a significant part of your work with listeners to small sections of music. Repeated listening and discussion of what actually goes on in the listening encounter build confidence and awareness of skills. Just as we focus on parallel parking as a part of learning to drive, so we need to identify particular listening skills and practice them repeatedly, in small, focused experiments—but not to the point of drudgery. Then apply that skill to new and larger listening challenges.

Balance how you listen with what you hear.   This natural back-and-forth helps the listener discover and expand his own listening habits. Be curious about both, and ask the questions you want the listeners to ask: "In what different ways did you find you were paying attention?" "Why do you think you're listening in that way?" "What other ways might you try?"

Ask great questions.   This teaching artist skill may be the clearest indicator of mastery. A great question is one that is inherently interesting (with some emotional or intellectual bite), has a rewarding relationship to the music, and provokes a lively answering process. Here is a question sequence I see too often: "What did you notice?" followed by a long, awkward silence, with the follow-up question, "Was it fast or slow?" These two are both weak after-listening questions—one too vague and the other binary. A question like, "How many parts would you say it had?" will model a much more invested exploration of how a piece is put together. Work on your questions to get the best ones possible, and then invest in them, which means to wait out some silence if the group is working toward answers. No need to bail out quickly. You might even need to ask it again, using slightly different words. Or if you really care about it, and they aren't getting it, explain what you are interested in and ask them to rephrase the question.

Connect impression with evidence.   Teaching artists are sometimes accused of being fluffy because we welcome a variety of answers to good questions. And we are fluffy if one person found a section "scary" and the next person found it "sleepy," and we say "great" to both and move on. It isn't that one is right and the other wrong—we need to ask both what they heard in the music that prompted the feeling of fear or somnolence. The great listener has that habit of mind to connect impression with evidence, and we foster this habit when we ask listeners to connect their impressions with aspects of the music that prompted them. Commit the time to do this often enough that listeners start doing it on their own.

Come back to the music.   Many listening impressions take us away, into memory or associations. This is natural and healthy, and yet we want to bring listeners back to the music as soon as it is appropriate, to affirm that the goal is in the music, not in the mental travels the music induced. Don't squelch, but don't indulge. How often I have seen someone tell a story that overwhelms people more than the music does! Bring the naturally wandering curiosity back inside the music. Get the gist of the extramusical trail and guide the discussion back into the music source. Given the natural tendency of the mind to wander off on a side trail of interest while listening, the skill is remembering to come back to the music as soon as possible; I refer to it as bringing the puppy back to the paper.

Document.   Setting things down clarifies. The medium matters less than the process of reflection and word or image choices we make. Listeners may respond with a journal, a poem, a diagram, a mind map, a series of notes—a variety of ways may be even better than just one. The teaching artist creates the prompts—great questions, reflective challenges—and the learner gets in the habit of specifying aspects of the encounter with music, building the quiet courage to document them. Over time, the process of documenting builds the reflective habits of mind and increases listeners' ability to assess the usually overlooked inner processes as they pass through the liminal zone.

Model the habits of mind/the law of 80%.   Teaching artists must be transparent and generous in sharing their own inner processes, in demonstrating the quality of their own attention and inquiry, their strategies and playfulness, their empathy and reflective interests. This teaching habit inspires great listening, just as musical virtuosity inspires others to play.

To some of the people I encounter in the music world, this focus on the quiet private place within which individual meets music seems overdone or dull. They prefer to deal with the beautiful and dynamic features of music and sharing their excitement about them. I share their delight and enthusiasm. However, a lifetime of experience has taught me that a teaching artist's love for musical features has limited impact on many listeners and doesn't usually succeed in nurturing those less familiar with the kind of music we love. What works, over time, is strengthening the listener's repertoire of ways to make her own meaning—developing the habits and getting the experiential rewards they produce.

9

The Essential Skills of the
Twenty-First-Century Artist

The headline might read: "Conservatory Top Dogs Talk to One Another."
That *would* be news, but not front-page news because no one got bit-
ten. In 2002, leaders from ten major conservatories, from the major arts
service organizations, and from large foundations, and some young artists,
spent three days in a cushy conference setting answering this question:
How are we developing artists for the twenty-first century?

I was designated to facilitate this herding of the cats sponsored by
the Kenan Institute for the Arts (my role fell somewhere between that of
Charlie Rose and Jerry Springer), and a blind goat would have recognized
that this was an ensemble that had never played together before. There
was much goodwill in the room (covering occasional flashes of anxiety
and irritation), but huge gaps in basic understanding appeared. Few of
those from outside the conservatories had any real sense of what actually
happens inside—although they certainly had a lot of opinions about conservatory training nonetheless. Even fewer had a sense of the constraints
and challenges conservatories face, and their firm judgments softened as
they got a sense of the inside realities. The conservatories recognized that
they are not aligned with the larger arts ecosystem in which they play their
part; they admitted to frustration that they cannot adequately prepare
students for the realities they face after school. The leaders wish to evolve
faster than they can.

One discovery emerged clearly. This insight affects every musician out
in the field, every presenter and educator, as well as future musicians still
in school. The group recognized a historic split in the mission of developing young musicians. The traditional goal remains primary: to develop the
best possible technical and artistic skills to launch successful careers in
music. This mission is clear and is arguably being fulfilled better in American conservatories today than at any previous time in history. There is
greater equality across training programs now—a music student can get

excellent training in many programs and institutions. Greater parity and greater quality, across the board—an accomplishment to celebrate.

The discovery was the admission of a second set of goals. Once peripheral extras, now they must be addressed as essential for building a fulfilling, holistic, fully expressed, successful life in the arts. The second set of goals is very different than the clear traditional goals; these are hard to define and harder to pursue. No one is clear about what this bag of abilities, understandings, habits of mind and heart really are, but we know they include capacities as educators and advocates, as entrepreneurs, as writers and speakers, as marketers and promoters. This is not news to those in the thick of creating a twenty-first-century musician's life; they live the demands and the crisis learning of the real world. The news of the conference was that those responsible for developing future musicians recognized and stated that these skills are now essential in the preparation for a musician's life. They defensively identified the ways in which they each try to address the need, even as they admitted their offerings were inadequate. They felt stuck. "Where do we find the time to include more focus on education, entrepreneurial, communication, and advocacy skills? Do we take it out of musical training time? That means our students are less likely to get good jobs. How you perform from behind the curtain is the only determinant of whether you get an orchestra job or not. What do you expect us to do?" The entire conference hit a wall at this dilemma. The president of the American Symphony Orchestra League (subsequently renamed the League of American Orchestras) threw up his hands. Literally.

Conservatories tend to be conservative; there is a reason they aren't called *progressatories* or arts *experimentariums*. Yet these institutions, dedicated to retaining the best of the past as they move forward, are now recognizing what working musicians have long known—the skills to draw people into music and educate them effectively about music are not afterthoughts, are not luxuries for the few who get famous or the few who are naturally outgoing or garrulous or happen to like teaching. Advocacy is a responsibility for all. We all are educators all the time. And these abilities are not just natural gifts, personality tricks, or the refuge of the musically less gifted.

Advocacy, entrepreneurialism, and education skills can be taught, can be learned and developed for a lifetime to enable even the shy or tongue-tied musician to become comfortable and effective in those roles. Conservatories are exploring this new kind of training; each one at the conference had examples of ways they are experimenting with increased emphasis on these skills. Teaching artists are beginning to find ways to share their techniques and successes with one another. Presenters are hiring those who have these "extra skills." The development of future audiences depends on these extra skills as much as it does on the traditional skills of great musicianship.

Working musicians already apply these skills out of necessity and advocate for music when they can—usually advocating for their ensemble, drumming up business (always a good thing to do). I believe our responsibility goes further. We are *all* responsible for drawing people into the fun, the excitement, and the essential human importance of concert music.

The people sitting next to you on the train or standing next to you at the grocery store checkout are a potential audience for our music. It is our responsibility to draw them in. When I taught advocacy skills at Juilliard, I sometimes gave musicians the following assignments. One experiment was to get on a New York City public bus and engage people in substantive conversations about classical music before they got off. They were terrified (lying awake in bed the night before in fear, I was told), but they did it!

It meant a real shift in the way they thought about relating to that old lady next to them or the bored office worker on her way home. For many it was a real challenge to their personalities—but they all survived and succeeded, and none got slapped for impertinence. They usually came back saying something like this: "I found that if you talk about *music* first, you have common ground. Everyone has a big interest in music. And once we have that common ground, they got really interested that my whole life is inside music."

Another assignment fell over a holiday break. They were to identify the biggest philistine, classical-music-hating person in their family and plot out a strategy to draw that person a little bit further into classical music over the holiday. They planned out a strategy, wrote it up, and then enacted their experiment at home to see if it worked. Almost invariably they found some small evidence of success, and how a sustained campaign just might work, for the same reason as the bus discovery, I believe. If you establish common ground in the love of music, using a big, genuinely inclusive definition of music, then your attitude evokes the other person's curiosity rather than prejudice. The moment you believe classical music is better than other music, you not only come off as elitist, you *are* elitist. I don't believe all music is equal, but I believe there are many kinds of music that can excellently deliver exactly the many kinds of experiences listeners seek. As Duke Ellington said, "If it sounds good, it is good."

The purpose of these two experiments was not to torture the shy but rather to build up the advocate's mind-set and courage. I wanted my students to be poised to take advantage of every opportunity to build interest in other people, even people they would normally ignore or give up on.

And nothing awakes interest better than a one-on-one connection with a living, enthusiastic musician.

A job satisfaction survey done a few years ago listed several hundred jobs in America and rated them according to how satisfied their practitioners were with their work. Unsurprisingly, low on the list was prison guard, and just underneath prison guard was orchestral musician. Quite high up in satisfaction was chamber musician. This suggests an enormous opportunity for the chamber world, and a cautionary note for orchestras. We need to capitalize on this truth—we need to resonate with the benefits of a life in music. We need to share our genuine enthusiasm and fascination, because they are known to be among the most powerful ways to draw people into our world. You know this is true from your own experience—whenever someone speaks excitedly and with delight about something they love to do, you want to experience it too. And the cautionary note for orchestras is that unhappy musicians do not draw people in as effectively. All musicians must be resonant with the benefits of life in music to draw in more Americans.

The current generation of musicians didn't get much dedicated focus on these additional skills in their training. They pick up skills as they go, or get bits from workshops, from colleagues, from people in other fields, from opportunities that require them to learn fast or else. It takes enormous motivation to learn in this way amid the pressures of our overstuffed lives, and it takes practice to bring these complementary skills into balance with great musicianship. Future musicians may be fortunate enough to be educated into a balance of musical and additional skills goals in their training—to make their transition into the real world less like entering a new, and daunting, plane of reality.

The conservatory honchos were sensitive to these necessities, but they never did find any answer to the time question mentioned earlier: Given that conservatories have a limited amount of hours to develop these young artists, and they are already working them hard, where does the time come for the focus on these additional skills? Do they give less time to developing musicianship? Do they reduce liberal arts classes, encourage less practice time? Do they eliminate sleep? They identified some "entrenched faculty" as a major impediment to internal change—they felt senior faculty didn't want the training practices to change in any significant way, and they admitted senior faculty was often pretty removed from the realities of the current marketplace for musicians. They also noted that younger faculty tended to feel quite different, being closer in touch with the everyday realities of the real world and more open to experimentation and change. The conservatory leaders did state clearly that they could bring about change much faster if the orchestra audition process opened up to consider education, communication, advocacy, and entrepreneurial skills as an element of hiring. Perhaps I will see consideration of such skills in the interviews of final-round auditionees in my lifetime.

I know I will live to see a change in the nature of the probationary time in orchestras, because it is already beginning. Probation will become a period of intensive professional development in these "extra" skills areas, to make sure the musician is a good educator and advocate before getting tenure. This is one way orchestras can embody their stated commitment to the importance of these skills to the future. Is it fair that previously tenured musicians didn't have to jump through that training hoop? No. But we have to start somewhere, and changing the audition process is going to take longer.

Since that conference, I have heard one solution offered with increasing frequency—to add project-based learning to all musician training programs. While students are learning their craft, challenge them to apply it in ways that mirror what will happen when they leave school. Have a project for all students that requires each to produce a concert in the city. Have a project to prepare a class of middle school students to see a live concert. Have a project to make a presentation to a Rotary Club or business group. Include required projects regularly throughout the years of training, not as separate electives on the business of music or pedagogy. Let projects provoke students to learn from doing, and learn fast, as we do when our butts are on the line—let this be a regular part of the preparation of young artists to succeed after school.

In the meantime, musicians continue to develop these essential skills in a disorganized but determined way—because they know they must for the good of their careers, their students, and the field. Those who succeed as advocates, educators, and innovative entrepreneurs change the ecosystem in which conservatories function. Those musicians who dedicate themselves to continually developing as advocates and educators contribute to future generations of musicians as much as they contribute to the present-day audiences—helping their own bottom line along the way.

10
Creating the Playground

A man's maturity consists in having found again the seriousness
one had as a child at play.

—Friedrich Nietzsche

Men do not quit playing because they grow old; they grow old
because they quit playing.

—Oliver Wendell Holmes

Play, art and religion are the acts or thoughts that incorporate the
rational without being bound by the rules set down by the rational.

—Lynda Sexson, *Ordinarily Sacred*

Gary Larson's *Far Side* cartoons took center stage at a Harvard lab. In the
experiment, psychologists Helen Langer and Sophia Snow randomly
gave adults one of three tasks involving a stack of pages from a *Far Side* cal-
endar. One task was a simple categorization into odd or even days, months,
and counting totals. The two more complex tasks were to change a word or
two to give the cartoon an entirely different meaning, and to recategorize
the cartoons by some scheme of the participant's invention. The researchers
split each of the three task cohorts into two groups. The task was described
to the first group as "work"; the instructions to the other group contained
the word "play." Everything else was the same; only that single word was
changed. The researchers' discovery? Equal numbers in the "work" and
"play" groups reported enjoying the simple sorting task, but significantly
more in the "work" group reported that their minds had wandered. As for
the two more complicated tasks, more people in the "play" group said that
they had enjoyed performing them, and twice as many in the "work" group
reported that their minds had wandered. Inescapable conclusion? When we
approach complex tasks playfully, as opposed to working at them, we focus
better and enjoy the experience more. Take note for your teaching.

Americans tend to view work and play as polarities. Our culture's
Puritan heritage leaves us feeling one is productive and the other is

frivolous. (I recall the headline of an Australian newspaper during the Clinton-Lewinsky scandal—"Thank God We Got the Criminals and They Got the Puritans.") Work is for the serious business of life; play provides the fun and balancing richness of life. We are a hardworking nation, averaging more work hours per week than any other; we average more hours of work than medieval peasants did.

Our formal schooling trains us to work at learning, and we carry that weight for a lifetime—learning takes effort, the harder the better. Most students will tell you they learn far more outside the hours of formal instruction, when they are messing around with things that interest them. That kind of interest-driven play happily fuels our lifelong learning.

I would go so far as to say that the *essential* experience of learning is playful. We may apply a lot of effort to many of the tasks that pass for learning in institutional settings—memorization, skill development, performing a task, regurgitating and applying information—but play is the natural and often faster route to mastery of new skills, new information, and greater accomplishment. In a famous experiment of the 1970s, psychologist Mihaly Csikszentmihalyi (now at Claremont University's Graduate School of Management) gave a pile of objects to a group of promising young professional artists, asking them to select and arrange some items and draw a still life; he videotaped and analyzed their creative process. The completed drawings were submitted to a panel of art experts tasked with selecting the best. The winners were not those previously deemed to be more talented or experienced. The researchers found that the highest-ranked artists were those who had handled the greatest number of objects before starting to draw, and those who had adjusted the arranged gizmos the greatest number of times *as* they drew. Csikszentmihalyi concluded that, more than innate talent, playing within the process produced the better art.

An endeavor that requires sustained effort, such as learning to play an instrument or learning to appreciate "boring classical music," goes much better in a framework of serious play. Children's work is play; that is how they learn to grow up and become who they can be, just as lion cubs and baby chimps do. Throughout our lives, we learn fast, and perhaps best, when we are invested in "messing around with" and "experimenting" and "playing with" something that has caught our fancy. Einstein did his breakthrough work while playing out thought experiments in his imagination. Let us not forget we play music for a lifetime.

Gustavo Dudamel, the music director of the Los Angeles Philharmonic, is a product of the remarkable music learning system in Venezuela, called El Sistema. In the program, hundreds of thousands of the poorest kids learn to play instruments and perform in youth orchestras;

El Sistema's top orchestra, the Simon Bolivar Youth Orchestra, composed of fifteen- to twenty-five-year-olds, plays as well as or better than the best professional orchestras in the world. How is this possible? Dudamel says the key is that they never forget that fun is the most important thing.

Play is one of the teaching artist's most powerful tools. If we can engage learners in the serious play of a musical challenge or game, problems of classroom control and student engagement diminish dramatically. I have noted that good teaching artists naturally devise games and playful ways to pull students into musical activity. More than just a particular game or an activity adopted for the moment, play is their entire style. Imagine the difference in a lesson on music history:

a. You stand in front of the room and play the same four bars of music on the violin in a classical style, then a Romantic style, and then a "modern" style—and ask students to point out the differences.

b. You play a boring/flat version of those four bars and then ask the students to give you suggestions for how to play it in a Romantic style, and you try out all the suggestions you get. After a lot of suggestions, you play four bars of Sibelius and ask what choices both the students, in their four bars, and Sibelius, in his, made as composers. Then play four bars of Mozart as boringly as you can and ask the students to transform that passage into four bars that sound like Wolfgang's.

Etymologically, the word *play* derives from the words meaning "quick movement for recreation or joy." Good teaching artists infuse their work with this energy and prioritize intentional fun. These are some of the tools they use:

- *Guessing games:* "What emotion am I feeling when I play the piece this way, and what do you hear in the music that gives you that impression?"
- *Secrets:* "Let us guess the three kinds of left-hand accompaniment written on your hidden card, by the way you play the air piano."
- *Hard challenges:* Start with a simple call-and-response format with a rhythmic pattern to clap and escalate to more and more difficult clapping challenges. Composer Tom Cabaniss (who led the teaching artist program when he was education director of the New York Philharmonic) has his recorder beginners turn their backs to a lead player and try to match the note sequence without looking until everyone has it right.

- *Body language and role play:* "Reenter the room one at a time, and in the way you move, try to capture the feel of the music I am playing," or "Write a dialogue that captures as much of the feel of the 'argument' between the two instruments as you can."
- *Playful formats:* Give instructions without saying a word, hide something, keep a top hat with ideas to draw from it, make whopping mistakes yourself, make a phrase go faster and faster, and so on.
- *Adapting known games:* Play charades, Family Feud, copy cat, or "May I?" Or try pretend arguments, interviews, and so on.

Good teaching artists inject playfulness into everything they do, even into performance settings. For example, violist Rachel Shapiro was performing a composition exercise for a middle school audience. She was eliciting good subjects from students, and one student suggested: President Bush choking on a pretzel while watching television. Deciding to go with the unexpected idea, Rachel challenged herself and her audience to create such a piece, with hilarious results.

When Misty Tolle was performing with Ariel Winds, the ensemble would explore each instrument's timbre with elementary school students and then test kids' ability to identify the instruments in a game. She would announce, "In this next piece, it will look like all five of us are playing, but in fact only three of us will be playing our instruments. At the end, you can tell us who was playing and who was faking." The musicians would ham it up, some pretending to play while three actually played; the entire time, the kids were listening hard and pointing out to one another who they thought was playing or faking. To wrap up the activity, the teaching artists listened to the students' guesses and reasons and reviewed the timbres of all five instruments.

Students, like most people, pour their best energy into their play. The pace quickens, and the stakes change. Play encourages risk taking, eases the pressure of challenges that demand right answers which dominate the schoolday. Playfulness allows the generative thinking of multiple-right-answer suggestions and the examination of the quality of ideas rather than their correctness. In play, surprise, cleverness, coolness, funniness, beauty, and so forth, become highly valued attributes. Learners naturally make decisions based on these criteria when playing seriously. It is useful to unpack their ideas sometimes—"What made us laugh at that musical phrase?" "Why is it more interesting to have the melody go like this than like that?"

Play is powerful because it feels good—we naturally like to do it. Very different stakes emerge in play—we engage in it for its own sake, not for a payoff for having done it. Art (not necessarily artistic media, but the art experience) is based in the pleasure principle, and part of our challenge is to expand the repertoire of experiences that give pleasure to our future audiences, so they can discover the joys of Bach and Bartók, along with the easy play of pop music.

When we work, we feel we've succeeded when we perform a feat without any mistakes. When we play, we feel successful if we experience a few momentary highs, have some great laughs, or come up with one or two original ideas. The relation of effort to failure eases in play—there is less fear, more freedom to experiment and be different. Play loves bloopers and holds the healthy attitude toward them that (1) there is no such thing as a mistake, and (2) something good can come from every one; sometimes they are actually huge successes. Honor this truth by celebrating "mistakes" and by avoiding questions and challenges that have single, correct answers. With some classes I develop a practice of awarding a prize for the best mistake of the day, and kids can't wait to nominate their own whoppers.

People play only when they are inwardly motivated to do so. You can make someone join a game and follow the rules, but you can't make someone experience play. Teaching artists are good at creating experiential invitations that are so appealing that participants can't resist joining in.

Creating a play atmosphere is the key. If you can accomplish that, then almost anything you do within it becomes serious play, even activities that do not seem very playful. Once you have created an atmosphere, learners will play with you and come up with playful ideas—"Could we see what happens to the sound if you circle around while you perform?" I recall seeing two members of the Chiara Quartet working with a group of inner-city fifth graders. One student asked if the ensemble members would switch instruments, viola and cello, and try to play them. These fine musicians looked at each other, part horror and part amusement on their faces. They said, "Why not?" The next five minutes were delightful and so illuminating about musicians and music that I remember it ten years later.

We foster a playful atmosphere in two ways: (1) Honoring the law of 80% (80% of what you teach is who you are). If exploring music fills you with a sense of adventure and delight, others will join. If you genuinely want to play around in music with your audience members or students—discovering what *they* can do and *they* can hear—they will come to meet you. (2) Nurturing the sense of play constantly, even in small ways. A good teaching artist begins with small games or playful moments, within boundaries that entice interest, control energy, and build trust. This may be a quick clapping game warm-up or making funny sounds to practice the canon form—so the learners understand they can pour in their energy and have fun yet remain in control.

In the school setting, engaging in playful activities can be a delicate business. In a number of ways it is risky for both teacher and students, who are used to certain behavioral norms, rules for success, and learning practices. In interacting with the classroom teacher, be sensitive to the discomfort (and adjustments to previously made agreements) that increased focus on play may bring up. Such issues need to be addressed openly and resolved mutually. For the students, being asked to play rather than work in school upsets norms and makes some kids anxious; some may lose control. Indeed, part of the capacity to play is to be able to tolerate uncertainty; students have different comfort levels with this challenge. Anxiety may appear in students wanting to clarify a plan before an improv, or constantly checking and rigidly adhering to the rules of a game. Be sensitive to the level of anxiety this will bring up for some. Others, of course, will grab the opportunity to play, to figure things out as they go.

Boundaries are a big part of playing. If the instructions are too complex or overly rigid, they squeeze out the play, requiring compliance rather than invention; if too loose, they can elicit caution or produce chaos. The ideal instructions are instantly clear and so interesting that they make people want to join in. This is why adapting known formats—TV game shows, interviews, situations to enact, or familiar kids' games—often work so well. In play there is a lot of showing off and overt acknowledging of creative accomplishment. We laugh and applaud and interject naturally when the student thinks up a rhythmic pattern we never would have imagined. It is important to reflect upon these moments of delight-filled achievement. In "serious work" we celebrate accuracy, virtuosity, and capacity. In play we can celebrate idiosyncrasy, originality, eccentricity— the artist's essentials. This shift in value and recognition is greatly empowering for many students, especially those who feel they do not shine as the "smart" kids do when judged by the measures schools use to determine "success."

You may recall that I believe the ultimate benefit of developing education skills is that they make you a better artist. The commitment to and attitude of play is one of the power tools that applies most directly to a musician's life. Can you bring a wider range of experimentation to your ensemble's rehearsals to deepen and expand interpretation—ever try singing a difficult passage with your ensemble, in different musical styles, just to see what you get? Can you increase playfulness in your practice time? Can you devise ways to boost creative risk taking, productive messing around? Can you add more "quick movement for recreation or joy" to the atmosphere and daily work of being a twenty-first-century musician? As the Greek philosopher Heraclitus wrote 2,500 years ago, "Man is most nearly himself when he achieves the seriousness of a child at play."

Let's close this chapter on play with a great example of how play can infuse a serious musical lesson (Box 10.1). This activity is designed and led by composer and teaching artist Daniel Levy. He calls it "Mozart's Balloons." He has used this activity—a preparatory workshop before a performance of Mozart's Trio for Clarinet, Piano and Viola in E-flat Major—with groups of students from kindergarten age through grad school. It is an elegantly fun way to heighten listeners' awareness of the interplay of one theme among three instruments.

BOX 10.1 **Mozart's Balloons**

Line of Inquiry: What kinds of choices are involved when three musicians carry one tune?

Materials: CD with excerpts of specific themes and textures

Warm-Up / Sing Movement 1, THEME A [15 Min.]

How can we best describe Mozart's tune?

- Around the circle. All lead a physical warm-up; as we do so, THEME A plays over and over.
- Sing the tune, draw the tune.
- Note characteristics of the tune.

Carrying Balloons [30 Min.]

How can three people carry a balloon?

- Two tables 30 feet apart. One student moves a balloon from table to table. Another does it another way. Two students move a balloon from table to table. Another pair do it another way. Three students move a balloon from table to table. Another trio do it another way. "What have we been doing?" [10 min.]
- Trios of students plan a way to carry a balloon across the space and take turns demonstrating their ideas. Students notice and chart ways that three can work together. [15 min.]
- Optional extension: Each member of each trio must add a significant physical constraint (e.g., can only go on one leg; feet must never leave the floor; must have eyes closed) and adjust the plan of carrying. Show. Students notice and chart

ways that three musicians can work together. Trios explain how the constraints affected their plans and choices. [5 min.]

Trio-fication of a Single Tune [15 Min.]

How can we apply our knowledge of collaborative trios to Mozart's tune?

- All students sing the THEME A tune again.
- What are the possibilities with clarinet, viola, and piano? What are the limits of the instruments? How would you have these three instruments work together to play the tune? Describe and draw a "score" with representative marks and shapes on large paper. [15 min.]

Listening to Mozart [15 Min.]

What choices did Mozart make in setting his tune for three musicians?

- Listen to THEME A on CD
- What do you notice?
- Compare with a second setting of the tune.
- As we listen, compare Mozart's choice with our choices. Listen again as needed to support clarity and specificity in students' observations.
- What questions do we have right now about Mozart and this piece of music?

Source: Daniel Levy, composer and teaching artist (Lincoln Center Institute, Carnegie Hall, 92nd Street Y); http://www.daniellevymusic.com.

Part III Learning to Be a Teaching Artist

11

The Entry Point Question
Where to Begin?

Onstage, the string quartet is performing a complex musical work, say Beethoven's Quartet in F Major (op. 59, no. 1). In the audience is an adult who doesn't know much about classical music and has never heard a string quartet perform before.

> *The goal:* to help that person get inside that piece of music in a way that she finds meaningful.
>
> *The challenge:* to get beyond mere information delivery, a common enough approach and one that may help the unsophisticated listener admire the work from the outside, but one that doesn't tap the work's power from within or invite in the less-experienced listener.
>
> *The solution:* apply the *engagement before information* guideline, which requires selecting an entry point—a particular aesthetic feature of the music—that will draw the listener into the piece.

Sometimes it's easier to grasp a concept from the distance of another art form, so let me introduce the term *entry point* through theater, the artistic discipline I studied and lived for decades.

David Shookhoff (my first teacher at Lincoln Center Institute back in the late 1970s and now director of education at Manhattan Theatre Club in New York) illuminated the entry point concept for me on my first day. In a workshop for prospective teaching artists of all artistic disciplines, he demonstrated how to introduce inexperienced theatergoers to a complex play by leading us through a preparation for Shakespeare's *Macbeth*. He didn't pick ten important ideas of the play to tell us about; he didn't have us read from the play; he didn't even teach us about a few key characteristics of Shakespearean drama (such as iambic pentameter or soliloquy structure). Instead, he took a central question dramatized in the play and created an experiential way for us to explore its relevance to our lives. That question was: How far are you willing to go, how many of your principles will you compromise or violate, to get what you want?

David created a game for the workshop participants. It involved drawing cards that told us to improvise certain scenes at various stations around the room, which was configured like a game board. To get to our goal, we had to choose whether or not to betray a friend, tell public lies, commit murder (all of which are, of course, actions that occur in Shakespeare's play). At various points, he stopped us midaction and asked us to articulate our choices and to explain how we justified them. Sometimes he raised the stakes—to prove that some people were willing to go to extremes to gain a compelling reward. After reflecting upon what we had chosen, and after he had guided us through a consideration of the underlying moral questions, we went to see *Macbeth*. The play bloomed with new resonance for me (a longtime theater artist), as well as for the musicians and dancers and the first-time Shakespeare viewers in the group. I came away brimming with eagerness to read the play again to see how Shakespeare had pulled it off. I walked to the theater with a dancer who had never seen a Shakespearean tragedy, and we talked as equal colleagues, despite our differing expertise.

David taught me the power of selecting a single entry point—not several entry points, not a responsible array that "covers" the most important elements of the piece. He gambled all his teaching chips on one key feature, the metaphoric heart of the artwork under study. Then he led us through that entry point, into the world of that artwork, experientially, not didactically. Those are the keys: select *one* crucial entry point that lies at the heart of what you care about in the work of art, and invite people in *experientially*.

Entry points can also be effective in everyday life to transform dull encounters into lively personal connections. Here is an example from my life. I was at brunch with some friends of my wife's, a couple who were quite formal in their manner. We were all being polite, but the event wasn't clicking—basically it was dullsville, and I was just pleasantly waiting it out, enjoying the food more than the talk. The woman asked me to tell her about my last book, *The Everyday Work of Art*. I have a few standard answers, honed through the endless marketing process, but I knew that prepared material, even if fairly snappy, would kill further conversation on that topic. I took a chance. Instead of the standard gambits, I asked her, "What is the one thing that can happen in your day that elevates a good day into a great day?" She went with it, replying that it was having an exciting conversation with a friend or coworker. I asked her to name a few features that make for a conversation like that. She had some answers, the ones you'd expect—about content and feelings. She was growing leery of my personal, and seemingly evasive, interrogation. I said, "Here's my last question, to answer your original question: 'What are some of the things you find yourself doing differently in a great conversation than in the ordinary or good?'" She blinked as she faced the entry point I had offered. And then she moved forward. Reflecting, she found some new words and new thoughts to describe an experience that is important in her life, freshly rediscovered. I thanked her and said, "What you just did as you answered that last question—that is what my book is about." Her husband later e-mailed me to tell me that she made him stop at a bookstore on the way home to get a copy of the book because she was so curious to find out more.

All I did was take a chance on a single entry point, invite her to enter experientially with three questions, and point out the relevance of the activity. And grab a buck or two of royalties.

In music performance situations, we rarely have the opportunity to lead a preconcert workshop that would be the musical equivalent of David Shookhoff's *Macbeth* preparation. But these limitations make having an entry point even more critical to the audience experience. If listeners make a personal connection—if they feel successful and satisfied inside the music—they'll come back. If not, they may not. And we can't afford to miss a single chance.

The entry-point decision determines the focus and feel of the program, so it has to be good. It has to be true to the piece, effective at opening up the work, exciting for you and fun for all. I am often asked how to select an entry point. The selection process is itself a work of art. We need to line up three elements: First, reconnect with the work of art yourself, listen again, and notice what excites you in the piece. Look for elements that turn you on, at this time in your life, as an exciting element of that work. Second, pick one of those aesthetic features you loved that you have a strong hunch will also be exciting for the particular group you will be working with. You can't pick a subtle technical element if you are working with a general audience because the entry point won't be exciting for them. Third, you must pick a feature at the heart of the work, and one that is appropriate to the setting you will have. This third consideration prevents picking an interesting but esoteric idea as the invitation in, and prevents your picking one that jars with the point of the event. If the first two requirements—that it is *hot* for you, and you believe it will be engaging for your audience—line up, the third considerations usually present no concern. (The third angle reminds you not to select a topic like sensuality for a seventh-grade class, even though that entry point might be exiting for you and those students.)

I asked a few experienced colleagues to identify a work they would like to have on a program, and what a good entry point for that piece might be. Look closely into their ideas.

Kelly Dylla (a violist, teaching artist, and now a University of Michigan M.B.A. graduate entrepreneur) took on the second movement of Beethoven's op. 59, no. 1. Eight minutes of string quartet music is complex stuff; there are probably ten good entry points she might have chosen. She picked the simple rhythmic pattern established in the first two seconds of the piece. She gambled that if listeners were on top of that musical idea, and were allowed to play with it creatively under her guidance, they would discover how it is used throughout the piece, and consequently many of Beethoven's choices would be revealed. Kelly's plan involved teaching the group the pattern and giving them a number of rhythmic challenges to solve (challenges Beethoven takes on in the composition) before they listened to the piece.

Richard Mannoia (clarinetist and teaching artist with the New York Philharmonic, 92nd Street Y, and other programs) said that Bela Bartók's Contrasts—a hefty mid-twentieth-century work for piano, violin, and clarinet—is something he would love to work on with an audience. His proposed entry point? The work's color palette. He would design activities that explored the work's unusual tonal range, spotlight key phrases, and have the audience try out some of the tools Bartók exploited as he pushed tones to expressive extremes to sharpen the audience's recognition of those unusual tone colors when they appeared.

Airi Yoshioka (teaching artist, violinist with the Damocles Trio, and faculty member at the University of Maryland, Baltimore County) came up with four good ideas. She first picked the first movement of one of her all-time favorite chamber pieces, the Schubert Cello Quintet, op. 163. She noted that some of its soaring, expansive melodies could serve as entry points themselves. But more effective, she felt, would be the various forms of accompaniment that enhance the melodies and give them impetus. A few accompaniments to the second theme are three triplets arriving on an eighth (in soft dynamic, they give a bouncy quality), two eighths and a quarter (grounding), and continuous arpeggiated sixteenth notes. Each figure adds a different emotional sheen and propulsion to the melody, and it is illuminating to explore how each one works. Airi thought she might take this approach one step further. Since some of the figures are used simultaneously, the musicians and audience could experiment with various combinations and note their impact.

Airi also mentioned an eight-week project she had done with public school second graders. All activities were based on Beethoven's op. 122A, Ten Variations on Wenzel Müller's song "Ich Bin der Schneider Kakadu," for piano, violin, and cello. The piece is an accessible work with a jovial and lighthearted theme and ten clearly articulated variations. She made up words to go with the tune, and the children were asked to compose a set of five variations of their own—and even got to rehearse these with Airi's piano trio. After working on some revisions, they were rewarded with a performance of their work. According to Airi, the same project could readily be adapted to an interactive concert. The words she made up in the classroom to go with the melody could also be used to quickly teach the tune in a concert setting. Before hearing Beethoven's rendition, the audience could develop variations of character and emotion and articulate how each instrument should play them.

Airi also thought that the first movement of Zoltán Kodály's Duo for Violin and Cello is a perfect piece for investigating how two voices converse. The instruments' dialogue can be seen as question-and-answer, unison statements, disagreements, taunting, approaching, and moving apart. The entry point is clear in the music and invites entertaining and illuminating preparatory activities in conversational composition.

Airi also referred to her work with Mendelssohn's Octet. The layering of instrumental timbres is her entry to the fourth movement (presto). First she introduces the audience to a melody played by each instrument. Then she experiments with the overall effect, as when all instruments are playing the same thing, or when some are together and some not. She moves from there to show how to create different effects through layering.

Edward Bilous was interested in subtle colors of Elliott Carter's *Eight Etudes for Woodwind Quartet*—in his view, the best piece ever written for this configuration. One movement (less than two minutes long) consists of the group playing a single pitch: A 440, as he recalls. Because each player fades in and out at different times, the timbre of the note keeps changing. Also, since the piece is played without any sense of rhythm or meter, the very essence of the piece is color. He would love to prepare an audience to receive this work by engaging them in experimentation around this idea.

Last year, flautist Tanya Witek and her colleagues in the Teaching Artist Ensemble of the New York Philharmonic performed a slightly abridged version of Maurice Ravel's *Introduction and Allegro* (for harp, string quartet, flute, and clarinet) at their in-school concerts. Before the ensemble performed the entire work, students had the chance to listen to some sample backgrounds and excerpts and to orchestrate their own miniversions of portions of the piece. Ravel's way of blending timbres made a rewarding entry point because it is a sophisticated and rich concept that enables the listener to continually discover new combinations. This entry point also invites visual awareness—it can be difficult to tell which instruments are blending without looking at the performers.

Tom Cabaniss (a composer and former animateur at the Philadelphia Orchestra) told me of his beloved String Quartet no. 12 in C minor, D. 703, "Quartettsatz," by Schubert. One of the work's signature traits is its astonishing variety of musical densities, each used for a specific expressive purpose. Tom aspired to draw attention to Schubert's endless ingenuity by engaging listeners in a series of activities that explore the capacity of a small group to express strong emotions through differing density of sound. He thought he might start with one voice, add in one more at a time; then begin again with all the voices, subtracting one at a time; then use two versus two, ending with four voices together.

Do those fine examples give you some leads for choices you might make? Here are the guidelines I use to determine a good entry point—some already mentioned—and they are presented in order of priority, most important first:

• Pick an entry point you love. The best entry point is the one that is hottest for you, right now at this moment, in your musical and personal life. The relevance for you will enliven the whole of the event for us, including the information about the piece or yourself you may choose to share along the way. Your personal aliveness to this aesthetic feature will make it hard for others to resist crossing the great divide and entering into the piece. The entry point need not be one of the "most important elements" that musicologists would cite, but it also shouldn't be a completely peripheral notion.

• Pick an entry point that you that believe is going to be genuinely exciting and personally relevant to your audience. A clever use of retrograde in a piece may excite you, but select an entry point that you are willing to gamble will grab your audience where they live. The whole point is to support the likelihood that they will be able to make deeper personal connections inside the music, not that they will be able to identify more musical elements at work. Remember too that audiences differ—select an entry point specific to the specific audience. There is a big difference between a family audience and a Saturday night season subscription audience. There is a big difference between a second-grade audience, a sixth-grade audience, a tenth-grade audience, and a mixed-grade audience. (For those who quail at the mixed audience challenge—sophisticated and new adult listeners at the same time, or second graders and sixth graders at the same performance—keep an eye on this. That is a challenge I face on every page of this book. I am writing for an audience that includes America's best teaching artists, which makes them about the best teaching artists in the world, and those who are barely beginners, at the same time. I don't claim I am succeeding well in this challenge, but I am addressing it and giving it my best shot on every page—so keep an occasional eye on how I am doing.) A good entry point is selected and investigated for that particular audience.

• Pick an entry point that has the dual character of being specific enough to allow audience members a satisfying grasp through your experiential invitations, and concurrently has a connection to a rich and rewarding underlying concept. We hope the investment in the entry point will support their making fresh connections throughout the piece. It must be experientially graspable in an efficient way and must connect to something that matters deeply in the piece. This seeming paradox is what allows experts and beginners to be successful in the same room at the same time. For example, if I were preparing both Shakespeare scholars and Shakespeare-phobes to see *Hamlet*, I might ask everyone to remember a time they faced a personal moral dilemma. I might have them write down the two voices of that dilemma, arguing as a thought debate in their heads, and then read through an internal debate soliloquy of Hamlet's. The hope is that the activity enables both audiences to enter the piece more deeply from where they begin—the experts bring new personal nuance from the lens of their own experience, the beginners have some ways to hang in with a sense of what Hamlet is doing even as they sometimes lose their way in the language.

• Pick an entry point that is engaging, and perhaps even a little surprising.

12

A Teaching Artist's Curriculum

deal. Doesn't the word have a nice ring to it? "What would be the ideal way to learn something you care about?" Just considering such a question begins to make me happy. Of course, we rarely get to live in an ideal anything, but conjuring the ideal can clarify what we aspire to.

What would be the ideal curriculum for training a music teaching artist? In a best of all possible worlds, what would that young musician study to develop her educator's skills along with her artistic skills? The nationwide trend, widely referred to as "the professionalization of the teaching artist," invites us to consider the development of those skills and even indulge in the luxury of considering what might work best.

Almost all music teaching artists feel they have been thrust into the work before they are adequately prepared. Indeed, many feel they have had almost no training at all, and have to learn how to swim after being thrown into the water—deep water, and it feels like sharks are around, even if those sharks are actually a roomful of cute third graders.

The less-than-ideal real-world training curriculum for music teaching artists is always constrained by time—how ideal can you get when you have two professional development days a year, or several half days, or some other limitation that makes it hard to even cover the basics? Teaching artist training as a part of conservatory training offers more time to approach the ideal because courses can be offered—such classes are slowly becoming more available to music students in many music programs.

I got to develop such a training in the luxury of the Art and Education/ Morse Fellowship program at Juilliard for a number of years. Pretty close to an ideal situation—students in a three-credit-per-semester course for a full classroom year, with projects and practice in schools. Plus, a subsequent year for most as Morse Fellows practicing their skills in public school classrooms for a year and getting a reasonable stipend in the process. As I write this, I am designing and launching a new teaching artist training program at the Meadows School of the Arts at Southern Methodist University; it also includes an in-depth partnership/internship with Big Thought, a remarkable arts education organization in Dallas, so it too is close to ideal.

I am often asked to share the curriculum I developed to train those emerging teaching artists at Juilliard and Meadows. The students at both schools were fine musicians (and Meadows also includes actors, dancers, and visual artists) who were also committed to developing education skills. Many of those Juilliard graduates are now making their mark on the world as artists and teaching artists. Some have moved into arts learning administration and now lead major organizations.

In this chapter, I will lay out the basics of the Juilliard curriculum, which was unprecedented in its depth at that time. The Meadows curriculum is derived from it, but it is still too new to affirm its effectiveness. Stay tuned. I certainly don't suggest other programs need to adopt this approach; successful curricula are local and refined to fit the particulars of the setting and students. I hope the following description sparks some ideas you can adapt to your own ongoing learning. You may not be in the ideal learning situation, but you can learn from those who were lucky enough to forge this learning curriculum over time.

First let me thank my longtime colleague at Juilliard, Edward Bilous, who brought me in to Juilliard to co-teach the Art and Education course with him fourteen years ago. He had created and nurtured it, and he still teaches it there, in a one-semester intensive. The curriculum I share here grew during the years I led the program by myself, experimenting every year. I also want to thank David Wallace (one of the first graduates of that program, and now a leader in the teaching artist field, as well as a coauthor of chapter 26 of this book), who now teaches his own one-semester version at Juilliard of the course I will describe in this chapter. These colleagues are building upon and developing the ideas I offer here.

The Art and Education course was a yearlong, three-credit-per-semester course totaling twenty-eight class meetings and some outside projects. Its approach was based largely on principles of aesthetic education, which I had learned at Lincoln Center Institute. It was a graduate-level elective (although we found ways for motivated undergraduates to join), and it averaged an enrollment of about twelve to eighteen students. Up to ten students were awarded a Morse Fellowship (endowed by the generous support of Lester and Dinny Morse) in the year after their classroom year, based on their skill and readiness to take on the challenge. This paid fellowship placed them in two classrooms in New York City elementary schools, to visit the same students every week all year long. They had to develop curricula week after week, plan and coordinate with the teacher, and write up their lesson plans, and they were observed several times. The students who completed the fellowship left their two-year cycle (or more; a number of students were Morse Fellows for two to four years as their Juilliard studies move through a D.M.A. degree) with their skills fully ready for a career brimming with teaching artistry. Within those two years of in-depth thinking and practice, they forged a true and deep set of skills—I called them samurai teaching artists, who were able to enter any setting, from a kindergarten classroom to a corporate boardroom, and advance the music learning effectively.

Rather than write down a dull class-by-class syllabus, I will give you the general shape of the curriculum, including five key ideas that made the course unusual.

Work in other disciplines.   We began as learners in unfamiliar disciplines to refresh our sense of what it is like to enter a new art form. The first five weeks were led by teaching artists of disciplines other than music. Each week we learned as novices, going through the anxiety, embarrassment, and delight at small successes that count so much for beginners. We took a lot of time to reflect on each experience and detail the impact of the choices and style of the teaching artist: How did that work for us as learners? What are the most effective ways to engage, encourage, surprise, delight, challenge, and guide people new to an art form?

A set of essential guidelines.   From the explorations in other art forms, we developed a small set of effective working principles that we applied, and experimented with, throughout the rest of the year—and the rest of our teaching artist lives. Yes, those guidelines looked a lot like the set I introduced to you in chapter 3.

Work with reality.   We focused on the five most common kinds of teaching artist employment opportunities and addressed how our working guidelines applied in each: preparing people (students or grown-ups) to attend and make personally relevant connections inside a live musical performance; teaching about musical issues without a performance; creating interactive concerts; designing a skill-building sequence of lessons (including private lessons); and presenting lecture-demonstrations. In later years we also addressed the challenge of the arts-integrated lesson (when music is taught in conjunction with another subject, like history), which we will explore in chapter 20.

Hands-on practice.   When it comes to learning, theory is one thing, doing is another. We practiced what we theorized and found out how hard it can be to do what we come to understand as great teaching artistry. I always enjoyed the wave of belated appreciation for just how good the teaching artists they worked with in the initial weeks of the class really were. "They made it look so easy."

Context counts.   We needed to know something about learning theory, about American attitudes toward art, about schools, about the job climate, all of which inform the way we guide musical learning. And we needed to develop habits of lifelong learning as teaching artists: How do we keep ourselves learning in a field that offers little support?

First Semester

The first day I began with this challenge: "Give me one good reason an inner-city fifth grader should give a damn about Mozart." I always got a snort of derisive laughter—how could this guy (who is not even a musician!) even think such a thing? After a pause, I got an answer like: "OK, he is only the greatest genius in all human history." I responded: "Maybe so, but not to that kid." Another offered three reasons based on Mozart's contributions to music. I answered, "It may be true that he invented all those musical ideas, which we still use today, but to that kid he wrote tinkly little stupid music." A long pause. Someone offered, "Here it is. I would say, 'When Mozart was your age, he wrote the following symphony.'" From me: "Oh, so now the kid thinks, 'Someone my age wrote that endless boring stupid music. Big deal.'" A long, ugly silence ensued, as students realized they couldn't think of a single reason Mozart might be relevant to a twenty-first-century ten-year-old. And then we began our curriculum to discover how we can open up the relevance, the joy, the richness of Mozart to that kid, to everyone.

We began with our explorations in other art forms. Guest teaching artists led classes in which we learned the basics of choreography by creating small dances, and then we viewed dances and pointed out choices and successes and surprises. We unpacked a complex Shakespeare poem with an actor, acted in improvisations, and then directed professional actors. We made drawings that related to masterworks and spent ninety minutes looking into one Matisse painting. We wrote creative sentences and lines of poetry in relation to famous writing.

This series of activities served to do more than raise our anxiety, build our courage, and bond us as a group of brave learners; the work in other disciplines reminded us of what it feels like to experience something for the first time. We rediscovered how scary it can be, how tiny bits of learning and simple successes can feel powerful, and how we were able to perceive so much more in masterworks of that discipline after we had explored with our own hands. For example, the five-minute modern dance was attractive when we saw it at the beginning of the class; we were impressed by the dancers and the cool moves; we *liked* it. Then we worked with the dance teaching artist for forty minutes, using our own bodies to create choreography, making choices, and seeing the variety of choices our colleagues made, which were related to some of the same issues the choreographer was dealing with in dance we watched. Then we watched the five-minute dance again and were astonished to discover how rich and thrilling it now seemed. We *loved* it; we *got* it. We hadn't talked about the dance at all, but through our participation, even at our rudimentary level as total beginners, it bloomed with meaning and satisfaction.

At the end of each class, we reflected in detail on our learning experiences: How had the teaching artist worked with us? What techniques and moments had been effective for us and why? How had he created that safe-yet-charged atmosphere? Then we carefully applied each of the pedagogical lessons we had just learned in another art form to our challenge in music: What would that approach look like in music? How could you engage people in that kind of learning experience in music? So that at the end of our five weeks of experimentation outside of music, we had a fully developed palette of teaching tools and their impact, based in our gut experience, as well as a rich brainstorming of ideas for engaging people musically.

We then had two weeks of demonstrations of excellent teaching artist practice in music. I would bring in my star former students or colleagues I had worked with for years (especially Edward Bilous). We followed the same pattern of experience, reflection, and analysis to clarify their techniques as teaching artists and the impact of their many choices on us, the learners.

Context

We then spent several weeks looking into context. We explored the history of American arts education, the current standing and trends of the arts themselves (with research), the realities and trends in American education (we had a school principal visit, and often a school music teacher). We addressed two overlooked parts of most teaching artist training: (1) Understanding what a teacher's and student's school day is really like (Morse Fellows had to spend a preparatory day following a teacher around to see what her day was like—most students were shocked at how tiring and complex a day is for teachers, and had to rush home at three o'clock to take a nap). (2) Understanding what music teachers do, and what the teaching artist's particular and complementary role can be to maximize the partnership for the benefit of the students.

We began our readings of selections from important texts: *Multiple Intelligences*, by Howard Gardner; *The Intelligent Eye*, by David Perkins; *The Power of Mindful Learning*, by Ellen Langer; *The Courage to Teach*, by Parker Palmer; *Renaissance in the Classroom*, edited by Gail Burnaford, Arnold Aprill, and Cynthia Weiss; and, yes, my book, *The Everyday Work of Art*. We culminated this study with a formal debate, pro and con, as to whether the arts should be central in the schooling of every American child. (Most years the con argument won the debate, and we were infuriated that it had the better case—making us more committed pros.)

We rounded out the first semester with some practice. We focused on the key teaching artist guidelines distilled from our investigations in other art forms: engagement before information, tapping competence, using entry points, infusing reflection, scaffolding step-by-step success, giving clear instructions. Sound familiar? Students had a project to design lessons that included at least two of the pedagogical techniques we experienced this semester. We had students lead the class in warm-up activities. We practiced listening to musical samples and discovering good entry points for each.

One of our activities for doing this was to listen to the same piece (or segment of it) three times, taking notes on what we noticed during each listening, as ourselves, a ten-year-old, and an adult with no music background. We then looked for the key aesthetic feature of the piece to focus on as an entry point—a feature that turns on the musically sophisticated Juilliard student and that is also graspable by a kid or inexperienced adult—and design ways to experientially (not by *telling* about it) draw that youngster (or adult) into greater awareness of that musical feature through our activities. We extended our practice a bit by listening to some recorded student compositions to sharpen our perception of what students were working on and discovering in their compositions—taking seriously the efforts of beginners, believing they have valid, interesting musical ideas to share even without the use of standard musical notation. (Let me parenthetically address a big issue about which there is some debate in the field: standard notation. Of course teaching artists value and want to nurture literacy in standard notation—when students' musical ideas and curiosity are complex enough that standard notation helps them communicate what they have to say. I don't believe in postponing the musical exploring and creative success that is possible without knowing standard notation for them to learn it first. I think musical language works like foreign language—we learn it fastest and most excitedly when we are actively immersed in the life of it, not as an exercise apart from its vitality and relevance. Yes, teach standard notation at the teachable moment, but no, don't postpone the excitement until a level of mastery is attained.)

In addition to the classroom work, the Juilliard students had two hands-on projects I described earlier: the conversation on a New York City public bus, and the plan to bring a family classical-music-avoider a little bit further into it.

There were some quizzes along the way, to make sure students were keeping up with the reading and to provoke them to apply it to their own thinking. And the first semester's final "exam" was to design a lesson plan, using as many aspects of our learning as possible. There were three musical examples for students to choose from to design their lessons, demonstrating understanding of the guidelines in as many ways as possible.

Second Semester

The second semester started with school issues. We studied arts integration—ways to authentically connect learning in music with learning in other subject areas without diluting the musical engagement. We studied assessment strategies and possibilities, and national and state standards. We looked into partnering with educators and leading effective planning meetings.

We then had two more detailed demonstrations of exemplary practice around using homemade instruments and guiding students in composition. As always, we took time to reflect on the pedagogy we were experiencing, to elicit tools and mind-sets that constitute strong teaching. We invested two class periods picking apart some of the technical details of teaching artist practice: maintaining classroom control, giving clear instructions, bringing variety to a lesson, managing group dynamics, and leading effective discussions with students and nonmusician adults.

Early in the second semester we began our hands-on work too. In pairs, students had to plan a forty-minute lesson for a particular age-group and lead their colleagues in our class in a fifteen-minute sliver of it. We gave lots of feedback about their work—the clarity, impact, and artistic challenges of it. Students also made an appointment to watch a Morse Fellow lead two classes in their public school setting, and they wrote an analytic paper about what they observed. Students also had to interview a grade school student for half an hour about her musical life, her interests and understandings. Finally, students had to co-teach a class in a school with a Morse Fellow and write a self-assessment paper about innate strengths and skill/understanding areas that need development.

Around midsemester, we looked to the real world. We had a visit from a professional teaching artist trainer and several professional TAs to talk about the realities of the profession, about résumés, and about various kinds of music education programs. We addressed the musician as presenter, ambassador, public figure. We explored how to advocate effectively. We looked into the preparation of public education materials—what makes guidebooks effective, promotional materials compelling? We considered traditional and more imaginative ways to present and market oneself as a teaching artist. We looked into the design of education concerts and interactive concerts, looking at videotaped segments and talking through the basic design features. We brainstormed about the ways our teaching artist knowledge could enrich private lessons and lecture-demonstrations. With so many topics to address, we did little more than skim a number of them. How often I wished for a second classroom year to do every aspect justice.

Students were given a final assignment to design an interactive concert—one that includes music and dialogue—with a fun and rich educational component. They had to present a ten-minute "pitch" to the Centralia Missouri Arts Council (the rest of the class) about why their interactive concert should be included in the coming season of public offerings. Our class feedback addressed not only the program and education components but also the presentation skills—we took time to explore what makes a sales pitch work.

In our final class, we had an open dialogue about the relationship between the skills of a teaching artist and the skills of a musician. By this point, all had found the hoped-for synergy—discovering the individual ways in which these skills blend and support one another. And we ended back at the beginning—exploring the ways in which an inner-city fifth grader might discover the relevance of Mozart. We had a lot to say at this point. We knew we couldn't *tell* those kids what was relevant (relevance is only discovered, not taught), but we did know a lot of ways, musically authentic, exciting ways, we could explore with that kid so that we all find relevance anew in any rich musical exploration.

13

What Does "Better"
Look Like?

How did you learn to ride a bike? You may not recall your learning process, but here are a few things you probably *didn't* do along the way. You didn't get on, ride a few yards, get off, and then have an adult give you a long verbal analysis of how you had performed. You didn't read an instruction booklet on bike riding. You didn't even talk with your friends and figure it out in the tree house or your friend's bedroom. You certainly didn't do it at school to please the teacher.

You probably ached to learn how to ride a bike, nagging for that first two-wheeler. It took real courage to try, those first few scary times, but you were motivated. It was your first big personal freedom since walking, so, although you probably got some assistance and guidance from grown-ups, you got past that stage as quickly as possible. You learned by making knee-scraping mistakes and figuring out how to correct them, by doing, not by talking. You continued to improve, adding speed, distance, tricks, and other embellishments, discovering what "better" was in biking. You knew what better looked like by watching others—other kids, grown-ups who rode fast, trick riders, and clips of the Tour de France. You knew what great looked like, and you knew you were going to keep getting better.

They say you never forget how to ride a bike. After decades driving a motorized four-wheeler, you can still hop right on a Schwinn and get rolling. Some kinds of learning imprint for life.

The way musicians learn to play an instrument is a little different, but some things are the same. They don't read their way to competence; they learn by doing. And however much input they get from teachers, they still have to be self-motivated to sustain the skills acquired by practicing. They guide their own improvement to some degree and keep expanding their sense of "better."

Research on learning tells us that those natural ways of learning have intuitive wisdom. We learn best by doing, learning from mistakes and emulating those we care about and admire. Self-assessment is at least as important as being assessed by others. And learning requires internal motivation. Yes, "they" can make you do things that pass for learning (giving back information on command, performing the way they told you to, etc.), but *real* learning, making new connections and discoveries, only happens when you are personally invested.

What about education skills? How do teaching artists become effective teachers? Not as easily as they learned to ride a bike! Acquiring the necessary skills is a haphazard business at best. Most performing artists fall back on the same well-intentioned, but not-very-informed, educational practices that were visited upon them. I have heard many state defensively, "Hey, those methods aren't so bad; I came out okay, didn't I?" Yes, they did come out okay, but the challenge is greater now; we need to more fully engage a public that may not be inclined to care about our music. We need to turn on a public that has less interest and patience for the journey of mastering an instrument, and less public visibility and acclaim for examples of greatness. The radio (and television) program *From the Top*, which features young virtuoso musicians, provides a marvelous gift to classical music by showing delightful, accessible, accomplished youngsters modeling what is possible.

Few institutions offer relevant courses in pedagogy. (Note that by relevant pedagogy, we are not talking about programs that teach you how to be a school music teacher, but about skills that the teaching artist needs for opportunities such as workshops and residencies in schools, public preconcert events, community programs, family concerts, and public speaking during concerts, as well as private lessons, coaching, and classroom teaching.) Many conservatories and universities offer electives that address the skills needed to seize those opportunities and put them to good use. Such courses explore ways to effectively engage the public verbally and musically, to develop a lesson plan, to shape a workshop, to share musical ideas, to design an interactive concert, to script your speaking. There are places where teaching artists can take workshops or work in a program with a bit of training.

Still, teaching artists largely learn by doing. They must do this—because even after getting some training, each artist has to keep improving on her own, learning from her experiences and finding occasional support from books, colleagues, and education partners. There are few outward rewards for improved skills, so the passion to get better and better as an educator has to come from within. This can be tough when the money stays the same whether you are merely competent or brilliant, and in a cultural climate where education events are perceived to be of secondary importance. Most fields recognize greater skill with better pay. It sometimes takes heroic effort to remain motivated, because too many education situations can be uninspiring, repetitive, or downright draining.

As for feedback, there isn't much. Teaching artists rarely get thoughtful, consistent, supportive feedback from informed colleagues. Most professions develop ways to provide this essential component of continued improvement. Feedback from the learners themselves is usually a mishmash—from generic comments about how everyone loved it to remarks from the grouchy individual who didn't like what you did and who mouths off at length about your failures. So accurate self-assessment is crucial.

The field is beginning to address another key question: How can we get better if we don't know what better looks like? We rarely get to see great teaching artists in action. Sure, we can watch videotapes of Leonard Bernstein's Young People's Concerts (which were so effective that they turned on a whole generation of Americans), and we can see occasional star turns in master classes or movie clips. But the real work of teaching artists in classrooms, in senior centers, in workshops, is almost invisible to colleagues.

That's where mentoring and peer-observation programs come in, and these are becoming more numerous. Meanwhile, two national networks—Young Audiences and Crossing Paths—each created rubrics that directly address teaching artist practice. A rubric is a grid for self-assessment. In each case, teaching artists and program leaders of mixed artistic disciplines took eight critical aspects of teaching artistry (such as what you teach, group management, and interpersonal skills) and described what they look like at four different levels of development—from acceptable, to good, to excellent, to ideal.

Think of them as distillations of the distributed knowledge in the field; these rubrics describe what great practice looks like. They are the first to be crafted by large numbers of professionals. Young Audiences' national network of chapters is the largest arts education network in the country. Beginning on a long conference day in Saint Louis in the winter of 2003, I was able to guide teaching artists and professional developers (often working in small groups) to hammer out a draft of a rubric for performing artists with school residencies. For the first time in our field, colleagues hashed out agreements on key issues and language that captured everyone's understanding. Afterward, various chapters around the country refined the rubric through use and revision. (You can find a précis of that rubric online at http://www.kcya.org/documents/4pagerubric. pdf.) That rubric has been widely distributed and adapted and has sparked additional rubrics, such as one to clarify the quality of an in-school performance program and the quality of a residency design. I include just a section of it here to give you a feel for it (Table 13.1).

The other rubric in this chapter was created at the Crossing Paths conference in Charlotte, North Carolina, in November 2003. This gathering of education directors—from the San Francisco Symphony to the Alabama

Shakespeare Festival, from opera companies to ballet troupes—working with a decent sampling of teaching artists, drafted a surprisingly similar rubric about work in many different venues and all disciplines. The League of American Orchestras revised the draft of the rubric the conference created to more directly suit the perspective of orchestra education programs. With their permission, I have included at the end of this chapter the entire eight-page rubric, entitled "Growing the Capacity of Artists Who Teach" (Table 13.2). It will give you a much more detailed idea of the kinds of skill and knowledge the field believes music teaching artists need, and what those capacities should look like for beginners, right up to masters. A rubric like this holds so much knowledge and effectively displays what "better" looks like. It is interesting to note that when musicians alone are asked to create such a rubric, they feel the artistry page is the only necessary one; but when the group also includes those who lead programs and train teaching artists, the other seven pages of necessary skills gain priority as areas of essential skill. The League of American Orchestras continues to revise this rubric, so you may want to review any changes at the Web address at the end of the rubric.

One of the benefits of these rubrics is that they help teaching artists assess their own work and guide their own development—and talk with greater precision about their work to peers and colleagues. After all, good educators have skills—not just magic, charisma, or luck.

So the arts education field is coming to a consensus on what best practices look like. You no longer have to learn how to ride this bicycle without having seen someone else do it.

TABLE 13.1 Two Segments from the Young Audiences' Residency Rubric (for All Artistic Disciplines)

1) Communication Skills

Acceptable	• Can be heard clearly and is aware of audience's level of involvement and understanding.
Good	• Varied use of voice and body to capture audience interest. Checks in with audience for understanding and/or sharing experiences when appropriate.
Excellent	• Expressive use of voice and body at all times. Is in a constant dialogue with the audience to ensure full understanding and engagement.
Ideal	• Uses voice and body to captivate the group in a unique artistic way. Adapts style and manner to capture audience's attention and ensure understanding on multiple levels.

2) Relevance of Material

Acceptable	• Connects art form to students' and teacher's life experience and curriculum standards.
Good	• Connects art form to students' and teacher's life experience and curriculum standards and current classroom curriculum.
Excellent	• Encourages students and teachers to make connections between personal knowledge and art form.
Ideal	• Inspires students and teachers to continue to find ways to connect the art form to other aspects of their lives, both in and out of the classroom.

Source: Young Audiences National, 2003. Full version available online at: http://www.kcya.org/documents/AtAGlanceYARubric12.15.03.pdf.

TABLE 13.2

Growing the Capacity of Artists Who Teach

ARTISTRY

Artistry	Acceptable	Good	Excellent	Ideal
Engagement of Learner in the Art Form	• Designs a lesson plan that introduces people to some aspect of the art form	• Creates experiences that introduce the art form, includes the development of basic listening skills, and uses interactive and reflective elements	• Transfers ownership to learners so they apply artistic elements fluently	• Empowers learner to be/function as a self-initiator of the artistic experience whether as an active fully engaged listener or as a musicmaker
Knowledge of Artistic Discipline	• Well versed in his/her particular artistic medium	• Demonstrates fluency in the art form both as a performer and in speaking about the art form	• Connects his/her understanding of the art form to other art forms	• Relates his/her expertise beyond the art form to other areas of learning
Embodies the Marriage of Art and Education and Artistically Implements Learning Goals	• Is aware that a connection between the arts experience and the educational experience should be made	• Authentically connects and integrates the arts experience with the educational experience	• Both arts experience and educational experience maintain levels of excellence and are aligned with one another	• Creates a seamless connection between the artistic and the educational experience

ASSESSMENT

Assessment	Acceptable	Good	Excellent	Ideal
Learner Assessment	• Is aware that programs are not self contained and must answer to evaluation standards beyond the program itself • Agrees to participate in and be responsive to assessment strategies	• Demonstrates an understanding of and receptivity to vocabulary, concepts, and processes of learner assessment in the context of state and national standards • Initiates and designs assessment strategies	• Applies and adapts vocabulary, concepts, and processes of learner assessment in the context of state and national standards to individual programs • Incorporates the results to improve the teaching and learning process	• Creates a dialogue with learners using the vocabulary of assessment to propel the art of teaching in/through the arts • Teaches and mentors other artists in the assessment process
Self-Assessment	• Is aware of the need for self-assessment • Is aware of the skills and knowledge needed to conduct self-assessment	• Values and begins to apply self-assessment strategies • Uses self-assessment to improve the teaching/learning process	• Incorporates/demonstrates improved practices derived from self-assessment • Seeks out and responds to feedback from others	• Teaches and mentors other artists in self-assessment strategies and processes • Continues to conduct self-assessment in the context of personal values, artistic goals, organizational philosophy, and educational imperatives

PRINT AND/OR ON-LINE CONTENT

Content	Acceptable	Good	Excellent	Ideal
Support Materials	• Serviceable and relates to the lesson/learning experience	• Materials are engaging, illuminate learning, are replicable, and provide additional resources for follow-up	• Materials are substantive and evidence collaboration between teaching artist and partners	• Material empowers learners to continue to grow the work after the artist is gone
Knowledge/ Application of Art Form	• No factual errors; articulates and provides evidence of the art form; work presented is authentic to the art form	• Conveys aspects of the history of the art form; identifies relationships between art forms and addresses those connections; engages students in experiential, arts-based learning	• Reflects aspects of the creative process; provides sequencing of artistic development; provides tools for inquiry, context, and reflection in the art form	• Seamless melding of artistry and teaching; illuminates the creative process; shows evidence of the depth and breadth of the arts discipline
Lesson Design	• Identifies clear understanding of goals; content relates to the standards, and relates to the participants' lives	• Sequential design and delivery; links arts and other content standards to the experiential learning/understanding; uses discipline vocabulary and process, and vocabulary from teaching field/practice	• Repertoire of sequential and experiential choices; the work provides and promotes experiences of inquiry, context, and reflection	• Ideas taught through the lesson are internalized and applied to life by the learners

PLANNING AND GROUP MANAGEMENT

Group Management	Acceptable	Good	Excellent	Ideal
Time	• Starts and ends on time; no gaping holes; stays on task; has closure	• Flexible to changing needs	• Adapts and creates teaching moments from changing needs; processes connect to curriculum and life	• Uses all "teachable moments" masterfully; opportunity is created to reflect on project goals, accomplishments, challenges, and possible next steps
Materials	• Exposes participants to materials	• Demonstrates materials	• Students interact with materials	• Students and teacher partners create with materials and/or create new materials
People	• Greets and introduces self, lesson, and art form	• Shares passion and begins rapport with group	• Uncovers participant knowledge	• With teacher partners, an environment for personal sharing and risk taking is established
	• States expectations and objectives; gives clear instructions	• Maintains expectations and checks in on understanding (takes and asks questions)	• Encourages individual responsibility around expectations and objectives	• With teacher partners, group and individual responsibility for expectations and objectives is promoted and encouraged
	• Shows respect for students and adult partners	• Collaborates in planning and implementation; demonstrates modesty and humility in working with adult partners, acknowledges that ideas and learning come from others as well as the artist him/herself	• Is fully collaborative in all aspects of planning and implementation	• Collaboration between partners is seamless, spontaneous, equitable, and respectful

MOTIVATION

Motivation	Acceptable	Good	Excellent	Ideal
Interaction with Learners	• Arrives on time, ends on time; lesson and program are prepared with materials; TA is in control	• Sustains focus	• Engages all constituents in a meaningful way	• Creates environment for learner to be self-directed and passionate
Interaction with Stakeholders	• Represents sponsor in a positive manner	• Believes in mission and goals	• Advocates for organization, sponsor, and program	• Embodies mission/spirit/ goal of the sponsoring organization; inspires recipient to continue the program beyond the TA/ sponsor's involvement
Commitment	• Available, willing, and competent in art form	• Believes in art form and program; accepts program work over other opportunities	• Actively seeks the work; improves self/skills/craft; advocates for art form and program; exhibits drive, passion, and energy	• Compelled to do the work; teaching and creating are integral; takes initiative to help evaluate, continue, and improve program; inspires others' commitment
Desire to Improve	• Accepts external direction/assessment	• Engages in dialogue for improvement; attends professional development	• Uses all tools for self improvement; seeks professional development	• Constant learner; actively pursues tools for improvement
Sustainability/ Resiliency	• Completes task	• Recognizes trouble and welcomes external help	• Recognizes problems and initiates solutions	• Seeks out evaluation and renewal opportunities to maintain enthusiastic service

KNOWLEDGE OF THE CLIENT

Participant Knowledge	Acceptable	Good	Excellent	Ideal
Logistics	• Knows address, start time, participant ages, number, contact person, conditions of facility, and points of service	• Knows end time, has map, instructions, has knowledge of technical resources, did preplanning with contact, appropriate space is available	• Conducts pre-program site visit, debriefs	• Advanced, complete, and ongoing knowledge of scheduling and resources through site visits and productive communication; adapts to logistical circumstances
Learner Capabilities and Knowledge	• Knows the audience and uses age-appropriate language	• Accommodates special needs	• Gauges and relates to learners' prior knowledge	• Advanced, complete, and ongoing knowledge of learners' capabilities through communication with stakeholders; adapts work to meet audience need
Cultural Community	• Aware of socioeconomic conditions of participants	• Knows demographics, geographic environment, religion, and heritage	• Understands site-based regulations and norms for engaging with diverse populations	• A complete knowledge of how to operate within the demographics of the site and able to adjust successfully to those dynamics
Expectations/Desired Outcomes	• Knows teacher/leader experience; invites basic feedback from client/institution	• Participants assess/evaluate	• A formal program evaluation, including assessment, is done	• All stakeholders are satisfied with the experience due to advance articulation of expected outcomes; evaluation is positive, complete, and timely

PARTNERSHIP RELATIONSHIPS

Partnership Relationships	Acceptable	Good	Excellent	Ideal
Administration	• Aware of an agreement between the partners • Aware that there is a budget and knows budget limits	• Agreement has been seen, read, signed, and copied • Able to work within the existing budget; aware of budgeting process	• Understands the agreement and can work within it • Articulates/advocates for the program's funding needs; gives realistic numbers to budget creators, including time, supplies, and space	• Creates, manipulates, and adjusts the agreement within the partnership • Gains ownership of budget design; is flexible within the limits; constantly relates budget to content
Planning	• General goals and objectives are created with input from the artist • Aware of role in the partnership • Aware of need for assessment/eval. for partners each time	• Collaborates in goals and objectives that can be assessed • Knows strengths and weaknesses of each partner • Reports back to partners data needed for assessment/evaluation	• Aware of goals and objectives at all times and is able to sustain them in practice • Enriches the knowledge and capabilities of the partners and themselves • Articulates criteria for assessment and evaluation	• Assessment is seamlessly woven into the goals and objectives • Personal investment matches the partnership's goals • Helps to create the measurement tools with all partners
Communication	• Knows who to contact and what they need • Knows partners use different languages • Recognizes possible conflicts and has ability to work them out	• Facilitates communication within partnership and listens to partners • Knows some vocabulary of other partners • Anticipates approaching conflicts and works with partners toward solution	• Communicates proactively • Can speak the languages of all partners • Works toward resolving conflicts as soon as they are recognized	• Independently coordinates communication with all partners • Fluent in languages of all partners • Adapts to differing communication styles to effectively resolve conflicts

PRESENTATION SKILLS

Presentation Skills	Acceptable	Good	Excellent	Ideal
Interpersonal Skills	• Relaxed body language • Can be heard; speaks clearly; delivers anticipated content • Addresses audience respectfully (shown in tone of voice and eye contact)	• Flexible, comfortable body language • Articulate; able to present off notes • Invites audience's participation and acknowledges responses	• Expressive body language • Lively vocal inflection; shows enthusiasm and confidence • Consistently involves audience; inspires participants; demonstrates engagement with students and teacher partners, and is clearly "present at the event"	• Dynamic body language • Demonstrates passion through clarity and intensity • Immediately captivates and maintains the engagement with the entire audience for the duration of the presentation; provides lasting inspiration
Structure/ Organization	• Artist has a plan with enough content to fill the time; most basic goals are met; material is clear and organized	• Has a well-integrated plan; identifies and meets all established goals with participants; uses supplemental tools and materials	• Adapts approach to meet needs of all participants; flexible use of various resources and skills; use of full range sensory activities; achieves a sense of community	• Demonstrates transfer of skills and knowledge with impact on all participants beyond the presentation; demonstrates a masterful sense of flow, serendipity, and joy; experience is life-lasting

Source: League of American Orchestras, adapted from a rubric prepared at the Crossing Paths Conference 2003, with additional participants from Association of Performing Arts Presenters, Chorus America, Dance/USA, OPERA America, and Theatre Communications Group. Also available online at: http://www.americanorchestras.org/images/stories/knowledge_pdf/growing_capacity_rubric.pdf.

14

Mentoring

Myths and Mission

I took a walk in the woods. This was a needed break from developing a training curriculum for the first cohort of mentors in the Juilliard Mentoring Program. My head was full of thoughts about mentors—the ones I had wished for but had never found in my own artistic life and those I had heard about who had changed my colleagues' lives. I'd been studying the research on mentoring, frustrated that it is used as a necessity to developing leaders in many professions but is used only haphazardly in ours.

As luck would have it, way out there in the woods I bumped into a man who was an expert on trees, and we chatted a bit. In our brief exchange, he compared the fate of a young tree in the middle of a meadow with that of an identical sapling sprouting in a clearing in the woods. He said that a sapling in the woods would grow faster and stronger. This surprised me—wouldn't the open space without arboreal competition nurture a healthier tree? He informed me that young trees in a forest clearing have one advantage that makes all the difference. The tender roots of that tree will "find" the old roots of trees now gone, and then grow along those old roots to quickly reach deeper, richer soil.

What an astonishingly apt metaphor for the power of mentoring! By sharing our hard-earned growth, we—the experienced ones—invite younger learners to speed their growth into the deepest artistic satisfactions they can find. Mentoring is one of the ways teaching artists can use their education skills to serve younger musicians; they tend to be extremely good mentors. Even more important, in the adolescence of our field of teaching artistry, mentorship is the most direct way that experienced teaching artists can bring along the next generation, sharing what they have learned so that the next generation can take the field further. So, younger readers, study this chapter to learn how to make good use of a teaching artist mentor; and senior teaching artists, take notes on how to serve the young.

Mentor, a character in Homer's *Odyssey*, was the family retainer to whom Odysseus, when he set off for the Trojan War, entrusted the care of his son and heir, Telemachus. With those origins, the term *mentor* carries the connotations not only of a teacher but also of a parental stand-in or life adviser. We use the word in a more limited sense today, yet mentoring is far more than those rare occasions when an eager learner sits at our feet waiting for our offered nuggets of golden wisdom. That is only one (pleasant) extreme of the mentoring spectrum.

The mentor takes responsibility for the advancement of another's learning. Mentoring, a particular kind of one-on-one teaching, embraces a broader range of exchange than just, say, musical training. Essentially personal, it contains a strong dose of role modeling. Indeed, the way a mentor thinks, solves problems, answers questions, and deals with the world teaches as least as much as the mentor's words. Mentees drink in everything they can from your example—a promising and daunting opportunity for a mentor.

I also believe that mentoring is more than a one-way relationship. At its best, it is reciprocal. This is not just a touchy-feely sentiment from the artsy set. Indeed, corporate America has studied mentoring extensively, as have the scientific, medical, and education industries, and they all use mentoring structurally, faithfully. Because it works. It speeds advancement, leadership, and learning; it fills in the gaps in savvy about how to handle the complex and human problems that arise in any field; it advances the organization and the field. I have not heard of any Fortune 500 company that does not have a mentoring program as a significant part of its human resources development plan. Almost any organized group that wants to fast-track the development of young talent, or guide the growth of vulnerable children, or build community capacities uses mentoring. MentorNet (just one of hundreds of similar programs), for example, focuses on the retention and success of women in engineering, science, and mathematics.

Mentoring creates an atmosphere conducive to reciprocal communication and encourages certain habits of mind in the teacher as well as the learner. Good mentoring is more about asking great questions than telling great stories. The mentor's crucial skill is listening.

Listening is to mentoring what love is to marriage. Or as Dr. Joyce Brothers wrote: "Listening, not imitation, is the sincerest form of flattery." Fully focused listening holds an open space in the mind that is without judgment, free (as much as possible) of encumbrances from the listener's past and unclouded by personal preference. Aesthetic listening brings our whole selves to hearing not only what is said but also what has *not* been said. Does that sound difficult, perhaps even a little Zen? Good, because the quality of your listening determines the quality of your mentoring. It is well worth spending a lifetime getting better at it. When your mentee can put answers together in your presence without your saying a thing, you have achieved great mentoring. (I promise a big reward for anyone who can provide a better word than the inelegant *mentee*.)

The rule of thumb I offer mentors-in-training is to listen until they have the urge to speak, and then listen some more. The time to speak is when you have ascertained where the mentee is coming from, and you are reasonably sure that what you have to say is just what she needs. A recent example from my life. A young administrative assistant asked me a professional question: How do I start new books? I began to gather my thoughts; I was going to take a fresh run at the question for her benefit. How generous of the mentor, me! I felt I was doing her a favor by applying creative energy to her question. I squinted and looked toward the sky, my lips pursed almost invisibly (a posture I recognized as typical of one of my own former teachers). The self-important pleasure of *telling* was rising in me. I recognized that; and just before I began to speak, I stopped. Instead, I asked her why she had asked. Startled, she said she was just curious. Detecting something more in her tone, I didn't take her comment at face value and asked a mentor's question: "Do you write, or have trouble starting big creative projects?" The door began to open, slowly at first: "Well, yeah, I kind of write, and I have this idea about a series of children's books on adventures through art…" I drew her out. When her specific curiosities were clarified, the "teachable moment" appeared. (Educators use often the term and understand it as that occasion when the learner is exactly ready for what the teacher has to give. The teachable moment is sweet and resonant—and happens only when the teacher listens well.) She had lots of questions about the children's publishing business that I couldn't help with at all. But I did know some things that might help her solve one or two pieces of her puzzle—how to build the habit of writing into the structure of overly busy days, and ways to organize big projects so they don't seem so overwhelming. That made a difference for her and was great for me. Had I just answered her initial question, she wouldn't have heard much of use; she would have been polite but disappointed, and I would have failed as a mentor.

Good mentors invest in such opportunities when occasions arise and time allows, and they often make time when time doesn't seem to allow. This supports the courage of others to look for the learning potential of every occasion, even of their mistakes. People tend to pass such gifts along, so—even as we have a good personal moment ourselves—we make a small contribution to the fabric of our culture.

Much of the success of mentoring has to do with creating just the right atmosphere. Mentor relationships are idiosyncratic. Both mentor and mentee bring a lot of hope and need to the relationship, so expectations must be articulated and matched—no good can come from misaligned expectations. For example, the mentee expects the mentor to weigh in on personal problems, and the mentor doesn't want to; the mentor thinks the mentee will respond quickly to an email, and the mentee doesn't. Clarify mutual expectations and establish how you will communicate. Your attention to the nuts and bolts builds mutual respect and confidence in the mentee and may help set a lifetime pattern. Of course, expectations can and should change; by being open about this as well, you help the relationship evolve. Concurrently, you can communicate your high expectations for that learner. The ideal relationship is safe and respectful, challenging, fun, and inspiring.

Mentors model habits of mind essential to every artistic practice: attention to process (asking about the *how*, as well as the *what*, of the learner's artistic work); self-assessment (showing how to question oneself in an ongoing, nonjudgmental way); inquiry (demonstrating a curious mind that reaches beyond narrow professional concerns to values in the arts and in life). Mentors model not just how to solve problems but also how to think about problems, and how to turn them into learning.

The Juilliard Mentoring Program has been particularly illuminating for me because it pairs interested students with trained faculty mentors from a different discipline. The policy of cross-disciplinary pairing sets the program apart from the mentoring that goes on within the music, dance, and drama departments, allowing an emphasis on creating a big, curious, exploratory life in the arts. A pianist mentor may not only take the dancer mentee to concerts and museums but also attend the dance performances of that mentee. A dancer mentor may invite a violin student mentee to watch him choreograph a ballet. The rich dialogue that emerges around those experiences can reveal new ways to experience and make meaning of art. They may end up at a Yankees game, where neither of them has much expertise.

Does mentoring sound like a lot of work? The only work is paying attention. The rest feels like play. Being selected, formally or informally, as a mentor is a gift—to the learner and the mentor.

Can you seek mentees? Yes and no. Formal and informal setups exist that allow for mentoring to unfold well. Try to become part of a program of official mentoring if you know of one—they usually attend to the basics: mentee selecting the mentor, establishing clear foundations and expectations, setting goals (for both mentor and mentee), getting things off to a positive start. But formal programs are only one way. In informal mentoring, the learner needs to select the mentor, having identified that person as having something essential for her. Even though you can't walk up to likely prospects and say, "Hey, how about opening your heart to me as your mentor?" there are things you can do. You can be available, with an open heart, taking active interest in young or new colleagues, wherever you go. And I mean *all* the time, even in settings that are difficult: mentees often identify a mentor through her handling of stress. I think we do well to be aware, all the time, that we are modeling what we would like mentees to see. You also can respond to the tentative expression of interest about something you know—even if you are busy. It may be his way of sounding out a possible affinity.

A friend of mine once said, "Lord, please make me the man my dog thinks I am." By embracing the responsibility of being a mentor, we commit ourselves more fully to walk our talk, to live what we say we believe in. Mentoring is the performing art that creates the future of our art, one deep relationship at a time.

Part IV The Fundamentals of Working in Education Settings

15

Truth and Dare in Education Programs

Let's start with a word association game. I'll write a couple of words, and you notice your response. For example, if I write *dog*, you might respond with *cat* or *Benji*. If I write *viola*, you might respond with...no, let's skip that. Ready? Here we go with a term most musicians know well: *education program*.

What is your answer? Based on my experience, I would guess many readers cringed slightly. Some felt the drop in the stomach that goes with the grudging compliance of a "should." A few may have felt upbeat because they love that part of a musician's work. It's no surprise that responses vary. Musicians and ensembles *should* develop strong education programs—for reasons of advocacy, audience building, artistic generosity, and a broader range of musical expression. But I don't want to "should" on you.

There are also practical reasons to dedicate serious creative energy to developing strong programs—good reasons like cash, better bookings, requests for longer residencies. Yet few musicians are trained in the skills and thinking needed to design and deliver strong education programs. Usually, the education program "problem" falls into the laps of those ensemble members who have "natural" educator's gifts, and they carry the group. While the development of education skills is slowly finding its way into conservatory training, active ensembles need to create and expand their education programs now, not wait for future generations or get by on current versions of the "should."

Let's look at what education programs are and what common misconceptions about them tend to be. We speak of education programs that ensembles should develop; we don't usually speak about what we mean by *education program*. The instinctive definitions that arise in our word association game vary widely in our field. Some picture a concert in a school auditorium in which you also talk about the music and your instrument and pray for attentive students—and often do *not* have your prayers

125

answered, at least not fast enough. Some picture a workshop or "petting zoo" in which you interact closely with young people. Some picture a series of classroom visits in which you teach about music, or even connect music to other school subjects. Some think of a lively preconcert lecture-demonstration or other adult education situations. Some picture guidebooks or meetings with teachers to prepare them, or even instrument instruction, coaching, or master classes. These are all good parts of education programs, and each taps different skills and invites different kinds of program design.

What they have in common is that they are mostly about moments when art meets not-art, when musical insiders try to draw outsiders another step in. There are common principles that apply in all these education occasions, and those guidelines, like "engagement before information," "tapping competence," and "opening up processes," form the basis of all teaching artist work.

So let's leave the definition broad: education programs include many kinds of events, the more the better. We are all educators all the time. You needn't embrace my pan-educational view to create good education programs. Whatever the term conjures for you, however, you do need to shed the following misconceptions.

Misconception 1: Teach means tell.   Many people think that because they said something, they have performed an act of education. If I rattled off the batting averages of famous baseball players of the 1970s, would you have learned them? No, not unless you were already invested in the subject, and my information was relevant to your interests. It is similar with music information—people take it in and make meaning of it only insofar as it is relevant to them personally. Information about composers, about the structure or history of pieces, is not necessarily something I am going to take in and "learn" from unless I already have a personal involvement in such topics. And even with those participants who are information-oriented, and do love to retain new facts, it doesn't mean they care a lick more about the music you are there to share.

Misconception 2: The goal of an education event is to teach.   I believe that learning is a by-product of a more essential goal: guiding people to be successful at making musical connections. We are successful teachers to the degree that people can individually make personally relevant discoveries in the music. That is why giving information doesn't necessarily make for a strong education program. However interesting the information may be, it needs to be part of an event that helps each learner experience the excitement and reward of creating personal connections to music. Having students learn that Mozart was as young as they are when he wrote a piece is not the goal; having them discover something relevant to their young lives when they listen to Mozart is. Since my maxim "engagement before information" works, we must focus on ways to engage participants first, in order to catalyze the learning chemistry.

Misconception 3: If we call it an education event then it is one.   People learn only when they individually choose to invest themselves in the learning. Sure, people will regurgitate information on command or perform tasks that show what they can do when compelled to, but the act of learning, making a new connection, happens only when we choose to invest ourselves in it. (Indeed, I think learning, creating, and loving are the three areas in life that happen only with intrinsic motivation. Have you ever succeeded in making someone love you?) This doesn't mean education is hopeless, or that it can happen only with an already-interested learner. There is much we can do to increase the likelihood that an individual will undertake that act of courage that creates new meaning. What can we do? We can create an atmosphere that is safe, dynamic, fun, and playful. We can make sure that the material we share is inherently interesting to that particular audience. We can make sure we know the developmental levels and interests of each audience. The environment we create for the "educational" action is as important as the activities that happen within it. I don't care how brilliant your information is; if the occasion is not conducive, safe, irresistibly fun, alive, and fully engaging, little learning will unfold.

Misconception 4: Some people are educators, some aren't.   Sure, some musicians are better talkers in education situations, and others may be better planners, but everyone has the responsibility and the ability to contribute to the education endeavor. Some musicians are excellent demonstrators, able to clarify a point with a lively musical example. Some are good improvisers, able to take an audience suggestion and apply it immediately to show how that thought works out musically. Every member of an ensemble must be fully invested in the education occasion; no one can merely coast on the voluble charm of the designated talker. I worked with a quartet with one player who just could not contribute verbally. It was excruciating to watch. So we did not draw her into full participation through words. We arranged that she spoke as often as everyone else, except that she always spoke with her instrument—it turned out to be personable, fun, and often hilarious. She got wickedly good at stealing the show without saying a word.

Misconception 5: The quality of the music is the key to success.   Of course, the excellence of the music is crucial, but the key to success is the authenticity of the whole event. Great music with inauthentic presenters equals a bad education program. The event must express who your ensemble is, what each of you cares about, and the joy you take in the education opportunity. Yes, 80% of what you teach is who you are, and the remaining 20% of an education program—the script and activities and demonstrations, the stuff you do—is important. What makes us care, bother to attend fully, go with your intentions and ideas, is the quality of the 80%—the live people in front of us. You must bring wholehearted enthusiasm and your active personal interest into every education opportunity, or you undercut your chance to make the event work. This can be a tall order when you are doing a lot of student concerts, or when a school situation is bad—and in reality, we can't always succeed. But the truth is always there—our inner state is loud and clear to everyone, even if we think we are covering it. Therefore, we must create programs we are wholeheartedly enthusiastic about, musical adventures that are fun, important, rich embodiments of our real passions in music.

Get rid of those misconceptions. Polish up your 80%. Create the programs that share your musical passions, pleasures, and current musical interests. And before you know it, your word association to *education program* may become "How soon?"

16

How to Succeed in School Environments

We all know how to do gigs. We prepare. We show up on time. We deliver the artistic goods. We have expectations of the presenter and the venue. We are rightly miffed when the basics are not well handled. Distracting noises, lighting difficulties, bad house management, awful backstage areas, stale coffee—all affect the quality of the musical engagement we want to have with the audience.

Got a gig in a school? Suspend your expectations of the norms. Both the goods we deliver and the realities of school environments dictate that we think and function differently there. You may find after-school situations different than school-day norms—many teaching artists prefer the extra time, relief from curricular demands, and self-selection of participating students in after-school programs, finding it easier to manage and succeed within such programs. Since there is so much variety in after-school programs, we will focus on the usually more challenging in-school setting to establish realistic expectations. These suggestions apply to all school settings but may be less crucial in after-school workshops. If you can succeed in the school-day realities, you are definitely going to succeed in after-school hours.

There was a time in American schooling when teachers had enormous discretion about what they could do once they closed the classroom door. (This autonomy was not always good news for students—many of us will never forget the harsh or unfair teachers who controlled us for an endless year of our young lives.) In the No Child Left Behind era, far more of school life is controlled and monitored from outside the room. Preoccupation with testing pervades school life. In many schools, it is now an act of personal courage to bring a visiting artist into a classroom or assembly. In some districts, teachers may not take pupils on a field trip (including a trip to a musical performance) without certifying in writing that it will directly contribute to raising test scores. Bringing artists into the school takes nerve and commitment on a teacher's part. The artist's very appearance there runs against the current. As for the students, your offering is so different from what they are used to, it may take them a while to sense its value.

To learn more about this topic, I did an informal survey of eight schoolteachers I know. These dedicated pros from all over the country (urban and rural) have worked with artists for years (some for decades). Mostly they had praise for the musicians they have gone out of their way to introduce to their students. But, assured of anonymity, they also let fly with some spicy comments about the downside of working with visiting musicians; indeed, several comments would get them kicked off children's television. Repressed grudges burst out about having been disappointed, frustrated, angered, and downright insulted. I have distilled some of their shared complaints and balanced them with observations from my own experience to give you some pointers about succeeding in schools.

The first and most important thing that school professionals want from musicians is *respect*. They know schools are not your preferred performance venue, and they know there will be a lot they can't give you. They ask that you be a gracious guest who understands the limitations going in and who doesn't complain or get disheartened by them. Cut them some serious slack.

Respect is a by-product of understanding. Whenever possible, I require a teaching-artist-in-training to spend a whole day following a teacher in a school. And not a cushy well-funded school with lovely arts programs, but a typical school where music and art are absent or struggle for a tiny toehold in students' lives. The experience is powerful. Not only do the trainees come to appreciate the physical and mental stamina required of a teacher in a typical day; they also are impressed by the often near-overwhelming number of issues a classroom teacher deals with every hour, every minute. The result is a respect that gives teachers more leeway—extending even to those teachers whose style the teaching artists may not like, and to those who sometimes let them down.

I urge you to spend time in schools, just watching—it will teach you more than a book chapter ever could. For those who can't manage that, take the following requests seriously:

Have appropriate expectations. The students probably won't be beautifully behaved or well prepared—possibly not prepared at all—even if you have made previous contact with the school and described the preparation you would like, and given them a handout or guidebook. Motion and noise and interruptions are typical. The auditorium may be seething with movement, and the noise a constant murmur. At one school where I performed in a play, the students were rapt. But during the climactic scene, a janitor wheeled a garbage can across the stage behind us without a second thought. That was his routine, the shortest route to the dumpster; the fact that there were actors doing something on the stage and a few hundred students watching didn't seem important enough to him to demand the longer route with the trash. I was outraged, but the teachers told me that they and the students had barely noticed. If you happen to be in one of those unusually well-focused situations, great; if not, great, too—the students need your best even if the circumstances are pretty bad.

It's about more than just the music.   My teacher respondents asked that you share more than music. Students are fascinated by you, as well as by the instruments and their sounds. Share all this generously; it is all part of learning about music. The vocalist, conductor, composer, and educator Bobby McFerrin does this in a lovely way you could borrow. He invites questions and answers of students, but the musicians must answer with their instruments. A student asks, "When did you start playing the cello?" The musician must decide if she wants to play seven notes, or play a child's tune, or capture the feel of being seven in an improvised melody—whatever the choice, the audience listens hard and appreciates musical playfulness.

Anticipate the double whammy.   Students are one of the few audiences you'll have that did not choose to be there. Most would probably *not* be there if they had any choice. Worse, most meet you with the belief that your music is boring. During the honeymoon period with them (the first few minutes), don't assume they will love just anything you play. Select music that you love and that is likely to be interesting to their ears. They're typical American kids; it isn't their fault that they have no initial feel for your music. That's the reason you are there. So meet them, with enthusiasm, wherever they are coming from.

Love kids.   They can tell how you feel about them, and they respond. How would you like to be required into an auditorium for a long speech with PowerPoint slides by a microbiologist who didn't like musicians? Musicians who really like young people find things go so much better; students respond if they can feel you are having genuine fun with them. Even if you are not especially good with kids, make it okay for them to be something other than short adults. The vast majority of them are excited that you are there—you are a novel and interesting break in their routine; they usually have charmingly open responses, often hilarious, to your musical offering.

Respect the schedule.   Show up early and don't run long—even though the teachers and students may not follow the same rule. Even a minor infraction on either side creates real problems for teachers. Don't give homework that is not previously arranged with a teacher. Don't assume that a teacher will have done substantive preparation, unless your work is part of a program that invests in real partnership—and even then know that sometimes even committed partners won't be able to do their part of the prep. Finally, don't expect the teacher to follow up, complete things, or build on your work after you are gone. It might happen, but don't count on it.

Clarify. Write key words on a board, or even better, bring a handout. Have simple definitions of key terms at the tip of your tongue. I have watched musicians caught off guard, fumbling to define the difference between meter and rhythm. I have seen terms defined wrong—often. Do your homework, so you can make your points without jargon, and in simple, age-appropriate language. Plan the few musical terms you want to introduce, build your program around them, and don't use others.

Appreciate where the power lies. Go out of your way to introduce yourself to the administrative leadership (especially the principal), as well as to the teachers and support staff. Respect the school secretary and janitor; they don't report to you, and they have plenty to do. If they're on your side, communication, problem solving, and a dozen other intangibles will go better. Sure, you can *politely, respectfully, apologetically* ask the janitor or secretary to help you if you need to, but offer to help that person help you.

Plan age-appropriately. The single most common complaint against teaching artists is that their activities, language, and expectations are not attuned to the particular young audience. If you are going to be working with ten-year-olds, you need to know what ten-year-olds can do, like to do, find interesting and funny. If you don't know any ten-year-olds, go find some and talk to them. Students (and teachers) can tell if you have a feel for them as people—it makes all the difference to the quality of their engagement with you. Teachers are a huge resource about student interests and capacities—use them in your planning. It is true that teachers frequently underestimate what their students can do and can hear musically, but the teachers have an abundance of accurate knowledge about interests and group dynamics.

Manage the group efficiently. Whether in a classroom or a larger gathering, be enthusiastic and clear in your instructions, be crisp and loud enough in your delivery. Musicians frequently speak a little too softly, and this is a signal to students to tune out. If you worry about being able to manage the group, ask for a teacher's help. This is the area that generally concerns teaching artists the most—with images of uncontrolled chaos haunting your dreams. Don't worry, it isn't about shouting or imposing discipline. It is about clarity, intent to be heard by everyone, working with teachers. This is a skill that grows with practice, and nothing helps you more than a good attitude and a dynamic program.

Be conscious of the group's energy.   Don't get them too worked up (or too loud) during your time with them, and leave them calmed down so the teacher doesn't have to impose strict order to get them back to work after you leave. Shape the energy so that they do get excited within control, so that they participate actively, but not in ways that invite chaos, and include a calming closure that brings them back to focus for the teacher.

Connect to the curriculum.   Plan with teachers or administrators beforehand. Planning supports the brave teachers who go out on a limb to bring you in. It is rarely difficult to find natural extensions of your work that make authentic links to other active classroom subjects. This interdisciplinary connection affirms the relevance of music and the value of the other subject. I do not advocate that you teach science through music, but making references and connections helps the students hold your information and helps the teacher connect back to the music after you are gone. For example, if you are describing something cyclical in a piece, it helps to mention that you know the students have been learning about the water cycle and to make some analogies. If you are discussing theme and variations, find out what they've been reading that uses that form, and refer to it.

Educators wangle scarce money to get you into their building because they believe in the importance of music. They want their students to see live artists and to discover that you are bright, personable, and interesting. They want their classes to have fun with you.

They have heartfelt but probably unrealistic expectations for your time with students (unless you have planned multiple visits). They're hoping you'll tap creative instincts, affirm the importance of personal voices, excite the desire to play an instrument. They wish for a miracle: that, during your short interaction with their students, the power of classical music or jazz will somehow be transmitted, because many will never have such a chance again.

A final note on my own wishes. Be an ambassador for professional musicians in the way you relate to everyone in the school. From the teachers in the faculty lounge, to the parent who shows up, to the gruff assistant principal—from the tenth grader who hates your music to the eager eight-year-old who plays violin—radiate enthusiasm (even under challenging conditions), be actively friendly, and be grateful for the chance to share with them. You may be an alien presence to many of them, but please have everything you do communicate what a great planet you come from, and how easy it is to start the journey there.

17
Getting Schooled on School Performances

Agreed: the field of teaching artists is disorganized, making it hard to learn how to create effective, original education/youth/family concerts—let's refer to them as e/y/f concerts. To reap the benefits of being a skilled e/y/f presenter, take an honest look at your offerings. Even ensembles that feel adept at the e/y/f game always have the challenge of getting better. And did I say benefits? Yes, both tangible (more bookings, financial viability, responsive audiences) and intangible (building future audiences, exploring deeper ways to share your artistry, enriching your understanding of the purposes and pleasures of music).

To examine some common misconceptions musicians have about e/y/f concerts, in 2005, I teamed up with Ariel Winds, a woodwind quintet (now sadly gone) that developed great e/y/f expertise. Many other ensembles have exemplary programs we could highlight, but I am focusing on Ariel Winds for two reasons: (1) they made an extra effort to develop effective workshops for other ensembles, and (2) I have worked with several of them since they were my students at Juilliard. A teacher loves to stay close to the work of his students.

Misty Tolle (Ariel's horn player and now the director of School and Family Programs at Carnegie Hall's Weill Music Institute) pulls no punches about the necessity to hone your presentation skills: "Everyone is raising money for music outreach, sending out ensembles from within the ranks of our symphony orchestras. Chamber ensembles are going out into schools. The musicians assume that they know how to make these events work. Unfortunately, many of them spend more time unintentionally alienating audiences than building them."

The members of the Ariel ensemble and I agree that the most common mistakes musicians make in e/y/f concerts are as follows:

- Thinking of them as "education" concerts
- Assuming that education programming must be "dumbed down"
- Planning with no plan
- Coming across as elitist
- Using vocabulary that students and nonmusician adults don't understand
- Including too many ideas
- Using only one spokesperson
- Assuming that speaking skills cannot be learned
- Forgetting fun
- Asking the wrong kinds of questions
- Setting a program in stone

Thinking of Them as "Education" Concerts

Seeing an e/y/f concert as a different category of performance weakens its design and the pleasure you take in it. Such events are really *expansions* of what the musician or ensemble already does, not a reduction of what it prefers to do.

Think of an e/f/y concert as a distilled, inclusive concert, so that everyone in the room—adult or child—is engaged and challenged. In one of its demonstrations of musical structure, Ariel Winds chose an interesting work—Gabriel Fauré's *Pavane*, for instance—and then analyzed it, using the metaphor of a pizza and doing demonstrations to "build the pizza." First comes the crust—the sometimes monotonous but crucial bass line played by the lowest-pitched instruments in the ensemble. Then they add the sauce, the accompaniment, which adds a little flavor and moisture, but—as they also demonstrated—isn't all that interesting on its own. (You wouldn't drink the tomato sauce by itself, would you?) Next comes the cheese—a melody beautiful on its own (cheese is, too), but when added to the crust and sauce, it is even better. And then there are the extras—like harmony—which, like pepperoni or mushrooms or basil, add depth and complexity. Such demonstrations open up young ears, yet the analysis is substantial enough to expand the awareness of adult ears as well. A performance of the work follows, illuminated by the preparation.

Assuming That Education Programming Must Be "Dumbed Down"

If you present music you're not excited about, everyone senses it. So instead of dumbing down the music, seek to "smarten up" the audience.

Help them "get" a piece they might otherwise find threatening or difficult. Choose works you really love, and look for inventive ways to use the pieces' best features to draw the audience in. That way, you won't be lecturing about why the piece is cool to you or other music experts; you'll be helping audience members discover their own excitement in the listening.

Elliott Carter's *Quintet* is a stretch for most ears. Few ensembles would even consider playing it for kids, but Ariel wanted to share it with everyone. Its pace is fast, sometimes manic. Squealing high notes from the woodwinds allow scant respite for listeners, but the horn continually interjects with a fanfare that momentarily stops the commotion. Ariel taught the audience this horn part and had them practice—singing along with the horn—the words "I IN-TER-RUPT!" Then the passage was performed, with the audience joining the horn every time it appears. This exercise sparked active, involved listening and playfully revealed a key structural aspect of the *Quintet* as well.

Misty says she learned the "don't-dumb-it-down" lesson from her work with the Albany Symphony in Albany, New York. "Standard fare for a concert in Albany is American music of the last hundred years. The concert halls are packed with people ready and willing to listen to the music of Persichetti, Torke and Carter. Why? Because David Allen Miller has a way of making his audience feel smart, because they 'get it.' This is the mentality we should use in approaching 'ed' concerts. . . . We are there to challenge and inspire."

Planning with No Plan

Sometimes a concept shapes a program, and the ensemble seeks the music that best embodies it. Sometimes the music itself suggests the shape of a program. No design template assures success, but keep in mind that each program must be a journey—an authentic musical exploration that travels an interesting, cohesive path and satisfies by arriving somewhere at the end. Too often, I see a good program idea undermined because the ensemble couldn't resist sticking in a piece it just loves to play, even though that piece didn't really fit. I also see programs full of good music that lack the cohesion to pull the parts into any kind of effective whole. Am I saying that great music is not enough? Yes—the opportunity for excellence is great music pulled together in a theatrical whole that is greater than the sum of its good parts. Musicians seem to forget that nonmusicians need the pieces on a program to make theatrical sense together more than those familiar with music do.

Coming across as Elitist

Musicians don't feel they are stuck up. Hardly! They usually feel underpaid, underappreciated, and pooped. However, they forget that most Americans bring a knapsack of preconceptions to the performance hall. Musicians—especially classical musicians—are seen as the heroes of a cultural elite, and most Americans feel decidedly nonelite. In e/y/f concerts we must strike a delicate balance, being neither too familiar nor too distant. You can't pretend you're a blue-collar football fan if you're not, nor can you afford to do anything that confirms the prejudice that you think of yourself as superior.

Be who you really are. Allow your real personality and feelings to come out—but in relation to the music. (I cringe when I hear musicians telling their favorite colors, or what they ate for dinner last night. I heard one refer to the school by the wrong name.) Misty notes that "musicians are taught to put on a 'mask' when on stage. Never show a mistake, never show elation at getting something right. Even personal interactions between members of an ensemble are often kept to a minimum."

The open canvas of an e/y/f concert gives you plenty of music-related ways to connect. Ariel audiences were especially drawn to the interplay of ensemble musicians; they enjoyed seeing the smirks, smiles, and nods that pass between players during a performance. Ariel's players talked between movements and between pieces, explaining certain aspects of what is going on: for example, "We're swabbing out—emptying our instruments of water." In one activity in their program "Workout in the Musician's Gym," each quintet member auditioned to play the melody from *Le Tombeau de Couperin*. As the players vied for approval, the audience became personally invested in the instrument each person liked best. The voting can get passionate—removing another layer of the wall between the audience and performer, while still sharpening the listening and willingness to attend to unfamiliar music. I confess their shameless ploys to woo voters to their instrument were downright hilarious.

Using Vocabulary That Students and Nonmusician Adults Don't Understand

This is a common mistake and inadvertently confirms people's preconceptions that concert music is not for them. Misty wishes she had a dime for every time she has heard performers use words such as "dynamics" or "tempo" or any of a dozen everyday musical terms that aren't familiar to audiences. You may be surprised to find how often you revert to professional jargon in the e/y/f setting.

Use only those terms that are crucial to your program, and use plain English to distill what they mean. (This, by the way, is not "dumbing down"; it is being articulate, considerate, effective—using language your listeners don't understand is just plain bad communication.) If you find you need the jargon as a kind of shorthand, the solution is to simplify the focus of each concert so you have the time to thoroughly address your subject and open up any crucial musical terms, in everyday, conversational language.

Including Too Many Ideas

Less is more—perhaps not always, but often. Ariel focused on one main musical idea per concert and approached it from various angles. In her e/y/f workshops with other ensembles, Misty reminds them to apply the standard rule of public speaking: tell the audience what you are going to say; say it; and then tell them what you've just said. Leonard Bernstein built each of his Young People's Concerts around one focal idea, often a question that he answered in various ways, like "What does music mean?" and "What is the sound of an orchestra?" Ariel Winds built one of its programs entirely around one piece, Mussorgsky's *Pictures at an Exhibition*.

Using Only One Spokesperson

This strategy is usually adopted out of expedience—one of you is a good talker, and the others are relieved to be rid of a nervous-making responsibility. But if a silent majority sits onstage, politely waiting while the designated talker talks, an uneasy distance develops between audience and ensemble. Every member should find places to speak up—or even to actively contribute without words. One player in an Ariel workshop just couldn't bear to talk at all. So, using a strategy I have employed with other ensembles, they arranged for her to speak with her instrument—her musical "comments" became a running gag throughout the concert. (Hey, Harpo Marx was a talented musician too—he could play more than the honker.) Adapt your program to play up the strengths or quirks of your members; the audience needs to sense that all of you are eager to communicate.

Assuming That Speaking Skills Cannot Be Learned

Many musicians think the gift of gab is a mysterious capacity some have and some don't—just the way nonmusicians think about your ability to play your instrument. Well, you know how long it took you to learn how to play that thing, and I know speaking skills can be learned. Provide your speaking skills one sliver of the time and commitment you gave to learning your instrument, and you will be a powerhouse presenter. Here are a few basics for the beginners and the terrified:

- *Speak slowly.* Nervousness may cause you to race, and then you'll lose the audience.
- *Speak all the way through your thoughts.* Many uncomfortable speakers drop their voice volume at the ends of sentences because their minds have already moved ahead. Apply the same principles of *attack* and *finish* to spoken phrases that you do to musical ones.
- *Address the "um."* Ums betray nerves and lack of preparation. Practice, focus, *know* what you want to communicate. This prevents meandering, reduces the "um" count, and sharpens the message.
- *Pause.* Even allow bits of silence. Give ideas a chance to sink in. Research shows that as much as 50% of a good conversation is silence.
- *Rehearse, but don't memorize.* Practice your speaking out loud, several times, before you try your words onstage. But don't commit a speech to memory. That gives your delivery an impersonal, rote quality and invites a different kind of terror— what if you forget the exact words?
- *Enjoy the moment.* Easy to say, not so easy for some to do. Your onstage attitude? You are eager to share your ideas with people who want to hear them. It takes time (sometimes years) for some people to get that comfortable with the audience, but it is a goal worth aspiring to.

Forgetting Fun

Fun does not mean fluff. Playfulness (which Mozart's music, for instance, has in abundance) is a natural way to engage audiences—the challenge is to have play lead to learning. Games, interplay, activities are not extras used to pep up a dull concert; they can spark energy and discovery. My colleague David Wallace uses a giant, laminated score in his e/y/f concert on ornamentation. He invites students to come up and decorate his score with markers, and together they try to figure out how he might play each of their ornaments on the viola. Then, reading from the giant score, he plays the first movement of the Telemann Viola Concerto, once with the ornaments the students have added and once with those the composer wrote. Fun all the way, and a direct illumination of the ornamentation concept.

Another effective bit of Ariel's educational interplay illuminated a virtuosic piece by Eugene Bozza called *Scherzo*. It is basically a lightning-fast chromatic scale passed from instrument to instrument. Ariel played a game of "duck-duck-goose" in which Misty tapped each musician on the head as each took over the musical line in turn. The speeding music was no longer a blur to listeners; they had seen it clarified in a playful way.

Asking the Wrong Kinds of Questions

The best interactive presenters stick to open-ended questions—remember teaching artist guideline 19 from chapter 3. Closed questions have single correct answers and underscore the sense that the presenter knows everything and the audience knows a lot less—exactly the opposite of the "us" feeling we want the concert to create. Closed questions often ask "when" and "what" and "who," while open questions invite greater participation by asking "why" and "how." In Ariel's *Pictures at an Exhibition* program, a musician asked students to raise their hands if they had ever painted a picture, and then to name some of the tools they had used in creating their works of art. The answers flew forward, and the kids quickly made the connection with composing: "Just as a painter has tools he or she uses to create a piece of art, a composer has tools he or she uses to make a piece of music." Then they delved into the serious play of discovering the tools Mussorgsky used in *Pictures*.

Another example from the same program: an Ariel musician asked, "How could a composer make music sound busy?" Players jotted down suggested answers on a blackboard. Just before performing "Limoges (The Marketplace)" from *Pictures*, the ensemble encouraged the audience to do two things: to check the list during the performance for techniques the composer used, and consider some additions, based on what they were hearing. After the performance, the group revisited the list and added to it, expanding awareness of compositional tools.

Setting a Program in Stone

A good program is always under construction (and sometimes improvised, if a surprising opportunity appears). A set program *feels* set; it loses an edge for the audience and is less engaging for the players. Think about experimenting, switching roles—every time! A huge part of the success of an e/y/f concert is the subtle vibe of your genuine excitement. Audiences know it when you're just phoning it in, going through the motions. An overdetermined program is missed opportunity, even if performed well. We need you to be having genuine musical fun, right in front of our eyes, so you can authentically model for us the deep rewards of a life in music.

18
Art for Art's Sake or for the School's Sake?

Music and art were not officially recognized as legitimate subjects of study in American public schools until about 1900. The decision to include the arts in the curriculum was supported by two main lines of reasoning. One might be called the *inherent*, or *intrinsic*, argument (art for art's sake), and the other the *instrumental* argument (art for the sake of some other value, like workplace preparedness or improved test scores).

Back in 1902, educators could not fully articulate the case for the arts as an intrinsic value, nor did they need to substantiate it with research—society shared the belief that music and visual art were somehow important enough to the youthful citizenry to merit a defined place in the school day. This same consensus persists today, showing up consistently in public opinion surveys—even though we still may not be able to clearly articulate the understanding behind this opinion or support it neatly with compelling research. Nonetheless, our belief in the value of arts learning usually keeps music and visual arts in schools, even when the great budget ax falls. At the same time, we always have to justify them and fight for them, and they remain on the periphery of a young person's school life, usually given only tiny commitments of school-day time.

A century ago, the *instrumental* reason for bringing the arts into schools was driven by the theory that music and visual arts boosted the development of children's fine motor skills and therefore made them become better factory workers. In other words, the arts were practical; they produced benefits our business-minded society really cared about—manual labor skills for the workforce. Also, starting in the late nineteenth century, the arts were seen as a good way to socialize immigrants. To that end, New York City developed some of the best school music programs in the nation, which endured until the budget crises of the last generation cut them down to the small size we see in the rest of the nation.

I think of my late father in this regard. A product of the New York City public school system of the 1920s and 1930s, he learned to play violin in school. He dreamed of becoming an orchestra conductor all his businessman's life, even though he never pursued his music studies beyond high school. He was a lifelong subscriber to the New York Philharmonic and loved the art of music all his life because of his public school opportunities. (Just recently I had his old violin repaired and refreshed in order to donate it to a public school music program. The gift must keep moving.)

Today we still use instrumental arguments to affirm the value of arts in schools, often pointing to studies that affirm that art programs enhance kids' test scores, school attendance, parental involvement, and the like. We may disagree about how strongly each separate piece of research supports these benefits, but gathered together, the collage of evidence makes a strong circumstantial case for many benefits that accrue from good arts programs in schools—even a hard-bitten doubter has a tough time dismissing the research conclusions.

Even though we now seek different skills than those of factory workers and no longer use music to address the needs of new immigrants, research still affirms the workplace value of arts learning. In 1987, for instance, the Labor Department of the first Bush administration issued a report by the Secretary's Commission on Achieving Necessary Skills (SCANS), which identified five essential skills for a twenty-first-century worker: identification and use of resources; interpersonal skills; information gathering and usage; understanding and managing complex systems; ability to use various technologies. One of the authors, Arnold Packer, wrote that those skills are developed at least as well in the arts as anywhere else. The SCANS report also discusses the importance of developing less tangible (but no less important) abilities, such as self-management and self-esteem. Many arts advocates, in the federal labor and education departments and in the private sector, assert that the arts develop these skills as directly as any other area of school curriculum. Still, the arts remain on the periphery of school priorities.

A 2004 report, *Gifts of the Muse: Reframing the Debate about the Benefits of the Arts*, written by Kevin F. McCarthy, Elizabeth Heneghan Ondaatje, Laura Zakaras, and Arthur Brooks, funded by The Wallace Foundation, and researched and published by the RAND Corporation, rekindled old arguments. The authors propose that in both arts education and the arts in general, instrumental, utilitarian benefits have been overemphasized at the expense of recognizing the arts' intrinsic worth. The report reminds us that people engage in the arts for personal reasons and that personal, experiential rewards are the basis of other kinds of benefits:

By the early 1990s...the social and political pressures that culminated in what became known as the "culture wars" put pressure on arts advocates to articulate the public value of the arts. Their response was to emphasize the *instrumental* benefits of the arts: They said the arts promote important, measurable benefits, such as economic growth and student learning, and thus are of value to all Americans, not just those involved in the arts. Such benefits are *instrumental* in that the arts are viewed as a means of achieving broad social and economic goals that have nothing to do with art per se....But [this] argument downplays...*intrinsic* benefits in aligning itself with an increasingly output-oriented, quantitative approach to public sector management. And underlying the argument is the belief that there is a clear distinction between private benefits, which accrue to individuals, and public benefits, which accrue to society as a whole.

Along the way, the report challenges some of the claims made for practical benefits of the arts, pointing to flaws in the research used to demonstrate *instrumental*—that is, economic and educational—gains. *Gifts of the Muse* sparked an outcry from many who argue that the case for the arts' ability to boost test scores and produce other learning benefits is stronger than the report claims. Others argue that the economic and social benefits are real and proven. No matter which side of the argument you fall on, the debate was back. Perhaps it never left: Do we believe in the arts for their own sake, or for many sakes for which they have been used since human artists started painting on cave walls at Lascaux?

But there is another way to consider the relationship—which is, I think, the most useful reading of this valid report. One side will never convince the other, and we arts advocates need as many kinds of arguments as we can get. To those who passionately espouse the instrumental argument, I contend that the report has done us all a service by refocusing attention on the ways we can affirm the intrinsic benefits of the arts, the harder case to make, but the one that lasts longer and lives closest to our hearts. A figure that appears early in the text provides a provocative way of looking at the "worth" of art (Figure 18.1). Its two axes attempt to show where the various benefits fall.

The "framework" graphic has two important implications. First, it presents a fluid and overlapping spectrum of benefits, not an exclusionary set of boxes. This is fitting, because historically and experientially the arts include and welcome all benefits—and don't privilege one kind over the other. A personal engagement and pleasure in the arts, over time, naturally

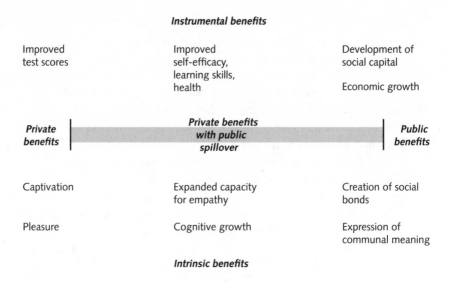

Instrumental benefits

| Improved test scores | Improved self-efficacy, learning skills, health | Development of social capital |
| | | Economic growth |

| Private benefits | Private benefits with public spillover | Public benefits |

| Captivation | Expanded capacity for empathy | Creation of social bonds |
| Pleasure | Cognitive growth | Expression of communal meaning |

Intrinsic benefits

FIGURE 18.1 Framework for Understanding the Benefit of the Arts

Source: Kevin F. McCarthy, Elizabeth Heneghan Ondaatje, Laura Zakaras, and Arthur Brooks, *Gifts of the Muse: Reframing the Debate about the Benefits of the Arts*, MG-218-WF (Santa Monica, Calif.: RAND Corporation, 2004). Entire report available for download at http://www.rand.org/pubs/mono-graphs/MG218/).

leads to a more empathetic connection to other people (which in turn enriches the community) and to more curious learning (which indirectly raises test scores). Second, it tacitly acknowledges that all the benefits of the arts have a basis in individual experience. People do not go to a chamber music concert to raise test scores or to boost America's economic strength. They seek a personally rewarding experience; indeed, that is the only thing that ultimately makes it worth the investment of time, full attention, and money in a world of so many options and enticements.

As you can see, I don't buy into the dualistic instrumental-versus-intrinsic argument, or the public-versus-private benefits debate, nor do I think the RAND report asks us to do that. I again apply wisdom of the great physicist David Bohm, who suggested that anytime we are faced with a seeming polarity, we should look for the larger truth that contains both extremes. To me that larger truth has something to do with the fullness of artistic experience. I believe that the discovery of meaning in art—an entirely personal experience that is often triggered by exposure to great works—is so powerful that it explodes into both intrinsic and extrinsic rewards. The person who is startled into a greater level of awareness by a powerful string quartet—or a great play, or a great painting—begins to wake up and to participate in life more fully. That participation may express itself in a richer internal emotional or spiritual life (intrinsic benefits), and/or it may result in a greater inclination to learn (higher school scores) and/or it may spur the impulse to communicate with or serve others.

The *Muse* report reminds us that it takes a personal investment to be able to tap into those rewards. A few disconnected encounters don't provide the sustained experience necessary to find personal enrichment in the arts, or the motivation to keep participating. To speed the journey to the promised land—full access to the power of art—we have to maximize the impact of each encounter, and to provide more personal reward all along the way. That is why I am so passionate about urging musicians (all artists!) to commit to learning the education skills that facilitate and intensify the experience of your music (of any artistic offering). Just playing the music, however brilliantly, is no longer enough. Most audiences for art, and certainly the audiences who don't currently attend, need a little support (often from teaching artists who are best prepared for this role) to have the experiences that count. And if they get them—and we had better do everything we can to make sure they do, because they may not come back if they don't—they will naturally become more curious and participate more—which will, over time, raise test scores, boost the local economy, build a stronger community, and keep the arts growing in our culture.

Gifts of the Muse tells us that people who have active, ongoing relationships to the arts are those who were artistically involved as young people. School programs and work with young people are not luxuries for the bleeding-heart types, nor are they the domain of those who can't build a high-flying concert career—they are the foundation stone of our future participants.

The teaching artist aims at intrinsic goals, especially dynamic musical engagement, and if she succeeds, the instrumental goals are also advanced. Good teaching artists can include some of those instrumental goals that count a lot for their partners in the school, especially in residencies that afford multiple visits. However, the Muse report implicitly warns us that aiming *primarily* at the instrumental goals means both kinds of goals are less likely to be attained.

19

Blind Dates, Steady Dating, and Musical Marriages

Education loves its buzzwords, and education in the arts is no exception. For music teaching artists who have lived through the rhetorical epochs of "standards," "authentic assessment," and "arts-integrated lesson design," we are now in the "era of partnerships." Partnerships of all kinds are proliferating throughout arts education—it is a veritable Reverend Moon marriage ceremony out there. What is this rush toward partnerships? Does it take a village to get students started musically? Isn't one good music teacher enough?

Back in my primary school days, every elementary school teacher was legally required to master piano basics as a part of her teacher training and to use music regularly in every early education classroom. We sang all day in Mrs. Newman's and Miss Mazden's classes (although Mrs. Newman could have used a little partnering help with those chords in "America, the Beautiful"— they were loud, not exactly majestic or fruited, and definitely plain).

Partnerships are more than a linguistic fad. They have emerged partly as a practical response to current conditions, and in their deeper expression, they are a quietly radical inquiry into changing the way arts connect to learning. The practical aspect of partnering responds to the scarcity of time and expertise for musical learning in many schools—and to the professional music world's need to be a part of young lives. According to the National Center for Education Statistics, while more than 90% of American schools say they teach music, only one in five elementary schools commits more than forty-nine teaching hours per year to music instruction. (That's about one-third of the average in other industrialized nations.) In only a third of elementary classrooms do teachers include music in their instruction more than "just a little." And in high schools, music learning has become rare, except for actively interested students who seek it out.

Bringing in outside expertise enriches the thin musical texture of schools and introduces students to music they would never otherwise discover. Most musicians have made school appearances and know that the educational quality of such events can range widely. Many occasions just click, but sometimes we have a hard time believing a significant educational event just happened. (These situations, more like arrangements than true partnerships, can resemble tests of endurance rather than significant educational experiences.) However, when partnership projects are well planned, and when students are prepared, every musician becomes an educator, everyone learns, and music takes a solid step forward in the minds, hearts, and awareness of students.

Many of the professional linkups that call themselves partnerships are really just cooperation—well-intentioned mutual accommodations that do not aspire to achieve something educationally significant or new. There is nothing wrong with two parties working cooperatively, but partnership represents a deeper challenge and potential. I classify the range of partnerships in three categories: blind dates, steady dating, and marriage.

The simplest kind of music-and-education collaboration is a blind date where you meet at the party where friends have decided you should meet. The more involved partnership is regular dating, which includes meeting one another's families and really getting to know one another, and doing worthwhile things together, but it stops short of the big commitment. Real partnership is a marriage.

"Collaborations" should bring teachers and presenters/arts organizations together to plan how and when a program can make a contribution, serving everyone's interests and students' needs. With a little more commitment, a partnership begins—the music professionals begin to listen to the educators, and jointly they consider the musical offering and the ways it can respond to needs and interests of the schools.

The "blind date" partnership typically has no goal beyond the presenter's making sure the musician or ensemble shows up and is engaging with the students, providing some appropriate learning along the way. Musicians know little about the students or the life of the specific school. (I have heard ensembles in their spoken introductions not only get the name of the school or city wrong, but even botch the name of state they are in. Everyone in the audience found this flat-out insulting.) All the arrangements are designed to make the event painless and pleasant for everyone involved—but "painless and pleasant" hardly sets inspiring educational or artistic goals. The quality of the occasion depends entirely on what the musicians have to offer and how well that offering fits with the occasion. In the name of expediency, everyone involved communicates only the necessities. This is pretty much the standard setup—not dissimilar from the old standard of twenty years ago, when an artist popped into a classroom to do a one-shot "Meet the Flute" event and then disappeared, leaving the students with no damage, no impact, and a vague sense of "what the heck was that?" While programs today rarely are so transparent in the marketing and description of their work, I confess I see a lot of musicians doing presentations that are exactly what one might have seen fifty years ago. I am old enough to declare that I *did* see such presentations fifty years ago! And they didn't do much for me then either.

The prospect of real partnerships raises possibilities and challenges for ensembles and presenters. In a full partnership, both sides share their aspirations, concerns, constraints, best ideas; they work over time to create programs that embody both unique features of each partner and overlapping, shared goals that are the target of the work. The possibilities seem limitless to me. Imagine if we could maximize the impact of each opportunity to change the way people (students, teachers, administrators, parents—everyone connected to the school) think about music and how it might fit into their lives. Instead of just "putting on that outreach event" and hoping good things happen, we actually create those events together to suit the unique configuration of the occasion. Imagine if everyone involved in outreach work actually thought about the learning goals of the occasion, discovered those that were shared, and emphasized those in the program they created. Also, what about partnerships with unconventional partners like museums and science centers and public parks—could we use the practices of partnership to create new audiences for our music?

Serious partnerships start by targeting modest-sized experiments. Partners seek that extra bit of funding needed to build something new. The challenges to this are real. Partnering in this way takes money and time; it takes a willingness on everyone's part to plan creatively (not just expediently), to rethink assumptions, to communicate patiently and well, and to experiment. Learning to truly listen—not just to nod agreeably as you really look to get what you want—to the many levels of concern, need, and interest on both sides is often the hardest part of building good partnerships. Because time and money limitations are so real, most partnership experimentation around the country is done in pilot projects—just one or two or a few parts of a program test out "going deeper," where the extra time can be dedicated without driving people batty. As the learning from that pilot program grows, the lessons are then applied more broadly—at least that is the plan and the justification for the overinvestment in the pilot project. This might mean that a presenter would seek to build real partnerships with only a couple of venues, of just a couple of classrooms, and have the ensembles work in greater depth only with them, until the lessons learned can spread.

What steps would be involved in creating such partnerships? One major step is to address the hard questions that lie at the heart of the future of classical music: What are the goals of outreach events, and what is possible if we are more ambitious? How could preparation for the appearance of a musician or ensemble (and follow-up) enhance its impact, and how can the visiting musicians adjust their presentations, without compromising their strengths, to more directly address the goals of the host institution? What do we *all* have to learn to build partnership skills? How might we find common goals with unconventional partners?

Let's not be naive. Most outreach concerts are not *bad* now, and we have little motivation to put them together differently. Why bother? Because the position of classical music in American life today is so peripheral that we have to become far more successful in creating major impact at every contact occasion. (It also means more gigs for individuals and ensembles that can do this well.) What is at stake is the future of the field, of the art form. Yes, it does take time, extra work, new thinking, and risk taking with new practices to push beyond the status quo, but the benefits are numerous. Not only do we expand as artists, not only do the musicians build new outreach skills they can market and cash in on, but the partner institutions have their goals met more thoroughly, and so become more committed to the value of music as an ongoing part of their institutional life.

Opera presents a good example of what can happen. One of the key reasons that opera has been growing in popularity, as other performing arts struggle, is the depth of its educational partnerships. Over the last twenty years, opera education has changed the way the art is introduced to American students, and this in-depth exploration has had serious impact. Opera education is much less about show-and-tell, and much more about hands-on creation. It has invested in create-an-opera partnerships with schools that are more complex and expensive to manage but leave a deep impact on students and teachers, one that is showing up at the box office, I believe.

Which brings us to money. Time is money, and it's unrealistic and inappropriate to expect professional musicians, presenters, or educators to give more than a little planning time without compensation. This is why serious partnerships usually begin by targeting modest-sized experiments. They heroically go out and create that extra bit of funding that provides the time to build something new. Partnerships are finding that many funding sources are keenly interested in this idea of going deeper. Indeed, in the funding community, "deeper" is the trend. Funders, who for many years loved seeing big student head counts for their program money, have come to admit that drive-by arts education, mile-wide-but-an-inch-deep programs, don't have any lasting impact. I have seen every kind of funding source—from state and local school budgets, to foundations, businesses, and individuals, from arts councils to PTAs—tapped to create pilot partnerships that go deeper. Partnerships are an effective way to go deeper.

Musicians and ensembles should know that thousands of schools and cultural organizations, teachers, artists, and administrators around the country are willing to pour in the extra time to create real partnerships because they believe that deeper arts learning relationships are necessary and worth the effort. Musicians and music organizations need to do the same. Presenters and performers must create pilot programs in which they take the time to ask the hard questions and listen to the real answers from everyone involved. What are the true goals of that elementary school, hospital, or aquarium in having an ensemble perform? They may not even know, so the dialogue might take longer than you expect.

What are the real goals of the presenter and musicians—not just the "get it done" and get the money goals but the deeper goals that got us into this field in the first place? Among all those goals, which are the ones that we all share most passionately? What matters enough to you to pour your time and heart into, to work with people (educators) who don't think like you do, so you can light up new understanding in young lives? Once those goals are identified, how can you and a partner shape a program that really meets them? How will you know if your project has met your ambitious goals? The word *partner* (which you notice has *art* right at its heart) has two derivations from Latin. One means "to divide up," and the other means "to hold joint trusteeship." Those seem pretty much like the options we face in creating classical music outreach events. We can partition the responsibilities, as is typically done, and get the job done as efficiently as a delivery service. Or we can take joint responsibility and work our way into dynamic partnerships that suit the aspirations of the presenter, performers, and host institution, and our art. Let's jointly hold a better future in trust. Let's earn that trust by bringing our most committed energies to our existing or future partnerships, listening, asking, and risking a chance to go deeper.

Part V Current Challenges

20

Arts Integration
The Hot Zone

Buzzword: integration, as in arts integration
Etymology: from the Latin, meaning "making whole"
American history: the civil rights movement
Arts education: bringing music into classroom learning
Arts integration overview: great potential and great caution

The largest area of experimentation in arts education across the country today is "arts integration." Schools and school districts, arts organizations and individual artists, enthusiastic teachers and model schools—by the thousands—are exploring the benefits of bringing more arts experiences into classrooms in direct relation to other curricula. On the surface, the idea is enormously appealing. Classroom learning can be revitalized with the excitement, fun, and fuller attention the arts often elicit. (Wouldn't you have welcomed an exploration of "description" in music as a part of your composition lesson in ninth-grade English class?)

Arts integration also means that the arts get taken more seriously; they are given a central place, right in the classroom, with an opportunity to engage great numbers of young people. Sounds like a win-win situation, especially when (in so many schools) testing mania deadens classroom learning and tight school budgets push the arts ever lower on the schools' list of priorities. That's why the arts integration idea has become a darling of grant officers and the focus of so much experimentation and research. So why do I suggest caution?

A little background. As you read in an earlier chapter, the arts came into the public school curriculum in the United States around the year 1900. The two motivations that drove this change—art for art's sake, and art for the sake of the workplace—are still with us. During the 1930s to the 1950s, the "progressive" trend in education emphasized the importance of the arts in awakening a youngster's natural creativity. Music, though rarely a central part of the curriculum, became a part of every student's life, and significant numbers of students joined the school chorus, orchestra, or band. (It's interesting to note that "creativity skills" have reappeared in education reform debates, and arts education is beginning to sense the rise of a new tide of interest, after music and art programs ebbed so low during the No Child Left Behind era.)

As for integrating the arts with the rest of the school curriculum, there has always been some of that—after all, how did you learn the alphabet? Thank you, Mozart. (To this day, I have to sing the planet song to remember whether Jupiter or Saturn is nearer Earth.) And many good teachers have always taken an interdisciplinary approach—my French teacher showed us paintings of French locales and had us follow recipes in French to make French foods. Unfortunately, my ninth-grade history teacher's bright idea to excite us about ancient Greece by showing the film of a production of *Oedipus Rex* backfired—the film was so stupendously boring, it made me hate any culture that could think that was a good night out.

Starting in the 1960s, the number of jobs for music and art teachers began to swing like a pendulum in response to economic recessions and national back-to-basics outcries. (Incidentally, I have come to believe that, despite whatever heartfelt talk you hear, what really drives those major school reform changes, what creates action, is the moment that American industry feels fear. When corporate leadership feels a threat, represented by Sputnik or Japanese economic growth, or, now emerging, the fear that business innovation will be taken over by China and India, we see school priorities change.) Since the sixties, the basic pattern has remained the same: elementary school students get some arts experiences; middle and high school students with a personal interest can follow a musical track of some kind, work in the arts studio, or be in a school play or dance. But integrated projects arising within a school's faculty are rare, left largely to the unsupported efforts of inspired individuals. Most such efforts are made almost impossible by teachers' schedules, which are diabolically arranged so that the music and arts teachers cannot meet to plan or talk with other teachers—one set is working while the others are on their break.

When the roster of school music and arts specialists was slashed during the recession of the early 1980s, many organizations jumped in to fill the vacuum. Cultural institutions (an orchestra's education department, a performing arts center's outreach effort, or an ensemble with a school program) and arts education organizations (independent groups like Young Audiences and Urban Gateways) increased their presence in classrooms. "Teaching artists" began to appear regularly in an increasing number of schools, and they brought a set of learning priorities that differed from those held by the departed full-time music and art specialists.

Initially, there was some tension between the remaining specialists and the TAs. Some music teachers felt their jobs were threatened; after all, the TAs cost schools comparatively little, and their brief stays were lively, and sounded good to administrators, parents, and school boards who wanted students to have some arts experiences but were hesitant to budget what arts teachers and programs require. The music teachers claimed, rightly, that the TAs did not do the foundation work of building skills over time. ("They breeze in, do all the fun stuff, get the kids all charged up and unfocused, and then they disappear, leaving me in a worse position.") The charming clarinet player who visited the class three times didn't teach anyone how to play an instrument or how to read standard musical notation. But she did get them interested in music and prepared for the performance they would see, if all went well. So despite the grumbling, most administrators and teachers who worked with the TAs saw their benefit.

For their part, the TAs expressed frustration with teachers' reluctance to engage creatively. As visitors to schools, TAs often felt disconnected. Yes, they provided a quick firecracker of experience to enliven a dull school day, but they knew they had no real artistic or educational impact. Teaching artists were not always diplomatic in the early years, sometimes bringing in an attitude about their specialness or condescension toward the music teachers.

Over the years, these anxieties and frustrations have diminished, as each side has come to realize that the other was not only *not* an enemy but was a potentially valuable partner. In the early 1990s, I began to notice that arts specialists were finding time to meet with visiting artists and that, in more and more places, the two groups were beginning to coordinate their work. Classroom teachers even began to vie to have artists join them, and they looked for ways to make the artist's focus relate to something else students were studying.

By the late 1990s, the integration experiment was under way around the country. Large, well-funded programs, as well as small experiments and conferences, began to address the key challenge: ensuring that art experiences in the classroom accomplish both artistic and scholastic goals. Many of the planning conversations of this time were awkward; teachers and teaching artists, basically unfamiliar with each other's methods and expertise, struggled to find common ground. Some experiments sought balance but erred on one side or the other. I personally witnessed the "Dance of the Fractions," in which movement was used to teach math. As cute as this was, it bent the arts too far toward the curriculum. The students did indeed learn fractions better, tested better on that part of their math curriculum, and even used their bodies in imaginative ways (a practice that often boosts learning)—but they didn't learn anything about the art of dance. Their choreographic and performing decisions were based entirely on representing math information accurately, having no personal stake in the choices. The students cared no more about dance after the project than before it. The most troubling aspect of this was that the school claimed it now had a successful dance program and an arts integration plan that worked, in a program that had little if any dance learning at all!

Conversely, I have seen classroom efforts that purport to connect art to the curriculum but that are really just pasted-on excuses for doing an art project. The "Rainforest Rag" was a project in a sixth-grade classroom in Georgia. The TA and the culminating class composition did make some reference to sounds you would find in a rain forest, but the project was really all about music exploration. It was a great art-for-art's-sake compositional project, and three cheers for such opportunities, but don't mistake that for an arts-integrated project in which both subjects are advanced. The students were no more invested in the rain forest at the end of the project than at the beginning, so the investment of time didn't pay off for the classroom teacher's environmental science goals. That is the gamble of arts integration—learning in *both* subject areas goes further as a result of bringing them together.

The "Polyrhythm Project," in New York City, is an example of successfully integrated music and history. Originated by teaching artist David Wallace, who has been mentioned often in these pages for his exemplary work, it has been picked up and extended by other musicians too. The visiting musician teaches the eighth-grade students about polyrhythms, of the kind that came across the ocean from Africa with the people who were taken as slaves. The students begin by exploring polyrhythmic play, first learning the way such play happens in African cultures (to this day), then invent their own polyrhythmic experimentation, including complex layering and jovial competition. Small groups practice and perform their own best work for one another. They then explore (with the history teacher and music teaching artist) how these musical ideas came across the ocean with these African people in such awful circumstances and influenced popular music in pre–Civil War America. What were the tunes of the first half of the nineteenth century? What social and political purposes did they serve? How were these rather simple (and dorky to our ears) tunes enriched by the cool and complex polyrhythmic ideas? Students see how the dopiest of tunes actually became less dopey as they picked up rhythmic complexity from the influence slave musicians were having on their culture. They find out that slaves played at the taverns, and even picked up American instruments like fiddles and played them with musical inventiveness never seen before. Students then move into small groups and select a pop song of the 1830s or 1840s and get a chance to improve it with some rhythmic and musical ideas of their own. And as they work on this project, they begin to notice that the rhythmic ideas they are applying appear in the music they hear on the morning radio. What a moment for them, to discover their active place in a gigantic historical continuum. To realize that "slaves" are not just facts on a test, but rather they were musically brilliant people who under dreadful inhuman conditions contributed to the abusing culture in ways so rich and delightful that their ideas still enrich out lives today. What a deepening of students' textbook learning—human understanding, possible only through the music integration.

I am convinced the reason the project has so much power for students is that it begins in musical engagement, not in the history study. This pair of partners, teaching artist and history teacher, creatively engage the students first, as the students create and play polyrhythmically. This enables the students to discover the relevance of the subject matter to their lives, before they deal with the facts. Engagement before information works.

To achieve such successes, American educators are now beginning to delve into the rich challenge of real integration of the differing priorities of the two cultures, arts and schools. There is a clear stylistic difference—teaching artists seek to excite and engage students in musical or artistic thinking and creating, often in an improvisatory "fly by the seat of the pants" style; classroom teachers have explicit, specific goals they must achieve, and they rely on sequential rigor, and documented accountability, to get there. Teaching artists emphasize engagement; teachers focus on achievement. The work of teaching artists is rarely, if ever, formally assessed; teachers are driven by test results—their jobs depend on them.

The arts integration experiment is by now far enough along that the field is beginning to learn from the findings. The discoveries are important for *all* teaching artists to know about—not just those who spend time in schools and are asked to connect their program with school curriculum. The key discoveries relate to all musicians' larger mission to discover more effective ways to draw all people into music. Here are some conclusions and observations I can report:

• Arts integration can work, but the field received an ice-water bath in 2000. An important study (from Harvard's Project Zero), the REAP report, from the Reviewing Education and the Arts Project, looked at all research from 1950 through 1999 that examined the claims linking arts in the classroom to testable academic improvement. While the REAP authors were observing only academic outcomes, not arts learning (and they admitted that much is absorbed that does not appear on academic tests), they basically said that many casual claims about the success of arts integration were baseless. REAP sparked new research and a focus on refining arts integration practices. (See chapter 31 for a more detailed discussion of the strengths and weaknesses of the REAP research.) Later research has shown that arts integration thoughtfully done *can* (but doesn't always) produce many benefits—from improved scores on tests to better socialization skills to a better attitude toward school. (To check out the latest music-related research, go to the Arts Education Partnership Web site and look up the organization's report *Critical Links* and its book *Third Space* at http://www.aep-arts.org.)

• It takes time. I have noticed that several years of partnering are needed for a teacher and a teaching artist to really understand each other. The difference is partly semantic (is what we mean by *rhythm* really the same in music and poetry?) and partly stylistic; but even more subtly, it takes time to fully grasp your partner's goals in enough detail to realize how your work can complement theirs. I find both partners are polite and casual in their listening throughout the early going, but they begin to *really* listen as the commitment to the work deepens. Casual listening results from the parochial mind-set that wants to do work that comfortably suits our preferred way of doing things, rather than listening to discover what the partner really means and wants, and stretching to find something new that accomplishes what both need.

• We are creating a hybrid. Arts integration is not just a polite accommodation of well-intentioned partners; it is a new way of teaching. It is a synthesis of pedagogies in which each partner adopts new, shared goals and coordinates teaching practices to make sure both achieve them.

• Arts integration is usually attempted in one of three ways: by content, by theme, or by process. Content connections (when both sides emphasize similar subject matter) look good on paper but are often information-based and not particularly engaging for learners. Students understand why you are listening to Gustav Holst's *The Planets* in relation to astronomy, but that doesn't mean either is illuminated or that the students are engaged. (I was very impressed with one Holst-astronomy project that culminated in having the students compose their own section about Earth, which Holst does not include in *The Planets*.) Thematic connection (in which both partners emphasize a theme that is central to their teaching goals, such as "theme and variation" or "patterns" or "American style") can excite new learning if the partners are passionate, clever, and well coordinated. Process connections (wherein both partners emphasize skills and practices such as "making compositional choices" or "decoding hidden information") are less common but often spark greater student involvement.

• Planning time is crucial. When a new arts integration plan is submitted to me for review, I no longer look first to see how bright the ideas are, nor do I skim for the names of the people involved to see how smart and experienced the team is. Instead, I flip to the back to see how much paid planning time they have allocated. If they wrote in an embarrassment of hours, it may be just enough for the program to succeed. There are plenty of smart ideas and people, but if there is not enough time to rethink, to go through the awkward process of evolving teaching practices and deep partnering, the program will not do much for student learning.

• Engagement is the sine qua non. My own experience has convinced me the catalytic fuse that produces learning in both art and other subject matter is lit only when the students are caught up in the *art* part of the project. Up front. When students "make stuff they care about," then that released energy springs into the connected curricular material, and only then do we tap the full potential of arts-integrated learning. Otherwise, the arts and the curriculum may be compatible—but not integrated.

We, as teaching artists, must focus on that core challenge—how do we engage students (and adults and colleagues and family and friends) artistically, musically, so that we can spark their curiosity to learn more? Many ensembles and musicians with outreach programs feel they are successful if they are charming, personable, and lively enough to hold the attention of squirmy youngsters in a cafetorium. That is certainly a good skill to have. But more is now possible. The opportunity to actually move music and art into the center of the learning in schools has been offered.

21
Reflecting on Reflection

Consider the following: Can anyone—no matter how gifted—learn to play a passage well without being able to hear how it sounds objectively and then extrapolate what needs to be done to improve it? Can a composer create a movement without the habit of noticing where it is going, and sensing better and worse choices a thousand times along the way? Good musicians work with those skills deep in their bones—so deep that reflection and self-assessment are not separated from musical action at all; they become fused with the acts of performance and creation. Yet teaching artists too often forget to develop these crucial reflection skills in their students.

Reflection and self-assessment practices can be used and taught in every setting—in private lessons, workshops, classrooms, master classes, even in conversations with colleagues and in performances. By modeling them and by weaving them into your instruction, you help develop the inner climate learners need for successful lifelong learning. In fact, fostering that healthy inner climate in learners may be a teacher's most important legacy.

Reflection

Back in our original guidelines, I wrote that the philosopher John Dewey told us that we do not learn from our experiences unless we reflect upon them—it's that simple. Musical experiences are particularly dense and particularly subtle. Music's abstract and ephemeral nature intensifies the learner's (and the listener's) need for reflective pauses. The word *reflect* comes from the Latin meaning "bend back toward," which precisely describes the reflective impulse—to take that vague body of an experience and bend it back into our view. Human experience is so densely packed with data—large and small interpersonal transactions, sensory stimuli, information coming in from all directions—that we require periodic pauses to scan our experiences and precipitate out what's important to us. In time, these grains become the pearls of our learning.

So much is going on in any chunk of complex music that, as listeners, we cannot take it in, or retain what it offers, without employing the process of reflection. The sophisticated listener does this naturally. Likewise, in making music, we need to call our own processes back into our awareness, so that we can see—and take note of—how we just did that, what was different than before, how it felt in the body, and so forth. Most teaching either "pours stuff in" or asks students to "put work out"; but helping a student learn how to reflect on his or her own practice creates an inner strength—learner-centered ballast.

American culture does not foster reflective practices; indeed, it squelches them. Because action, reaction, and stimulation sell so well and so widely, young people are not in the habit of reflecting on those often-subtle internal blips of curiosity, feeling, discovery, and uncertainty that pass through consciousness during complex experiences. They are conditioned to want and demand more input. Reflection attends to the messages and cues from our authentic selves; it provides the raw materials for creativity and the development of a personal voice. It's not just mainstream culture that suppresses reflection—American schooling also ignores it. The school day offers few opportunities for students to consider how they feel about—and value—the information being presented to them. Acts of reflection are private, fitful, unsupported, and not honored with the hardest currency of schooling—time. An arts course can be a haven where students are guided to notice their own personal processes and responses, but only if arts teachers put a high priority on them. As things now stand, the locker room—not the music room—is probably the most reflective place on campus, because only in the locker room is the study of and reflection on performance videotapes a regular and essential practice. Do we record, listen to repeatedly, and study our music rehearsals?

Consistently providing learners with opportunities to reflect builds habits of mind that students will rely on throughout their lives. We cannot stint them, relegating reflection to a group discussion left for the last five minutes of the class (which we often run out of time to include). When preparing for our performances, we cannot exclude reflection and just hope for the best. We cannot assume the private student is good at observing her own performance and progress, able to identify the elements of consequence. We must provide reflective pauses as teaching opportunities, at junctures when the learner would benefit from a scan of the experience to grab hold of the few key pieces to retain. We must model reflective capacity overtly, showing our learners how *we* reflect and learn from what we see and hear.

Do you take a moment to reflect on your work as a teacher in front of students and share your sense of how *you* did that day? Imagine it—at the end of a class, you say, "I thought the small group activity when we composed was the best part of the class today. The warm-up didn't seem to engage you much—my instructions weren't very clear, and hardly anyone was answering questions. But I noticed a lot of energy and imaginative musical choices being made in the small group work. What do you think?" If you are building a relationship with that group, you just made a bold demonstration of walking your talk, and I think you just laid the foundation for deeper work with them.

Reflecting is not navel-gazing. It is an active internal state in which we accomplish many personally crucial goals. Think about the ways you reflect in your own life: you sit and think, go for long walks or drives, write in a journal, talk to friends, swim, jog, sketch—I have even heard people mention skydiving as a reflective activity. Think about the *reasons* you naturally reflect, what you rely on reflection to accomplish—perhaps to solve a problem, figure out something that is bothering you, make a decision, clarify a confusing situation, more deeply enjoy something wonderful, learn from mistakes and successes. In modeling reflection for learners, you model the habit of mind—you pause and consider what just happened and share the process and observation. You speak the internal questions aloud, so the learner gets the feel for that inner work: "I never noticed before that Bartók did that in this piece"; "I wonder what the right image is for the phrase"; "When I get stuck like this, here's what I ask myself..."

It is the same in guiding the learning of others. We must invite learners to reflect in a variety of ways and for a variety of purposes. Table 21.1 illustrates some common reflective tools that I and other teaching artists use. The second column names some of the purposes for which you might use them. The third column provides an example of what the combination might look like. The list is certainly not comprehensive; different tools might easily be used for goals other than those suggested. Please use the table to spark your own ideas that best suit your own teaching goals, situations, and style.

The following are three guidelines for artists who would like to incorporate reflective activities more prominently in their teaching repertoire.

Regularity is key.   Model the way artists work at their best—asking reflective questions throughout the process. Hit the "pause" button in your teaching at junctures between one exercise and another, at the beginning and end, and any time a significant moment or part of a project holds a

TABLE 21.1 **Examples of Connecting Reflective Tools, Goals, Examples**

Reflective tool	Possible goal	Might look like
Guided thinking	Deepen musicality	Teacher poses a great question to think about, e.g., "What are some fresh lifeways we can bring to this passage?"
Dialogue	Dig into a problem area	Teacher asks illuminating questions and follow-up questions: "Talk me through your thinking steps when you work on this part of the piece."
Journal writing—free	Clarify response or feeling	"For the next 2 minutes write about one mystery you find in this section, and why it matters to you."
Journal writing—guided	Capture expectations	"Find at least three expectations you had before you listened/performed; where did they come from, and how they were met or surprised?"
Guided group discussion	Group takes ownership of a key idea	"What about this piece makes it sound American?"
Unguided group discussion	Uncover subsurface issues of importance	"What's the point of listening to a piece like this? Are the reasons important?"
Peer interview	Illuminate personal process	"Interview your partner about...the things she did while listening to that movement"; or "Interview your partner about the learning journey she has had in playing that passage."
Write a review	Focus critical attention	"Write a 100-word review of our performance of that piece."
Cross-discipline	Clarify complex ideas	"Make two sketches, one of the way you played [or heard] that piece the first time, and one of the way you play [or hear] it now."
Storyboard	Document process	"Create a five-cell storyboard that captures the key moments of the process we just went through this week."
Improvise	Switch perspectives	"Describe the performance, from the point of view of the music we just played"; or "Write a singles ad for this piece and the kind of listeners it wants to pick up."
Self-assessment notes	Embed habit of self-assessment	"Take a minute to jot some notes in your process journal."

message your learners need to grasp. Do it often, and do it with eager interest to see what you get. The attitude of curiosity about what you will discover is the healthiest soil in which to nurture the growth of reflective skills. These inquiries do not need to be long (although when you hit a juicy exploration, let it roll), but they do need to be consistent, always interesting, and rewarding to pursue.

And remember, as teaching artists we invite learners into the acts of reflection, trying to build a rewarding habit in them. Don't critique the quality of their reflection, or learners won't take ownership of the practice, which is how they get better over time. So don't respond, "The piece has other, more significant, elements than those you noticed," or, "I think you are missing some of the key weaknesses in your playing"—such criticism undermines the reflective habit. Accept reflective observations as true for the person, perhaps contrast the learner's with your own view on occasion, perhaps use it diagnostically to see where their understandings lie, but support their reflective effort.

Be inventive.   Many teaching artists are creative in the activities they design and lead, yet they are perfunctory in their invitations to reflection. Around the third time most kids hear "Take out your journal and...," they turn off. The third time they are asked to think about how they just did something, and then you move on without really listening to their answer, they are going to lose interest. Be as imaginative and entertaining with the reflective invitations as you are with other activities. "If that piece of music had a MySpace profile, how would it read?" "You *are* your emerging composition; what would you say to a neighbor composition about how the process is going?" Or even, "You are a reporter for Creative Youth Radio; using your pen as a microphone, would you interview your neighbor about her process of mastering that piece of music?" It is amazing how smart you become when the reporter brings the imaginary microphone to your mouth. To develop the habit of reflection in learners, it must feel good to do, and it must produce discoveries that consistently interest the learner.

Vary the modalities.   Don't overrely on the same reflective tools—group discussion or personal journal; vary the reflective invitations to include learners with differing kinds of strengths. Not everyone reflects best in writing or by talking. "Now that you can perform that piece well, please sketch a five-cell storyboard that captures your key moments along the way in mastering that piece." "If you were going to write a piece of music that captures your process of learning that piece, what would the piece be like and have in it?" "Show me, with your hand in the air, the shapes you find in that passage."

In the second paragraph of this chapter, I mentioned the performance setting as a place to include reflective activities. The idea is to find clever and effective ways to support the audience in reflecting on what they hear, because it deepens the impact of the music and what they take away and remember. I have a friend who distinguishes art from entertainment by the impact that is left after the encounter. He contends that experiences that linger and continue to exert an influence on us are artistic experiences, no matter what the music is. If we can inveigle a little reflective experience into a performance occasion, we support our audience's capacity to get more of the artistic goodies we are working so hard to provide. In what ways can you gently engage audiences in reflection on what they have heard without seeming weird or disrupting performance expectations? Don't say you can't think of anything and give up; persist in small ways, because it is important. Can you ask reflective questions once or twice in the speaking part of a performance? "I find the following piece reminds me of my childhood. What childhood memories arise for you as you listen?" Then ask for and hear a few examples from audience members after the piece—and see if they can bring it back to the music: "So you remember what you heard that sparked that recollection?"

I urge ensembles to include reflective activities in their adult programs as well as in youth and family concerts, where they are more common. Have you ever asked adults to turn to a neighbor and share things that really struck them in the piece you just played? Have you ever asked them to consider something about the piece you just played, and/or set up a particular lens for viewing the next. For example, "As we have rehearsed this Shostakovich string quartet in recent weeks, we have felt it was about various aspects of grief he experienced after his wife's death. What are some of the different emotions you, or people you know, have had during a period of mourning? Let's see if you find them in the piece as we have; and we will check in with you afterward."

During young people's concerts, I urge you to add reflective questions and challenges to the usual mix of introduction, information, and engagement. "Think for a moment...what are you expecting to hear in the piece we are about to play?"; and then afterward, "What surprised you in that piece?" "If you knew another student was going to hear us perform this piece tomorrow, what would you tell him or her today about what to expect in the music?" Ask interesting, artistically respectful questions of your young audiences; a question like "Was that piece fast or slow?" is neither interesting nor respectful; however, "Why do you think the composer used speediness sometimes?" is.

Do people leave your concerts talking about the music or about other aspects of their day? Can you encourage them to engage in dialogue about the music on their way home—"We are so interested in your response to that new work we just played, we ask you to pull your thoughts together and share them with us on your way out, either on the note cards we provided in the lobby or directly to us; and we will get to the lobby as fast as we can."

Lawrence Tamburri, president, managing director, and CEO of the Pittsburgh Symphony, is troubled when he overhears concertgoers leaving Heinz Hall *not* talking about the music they heard. To him, talking about the music is a barometer of musical engagement—the goal of any performance. So the Pittsburgh Symphony is seeking to enrich the performance atmosphere, to deepen the encounter, and it is keeping an eye on the natural reflective expression of dialogue immediately following the encounter. If people are talking piano instead of parking, Tan Dun instead of tan lines, good things happened in the hall.

Another habit teaching artists need to build is documentation— recording reflections in a way that enables them to stay there so you can come back to them later. Documentation supports self-assessment, and self-assessment is the natural way artists keep learning. Reflection, documentation, assessment—certainly not the three most exciting words in the musical lexicon, but three extremely important, almost overlooked, experience-deepening practices.

22

The Dos and Don'ts
of Assessment

As we did in chapter 15 to tease out embedded preconceptions about education programs, I invited a roomful of musicians to play a free-association game with me. I would say one word, and they would respond with the first words that came to mind. We warmed up with my saying, "Recess." They hollered out responses like "Playground," "Dodgeball," "Cliques," "Fights," "Escape," "Outdoors," "Running," "Friends," and even "Alcove in a wall." There's one in every group.

Ready to play for real, I said, "Assessment." They grimaced and barked out, "Test" "Judgment," "Failure," "Fear," "Unfair," "Institutions," "Dull," "Statistics," "Impersonal." Hardly a scrapbook of rosy-cheeked, gentle, learner-friendly memories. We all carry bruises from our past testing experiences, and so we are cautious or downright resistant about bringing assessment into our teaching situations. With such unpleasant associations, why impose assessment responsibilities on the already challenging aspirations of the music teaching artist? Because, if done right, assessment practices make the crucial difference, turning good learning events into real understanding.

I am the poster child for this topic. For many years, I was a passionate opponent of bringing assessment challenges into a teaching artist's work. I felt it was an institutional wet blanket on the fire we try so hard to light. Until...my pet program couldn't be funded unless it included a serious commitment to assess the student learning. So I was dragged kicking and screaming into the age of assessment—and that requirement taught me more about teaching and learning than any other challenge I had faced. I continue to learn so much through assessment thinking that I have become a zealot for it. Nothing is more intense than the zealotry of converts.

Assessment is a natural, authentic part of the artistic process. Musicians assess the quality of their work all the time, to determine how to get better. The years of training embed criteria of excellence in the very way we think and perform—so intimately that we do not separate artistic action from assessment of its quality. We can encourage new learners to absorb some of these criteria earlier, and can advance the musical learning of those who are not dedicating themselves to a musical track.

Assessment practices can illuminate *some* but certainly not all of the learning contained in our musical activities. They cannot affirm many core learnings teaching artists care most about—we cannot weigh a decrease in boredom at school or measure the joy of musical accomplishment. Etymologically, the word *assess* originally meant "to sit beside." It came to signify one who sat beside a judge in a courtroom and helped him enact judgments, eventually becoming the term for the one who collected the taxes the judge levied (where we get the term *tax assessor*). Loaded with the weight of judges, courts, and taxes, no wonder we grimace at the word. We do well to remember its gentle origins, "to sit beside," which feels very much like the kinds of work colleague artists do together, as partners in the art of learning.

Before looking at some specific assessment practices, let's clarify four key terms:

- *Documentation.* This is the process of setting down work so that it stays there, allowing us to reflect upon it and illuminate the learning it contains. "Documents" include journals and portfolios, but they can also be musical scores, drawings, video and audio tape—anything that stays there and allows us to unpack the learning its holds. Many teaching artists in the performing arts envy visual artists because their "documents" stay there on the wall for in-depth observation and reflection.
- *Reflection.* This was the focus of our last chapter—any process of casting the mind back across experience to accomplish any number of tasks like identifying relevance, figuring answers out, wondering, reviewing experiences, and so on.
- *Assessment.* This is the act of illuminating aspects of a learner's learning. A common misconception is: "I videotaped the whole process; I have done the assessment." No, that person has done some documentation on video, but she hasn't begun the assessment process, which works with those documents to illuminate the learning they contain.
- *Evaluation.* This word is used almost synonymously with *assessment*, but it means something different. We assess the learning of students, and we evaluate the effectiveness of programs. Evaluation of an arts learning program certainly includes assessment data to determine the program's effectiveness, but evaluation takes a different analytic

perspective—you don't "sit beside," you distance yourself and analyze bundles of data to make valid judgments.

Why do we assess? In programs I work on, I insist that the first and foremost purpose, the North Star to guide every choice we make about assessment, comes from this belief: *assessment is first and foremost for the benefit of the learner.* Self-assessment is the primary goal—to help the learner grasp more about what she is learning. This inviolable priority allows me to sleep at night while advocating more assessment in teaching artists' pedagogy. Second, assessment informs those who work directly with the student—the teacher and teaching artist—giving us insight into what the student is really learning. Third, the assessment produces some useful information for those who aren't in the room—for administrators, families, and others who care about that child's learning.

These priorities are the exact reverse of current schooling, of course, where assessment primarily serves the needs of those not in the room and is designed to be convenient, cost-effective, and focused for their interests. School assessments provide some information for educators and families about what the child is learning; but they care little for the self-assessment of the learner herself. So, always, *please*, teaching artists, assess primarily to help the learner to learn better. I know this makes for an awkward fit sometimes when you work in school settings. However, I believe we cannot compromise this fundamental artistic priority. Be as flexible as possible to accommodate school needs, but please don't allow your assessment work to whack yet another institutional bruise on young learners, laid to the blame of music.

Here's an example of how an assessment tool can work in a school or any setting. Figure 22.1 is a little graphic composed of four empty boxes for learners to fill in. If the players in an ensemble each filled out a sheet with these four boxes on a regular basis in rehearsal, it would help them capture and advance their grasp on how they are doing—self-assessment first! They should each fill in all four boxes immediately after a run-though or rehearsal, before they say a word to one another. Both top boxes invite the musicians to reflect upon and identify specific aspects of their individual work within the ensemble that might otherwise remain vague to them: How did *I* do this time? What do *I* need to do to get better? Both lower boxes invite them to take responsibility for group work: How did *we* do this time? What do *we* need to do to get better? After the musicians have filled out the sheets, they should compare their observations and ideas to guide the next steps of their work. If a teacher is involved in the process, this time of sharing observations and ideas is an educator's bonanza.

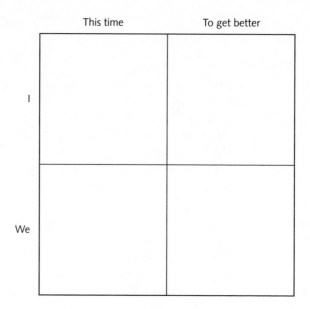

Read the four boxes as asking:
How did I do this time?
What do I need to do to get better?
How did we do this time?
What do we need to do to get better?

FIGURE 22.1 Self-Assessment Form

Source: Author's adaptation, with permission, from *Ensemble Rehearsal Critique*, Copyright 1992 by Educational Testing Service and the President and Fellows of Harvard College (on behalf of Project Zero, Harvard Graduate School of Education). From *Arts PROPEL: A Handbook for Music*, edited by Ellen Winner, Lyle Davidson, and Larry Scripp.

Teachers involved in a process that regularly uses an assessment tool like this learn a lot from studying what the young musicians have written. Finally, if you gather a collection of these sheets over time, they become rich documents to illuminate the growth in musical, rehearsal, and thinking skills over time—it is all set down to assess and communicate the learning that has happened.

I picked up this tool from Pittsburgh high school choral teacher Linda Ross-Broadus, who developed it in her work with Harvard Project Zero's Arts Propel research. It worked for her in chorus rooms, and I have seen it adapted widely, from first-grade classroom cleanup to descriptive essay writing (using only the top pair of empty boxes).

Another simple tool is a pre- and postdocumentation process—you ask students to undertake an identical task at the beginning and end of the work with you, and then the student and you compare those documents to see what has changed. (This is probably not a useful tool for a single visit with learners, where you can't expect much learning impact.) Say, for example, you are going to be doing some compositional work with students. On the first day, you give them a blank sheet of paper with a circle and the word *composer* in the center and ask them to write down on the sheet everything they can think of that connects to the act of musical composition. On the last day, you ask them the same thing. You then hand back their original pages and ask them to identify the differences that appear and assess some of their learning in this project. Second, you review all their documents to learn about the impact of your compositional residency. Finally, you draw valid conclusions about the learning that happened in the room to share with those who sponsored your compositional residency with the students.

This same pre-and-post approach can be used for other kinds of teaching too, like developing listening skills. You ask students to document what they notice and can hear in an excerpt of Ligeti at the beginning of day 1 with you, and a very similar piece on the last day, and then have them assess changes in their capacity to listen and notice and hear based on what they wrote down. If the documentation indicates they didn't get any better, that suggests that either the pre-and-post process isn't aimed right for your teaching, or maybe, less learning is going on than you would like to think.

Certainly you can use pre-and-post approaches in developing performance skills by recording work on day 1 and at the end and having the learners compare and document specific ways in which they got better over time.

Another common tool, akin to that last idea, is called "performance task" assessment. This involves documenting a natural artistic performance (say, videotaping a rehearsal of a piece) and guiding the learner to reflect on it by identifying (and setting them down so you can assess) specific aspects of it to detail what she can or can't do. This is entirely organic musical practice that we formalize a little to give it an assessment focus—merely adding the structure of studying the recorded document, setting down the observations, and assessing what has been learned. And we bother because it deepens the impact for the learner.

Connected to performance task assessment is the use of rubrics, or grids that describe what performance looks like at different levels of quality. We introduced a complex rubric about teaching artistry in chapter 13 (Table 13.2). I want to encourage you to develop simple rubrics that detail the areas of learning you care most about to support your learners' mastery of those capacities. In Table 22.1, I provide two examples that I made up to demonstrate how rubrics work: one is merely a single line from a larger listening rubric, and the other is one

TABLE 22.1 **Examples of Two Rubrics Teaching Artists Might Use**

Listening skill

	Acceptable	Good	Great	Masterful
Rhythm	• Can find and clap the beat	• Can find the meter	• Can find different rhythms and their interaction	• Can identify impact of the piece as a whole

Performance skill in learning recorder

	Acceptable	Good	Great	Masterful
Playing a single note	• Can sound it without squeaking to another note	• Can control attack and finish on the note	• Can control dynamics and duration variables	• Can control aesthetic nuance variables

line from a recorder-playing rubric. There would be several, or possibly many, such lines on a rubric you could use. You introduce these categories to help the learners self-assess where their skills lie, and what getting better looks like. You use the rubric consistently as a way for the learner to identify elements of her performance, and to give discussion and feedback a consistent way to clarify certain elements of skill. Of course, musicians do this all the time internally; this is how they guide their choices, how they know if something they are doing is better or worse, what they need to rehearse or get help with. Using the assessment tool of a rubric helps the learner embed those understandings of quality, grasp what getting better looks like, and celebrate her own improvement. I recommend that you create rubrics that focus on the elements you find most important, and even make them up in partnership with your learners, letting them help you fill in the boxes with their understanding of what increasing quality looks like in the areas you both care about. I have found this a powerful way to increase learners' grasp on what it means to improve in an area.

Finally, let me mention a very common assessment tool—the portfolio—which is a collection of a student's work. The most common kind is a "best work" portfolio in which students collect the documents of their most successful work. While this is fine, gathering does not equal assessment. Portfolios begin to prompt self-assessment more directly by having the contents be student selected. A prompt I use is: "Out of all the stuff we produced in this project, select the documents that are most eloquent in highlighting your learning journey." Or "Pick the documents that show where you learned particular things." I then ask them to include some writing (on post-it notes or additional pages) that helps others discover what the learner knows the documents contain. A scrunched-up score from a big mistake can be an eloquent document; so can three short audio clips of the same eight bars played at two-week intervals, plus a narrative description by the student about the learning she hears. (Harvard Project Zero calls these process-folios.) Portfolios are very common in the arts, indeed they originated in the visual arts; however, too often the portfolio process succeeds well in gathering documentation but entirely misses the assessment opportunity. We must reflect upon and analyze the learning contained in those documents to mine the gold they contain.

Let's close our speedy overview of assessment tools with a big truth about the whole process. Good assessment is more atmosphere than instrument. Creating a curious, conducive, safe atmosphere about self-assessment produces better learning than the best instruments used in an unconducive setting.

You can spot musicians whose learning did not contain or develop a healthy self-assessment culture. They need feedback from others to get a sense of how they did. They often overreact to input because they don't know how to fit others' opinions and observations into the more important context of their own understanding. They tend to stop learning on their own, unprompted by external demand or critique. They are a lot less happy inside a life of musical learning.

Your teaching sets that atmosphere—in the hundred ways you model self-assessment and use the habits of mind of identifying, documenting, and assessing specific aspects of your own work. Your questions of learners must consistently invite and respect the validity of student self-assessment. You must balance your own impulse to tell the student how he is doing with asking the student to identify aspects of his own work. Although it may seem cumbersome at first, make sure you use documentation—have students set things down. Learning blooms when we are able to take the time to assess documents that stay there long enough to unpack the learning they contain, so we can know it, own it, and look back at it comparatively when we have learned more.

The art of creating a good assessment environment is to keep the documentation elegantly simple, and the process of discovering what the documents contain interesting and rewarding. If we create the right atmosphere, we tap the natural human curiosity to discover more about ourselves and feel joy in affirming real accomplishment. It feels great to discover the ways we succeed and to be able to confirm that we are getting better inside the world of music. As thrilling as it is to have a teacher we admire tell us we did well, the habits of mind that enable us to understand for ourselves why and how we did well will take us much further as artists and individuals.

23
Feedback
Giving It and Getting It Right

Recall a time in your life when you learned something difficult, something that you really cared about, and that took time to learn. When
you have a specific instance in mind—anything from learning to ride a
skateboard to mastering an instrument—answer these four questions
about that learning journey:

- What helped you get better?
- What hindered your progress?
- How did you know you were getting better along the way?
- In hindsight, if you could redesign your learning process to make
  it optimum for you, what changes would you make?

I have led professionals in business, science, engineering, as well as arts
and education through that series of questions and have found that in each
setting—whether a corporation, a classroom, or an arts organization—
participants tend to write down pretty much the same answers. When we
humans pour ourselves into learning something hard over time, our wishes
and needs tend to be quite similar.

One answer invariably appears to each of the four questions: feedback.
It is cited more frequently than issues of time, resources, learning environment, or examples of excellence. For some people, feedback topped both
their list of most important supports *and* their list of hindrances. So let's
look at feedback.

As central as it is to the learning process, the art of giving feedback is
widely overlooked in the training of teaching artists. Yet instructing people
how to give and handle feedback is a major focus of leadership training
elsewhere, especially in the corporate environment and in education. You
would be amazed to learn how many millions of dollars are spent in those
fields training leaders to give feedback effectively. And you might also be
appalled to hear how few leaders (from middle management to the top

brass) in business, education, and the arts are more than halfway decent at it.

People in the arts seem to assume that we already know how to manage feedback well enough. We ourselves got a lot of it along the way, so we *must* know. Yet by falling back on our instincts and personal experience, we tend to give feedback the way it was given to us—forgetting that much of the time our own experience was less than optimal (and that may be the understatement of the month!). Yes, most of our teachers and coaches did give us effective feedback, occasionally or regularly, and those lucky enough to have been on the receiving end remember its power. But that's the exception; whenever I raise the topic with musicians, tales of feedback damage pour out.

Most of our feedback mistakes aren't horror stories. They aren't about gross insensitivity or insults. They are just mistakes of unawareness. Almost every time I have observed a teaching artist in a classroom, even when good activities are under way, I witness a parade of common (yet crucial) feedback miscues; for example, missing the right moment, not listening carefully enough to students, asking a question that closes down rather than opens up responses, inviting "open season" on the young artist and making her feel nervous about the feedback, proposing a feedback topic but bailing out on it when there were some seconds of silence.

Let's first agree that you *have to* include feedback loops in your teaching—learners require it. Let's also admit this is most difficult in large group settings, where we don't have much time for one-on-one attention. Too bad, but you have to provide feedback opportunities anyway. Why? Certain kinds of essential mirroring and guidance can only come from the outside. To build confidence, a learner needs to be seen and confirmed in her learning; she needs external affirmation to turn her experiments into reliable understandings she can build on. Without that confirmation by the right person (someone deemed credible and caring by the learner), the learning journey slows and becomes tentative, and the learner is easily knocked off her path.

Think of apprenticeship, perhaps the oldest form of in-depth instruction in human history—its success is entirely dependent on feedback, in context, from the right person. When done artfully, optimally, feedback comes from the right trusted person, in the right way, at the right time, in just the right amount.

The astounding sophistication and beauty of human beings' 30,000-year-old cave paintings suggests that art teaching must be an ancient human activity, and feedback must have been involved in the centuries that passed down the traditions. Feedback may be deeper than human, since other primates give direct feedback, naturally, patiently, successfully.

Many primate biologists (including Jane Goodall and Frans de Waal) have reported simian apprenticeship—with an adult chimp, gorilla, or baboon side by side guiding the learning of a task by a young ape, with feedback. Yet as humans, everywhere outside the nursery school and kindergarten classroom, we struggle to manage human feedback effectively. I am not sure quite how we got so blocked up, but I have a hunch it has to do with institutions and egos, with our culture's prioritization of product above process, with fear and ignorance. Let's address those last two causes just a bit.

Fear appears because it takes courage for the young (and not so young) artist to put her work forward. When a student presents her work in front of peers, and in front of a professional (the teaching artist), in front of a judging authority (a teacher), she takes a risk and becomes vulnerable.

We must handle this moment of courage well to tap into its full learning potential. This truth applies in more settings than schools. Whenever teaching artists (or *any* artists) share their work with one another, it's a high-risk occasion. What tools are out there to help us handle the occasion wisely and effectively? One tool is a formal protocol, which is a step-by-step process the group agrees to follow. For example, the Artist-to-Artist collaborative of teaching artists in Minnesota uses a formal "descriptive review" protocol for giving feedback safely and constructively in workshops led by teaching artists for teaching artists, to improve their work. The protocol's three basic questions for eliciting good feedback are:

1. What do you notice? Describe without judgment. ("I notice...")
2. What questions does this work, activity, or subject of inquiry raise for you? ("I wonder...")
3. What meaning or understanding is intended or conveyed in this work? Speculate on the meaning behind a work or what an artist, teacher, or presenter wants learners to understand.

> *For much more on the Artist-to-Artist protocol, go to http://opd.mpls.k12.mn.us/Descriptive_Review2.html.*

When I watch teaching artists give feedback in groups, it can get to be a mess. We get random observations; we call on the few with hands waving, while others judge. We can't hear from everyone; the discussion gets stuck in a rut that misses the main points. If the group is focusing on the work of one individual, it can get dangerous and scary. These are such common difficulties that educators in all fields have created protocols for a facilitator to guide the group through the feedback process.

Protocols are admittedly artificial in that they impose a fixed sequence of steps for giving feedback, and they can feel stilted at first use. However,

I find them so useful in minimizing danger and maximizing insights in risky situations that I recommend you consider familiarizing yourself with them. In this chapter I supply one example, the Tuning Protocol (Box 23.1). It is distilled from the online resources presented by the Perpich Center for Arts Education in Minneapolis, located on the school's excellent Web site, Artful Online (http://opd.mpls.k12.mn.us/ArtfulTools.html).

You can adapt your own protocol, a simple series of questions the group always goes through in feedback. Teaching artists tend to be good facilitators, recognizing that they are creating an atmosphere and a process through which others may develop their feedback muscles and sense of responsibility.

Many protocols are used in organizational settings when a group focuses at length on a single piece of work. I find the Tuning Protocol

---

BOX 23.1 **The Tuning Protocol**

When to Use It:

- An artist or teacher presents his work and wants more feedback about the process and content.
- A group of collaborators would like to get some feedback on a work in progress so they can refine it or take it to the next level.

Presenter Duties: Presenters provide work in its unfinished state for general feedback or specific feedback about areas of the work they are struggling with.

Time Needed: About an hour, or up to two hours. (Protocols need enough time to allow for meaningful, in-depth observation and reflection. An experienced facilitator can adapt the protocol to the needs of the group.)

1. Getting Started: 20 Minutes

Facilitator: Introduce participants to each other if needed and explain steps of protocol.

Presenter: Give a quick introduction to the lesson or work in progress or subject of investigation. State what you would like responders to focus on or what it is you want to get from the process. Present the work.

Responders: Ask clarifying questions. These are factual questions that can be answered with a short reply or a simple "yes/no."

2. Warm Feedback: 10 Minutes

Facilitator: Ask the group about what they observe, and then what they like or think is successful about the work.

3. Cool Feedback: 10 Minutes

Facilitator: Check in with the presenter to see if he or she wants more feedback. Ask the group about what aspects of the work might be improved or clarified. What questions do they have?

Responders: Frame response in the form of a question: *I wonder if...? Have you thought about...?*

4. Hard Feedback: 5 Minutes

Facilitator: Check in with the presenter to see if he or she wants more feedback.

Responders: Ask deeper, more difficult questions that get at larger, structural aspects of the work. Keep your feedback respectful.

5. Reflect/Respond: 15 Minutes

Presenter: Reflect out loud on the process, respond to any of the questions raised (if you want—you don't have to answer every question), or comment on anything surprising or unexpected that you heard. During this time the other participants are silent.

Responders: Reflect on how the protocol went and how it affected your understanding. Discuss implications for the work in question.

---

useful for a roomful of professionals who don't know each other and who are looking at one teaching artist's work, or at one musician's work—for a session that lasts up to two hours. It is considered a challenging protocol because it invites suggestions about how to make the work better. However, I find it serves well if the initial steps are not stinted.

Generally, a number of considerations are fundamental to providing good feedback whether you use a protocol or not. Here are the elements I think are most important.

The safe yet charged atmosphere.   First and foremost, we must support a student's (or a peer's) risk taking and turn it, over time, into a habit of courage. To do so, we must create the right atmosphere, one that is both safe and charged. You have heard the "safe and charged" paradox earlier in this book to describe any effective learning environment—learners must feel they will not be made to look stupid or required to do things that will embarrass them. But at the same time, the atmosphere has to be electric enough that they want to push themselves to reach for high-quality, personally satisfying answers to the challenges. For example, small groups have been composing variations on a theme the teaching artist presented. Each group must believe they can succeed and that their work will be well received (a safe environment); also the teaching artist must set the level of fun, challenge, even the playful competitiveness high enough that they want their group's variation to be better, or different, or surprising, compared with the others—better perhaps than the TA imagined. It is a skill of teaching artists to be able to foster such environments quickly and sustainably, even as the "judgment" of feedback raises the stakes regarding both safety and aspiration.

Attentiveness to the individual. The learner must feel, whatever the setting, that you actually *see* her and are paying full—even if brief— attention to her work. To accomplish this, build trust by stating specific details about the work. I always begin by pointing out things I see in the work, and I demand the same in group feedback (as do most feedback protocols, such as the Descriptive Review cited earlier). For example, "I noticed Mike's composition included five different notes rather than the three most of us were using." When managing group feedback, I always begin with, "Let's start giving Mike feedback by only stating things we noticed in his composition. No opinions. Nothing about what you liked or didn't like. Just point out things you find in the piece." I police the responses from the group, because people, young or older, can't limit themselves to observation; they slip into likes and dislikes fast. I pull them back: "You said you liked the ending. What were some of the things you saw Mike do in the composition that gave you that positive impression?" "You said you didn't like the beginning. Setting that opinion aside, please identify some of the choices Mike made in the first ten seconds of his piece." The guideline to begin feedback is always: *observation before interpretation or opinion.* Insist on it every time and model it yourself, build it in as a habit of mind. It's essential to good learning, to creating safe-charged atmospheres, to good parenting, and even to good citizenship.

When the learner believes she is really seen, she opens up—because she feels the connection between her intent, the work put in the middle, and the feedback coming from other people. She comes to trust that the feedback is not intended to judge her but to make her work better. Pretty soon she finds that good feedback *does* make her work better, as we all find out in projects that matter to us.

Perceptiveness of observation.   Learning zooms ahead when the feedback illuminates—and this is the value of perceptive feedback—things he didn't know, or, even more powerfully, things he didn't know he knew. When feedback is not perceptive—in other words, does not illuminate new learning for the artist—we earn the prejudice many people have of us in the arts: that our assessment is fluffy, that we say every performance is lovely, that the cow every kid in the room drew is good because everyone tried. If our feedback is off the mark or inaccurate, we confirm the widespread prejudice that because the arts are "subjective" we "lack rigor" because we can't give objective feedback or assessment. (This is completely untrue, even if the impression persists. For example, the College Board's Advanced Placement [AP] exam in studio art is the only AP exam scored by a rubric. Students take no test but instead send in a portfolio of their year's work. The scorers look at the artworks and writing and use a detailed rubric to score their elements, even for a quality as seemingly subjective as inventiveness. No test, no essay or short-answer questions, just artworks with no right answers. It turns out that this test has among the highest "agreement among scorers"—a key measure of an accurate and reliable test—of all AP exams. Yes, artwork can be assessed more precisely than tests in algebra or chemistry.)

The teaching artist is responsible for establishing the standard of perceptiveness the group should aspire to and for making sure perceptive feedback gets delivered. To deliver just the right next step in that individual learner's process, the teacher or teaching artist must be a good perceiver. That is our gift, and our responsibility; otherwise, we may create a positive atmosphere, but we miss the real learning.

Calibration.   A common weakness is the practice of giving feedback from the point of view of our expertise: "This is what I see, and so I will share it all." While certainly such teachers may give accurate and insightful observations, the most effective teachers see far more than they give feedback on, and they make their choices based on the needs and style of that particular learner. Both orchestral conductors and stage play directors see many more flaws in every rehearsal than they can constructively give feedback on; they advance the learning of the individual or ensemble through the elegance of their choices. A theater director once gave me 107 notes after a run-through (I wasn't *that* bad, I swear), and he expected me to enact them in the run-through that evening. This is feedback turned destructive. You may have been the recipient of feedback like that—you probably remember the occasion because it left a mark, as I do thirty years later. Giving an observation to a young violinist who isn't ready to receive it diminishes her enthusiasm and slows down her success.

Credibility. Your feedback requires credibility, which has two aspects for you as an artist and as a teacher: formal and personal. Formal credibility is usually conferred by background and credentials. Since teaching artists aren't formally credentialed, the mere fact that a sponsoring organization has given you the gig is about all we have, plus a track record of experience (which few will know about). This wouldn't work for a brain surgeon, but we must make do with it. (This lack of official stamp of approval is one reason so many cities are currently exploring ways to provide some kind of credentialing of qualified teaching artists.) Credibility as an artist or teacher can be undermined by poor performance, but most learners accept that whatever circumstance brought a TA to teach them is evidence of adequate skill. Play the violin fast for twenty seconds, and your art-cred is assured. It is interesting that formal credibility trumps personal oddity in many situations (we will put up with rude doctors if they are at the top of their field) and within the arts—a virtuoso can be a creep, and a destructive teacher, and some learners will beg for his feedback nonetheless.

Teaching credibility is far less automatic. Even a credentialed educator must demonstrate to learners that they should take him seriously as a teacher. Teachers must earn the learners' willingness to learn from and with them. Personal credibility as a teacher (and artist) is crucial in teaching artist work. Learners in a school setting must feel you are trustworthy, that you see and care about them, and that you are offering something that is going to be worth their risk and effort. They will often forgive nervousness and some odd teaching choices, but if they pick up any whiff of condescension or lack of interest—and they are stunningly sensitive to these, they can pick them up in one part per million—they are far less available to feedback.

Awareness. You demonstrate your teaching credibility by recognizing exactly where the learner is at. You articulate aspects of the process that they know only in doing it; you affirm their observations and experiences; you really listen when they speak and respond to exactly what they say. In group feedback, I always quickly repeat back a question or an observation from a learner: to make sure I got it right (their energy tells me if I have or haven't), letting them know they are heard, and also to slightly reframe or reword their input to give it more impact. For this same reason, we must begin feedback with observations before critique.

Matching feedback to the moment. A general rule: use the fewest words possible to say exactly what you see, responding to exactly where the learning is happening or heading. The common term for the ideal timing is "the teachable moment"—the learner is ready for exactly what you have to offer. More often, we just do our best to match our observations with what seems to be the flow of the learning, pouncing on any hints of specific issues that appear in the learner's mind or process. "Amy, you seem to be struggling with this issue; am I right?"

Listening. Although I have repeatedly said that observation is basic to good feedback, I have come to think that *listening* is even more crucial—that if we listen hard and perceptively enough, we can draw out (the etymological meaning of *educate*) the learner's ability to self-assess. To this we can add those few bits of feedback that target the exact places where the learning is happening. Whenever possible, ask pointed self-assessment question before giving feedback—to strengthen that skill in the learner, and to hear more deeply what she understands. Before you say to a group, "Our performance is weak in the following ways," ask, "How did we do as an ensemble that time?" Or of an individual, "What are some of the ways in which that performance could get better?" Or even, "Which parts of that performance would benefit most from my feedback?" I believe listening—not just to what the learner says but also to what is being said under the words and through the art—is the ultimate skill of feedback. The poet Audre Lorde says we can hear one another into being. Believe it.

Feedback is an art. Since we work in far less than ideal situations, we do the best we can, providing as many learners as possible with the best insights we can manage, being trustworthy and credible, providing some time for feedback within safe and charged atmospheres—always imperfect and always doing the best we can.

Part VI Bringing Teaching Artistry into Performances

24

Fuller Audience Engagement

What Does It Look Like?

"Enough with the theories; what does it look like in practice?"

Because musicians are generally polite by nature (no comments about low brass, please), they don't actually speak that sentence above—but they probably *think* it at some point in my workshops. Since I often teach general principles for drawing general audiences into satisfying musical experiences, it's fair enough to request examples of what those ideas actually look like in a concert. So let's get specific. This chapter will talk you through one concert I saw in 2002 that elegantly and playfully exemplified some excellent strategies that all ensembles can use to enliven their interactions with audiences.

Entitled "Samba vs. Tango: The Cultural Contrasts of South America," the concert was designed by two performers in the Oregon Symphony (OS). The symphony was working within a grant (The Magic of Music Initiative from the Knight Foundation) that supported the development of creative, unconventional chamber ensemble programs designed by their musicians. I led a preparatory workshop with a number of OS musicians in which we brainstormed dozens of ways we might engage audiences more actively in a concert setting. Chris Perry (percussionist) and Erin Furbee (assistant concertmaster) designed a program of music they shared as a passion, and an entire evening's event that sought to upset concertgoing expectations (without angering patrons) and to draw the audience in as fully as possible.

They and the OS Education and Community Programs Department selected a nontraditional location—the large, open central hall of the Pacific Northwest College of Art, which gave them an open space about the size of four basketball courts, with a balcony, and some side areas usually used for gallery display. The tickets said the event started at 7:00 P.M., and patrons arrived early to find the space filled by small round tables with red tablecloths, a rose on each table, and a couple of bars—to which people headed directly. The ticket *didn't* say the music began at 8:00 P.M. The first hour was unannounced preparation.

Around the periphery of the space were six activity areas. One area had a slide show loop of samba and Carnaval images, right next to some Carnaval costumes people could try on. A bandoneon player strolled through the seating area, going up to people, introducing the instrument and the music, and loosening them up with a mix of charm and fun. (I was flabbergasted to see how complicated that instrument is.) The three most popular areas were a samba lesson room, a tango practice corner, and the percussion zone. Arriving audience members adjusted to this unexpected setup quickly—no "Now I have to wait an hour?" grumblings; they grabbed the spirit of the event (and a glass of wine) and joined in.

Watching people arrive, I could see them take a minute or two to figure out and adjust to the unfamiliar setup and happily begin to choose what they would like to do. There was no clear guidance for where to start; it was like a fair. The atmosphere of that first hour was like an adult musical playground—grown-ups got to do the fun things that are usually reserved for kids. The unbelievably sexy samba dancers had a packed house of men and women practicing the moves, but more important for the concert that followed, they were physically learning the nature of the samba rhythms and the rhythmic structures of the pieces.

The tango group learned some steps but also learned what was distinctive about the tango rhythm that provides its flavor. The percussion group had a table covered in instruments that people were invited to play with. Audience members were tentative at the table at first, but with the players' encouragement, they picked up weird-looking instruments, found a way to use them, and got rhythms and questions going—eventually there were creating rhythm jams, performed by audience *and* musicians. I watched one man nearly jump with delight when he broke out of the rhythmic pattern and played a little riff on his clave—when the professional percussionist nodded approval, this guy's night was made.

The idea was to engage audience members physically in the fundamental nature of the music that would follow. Get them to feel it, learn a little of it, experiment within it, and *play*. The effect of this showed up powerfully when the music began because the audience was loose and already in the habit of participating, and they had formed a personal link with one or more of the performers in the warm-up hour. Also, the audience had already learned important things about the music that enabled them to go much further in their listening and responding.

This preparation carried into the performance itself. The audience spontaneously grooved in their seats, clapped, tapped, and nodded throughout—but there was more. The speakers, especially Brian Davis in the samba part of the program, invited the audience into active participation several times—to learn a clapping pattern, to learn a call-and-response sequence, practice it, and perform it with the band. The call-and-response was particularly effective. It was a last-minute solution to cover the dead time during a stage set change, but the ensemble instantly discovered how much the crowd wanted to join the music. Brian was strict with us, making us rehearse to get our responses right and tuning our ears for ways musical choices sounded better and worse. When that song came up at the end of the set, the audience was bursting to participate and wholeheartedly did.

Here are a few of our guidelines that this event employed effectively to enliven the concert. How might these apply to a concert of yours? Perhaps not in such radical ways, but in more modest changes to traditional format. Is it easy to change expectations and find ways to use engagement practices? Maybe not. But that doesn't mean you don't find ways to do them anyway, when the rewards of succeeding are so great. Experiment. Start small, perhaps, but start.

Engagement before information.   This concert brought audiences into the music through their involvement first, in a grand and dramatic way, not through information first. Information is fine, but it prompts a cerebral, distanced entry into the music; information is important, of course, but it is a lousy spark for the investment of heart and spirit and courageous willingness to give total attention. Certainly samba music lends itself to engagement in ways a Beethoven quartet doesn't, but the principle applies to all concert music.

Tapping competence.   The ensemble engaged audience members musically, getting them to accomplish musical things they could successfully do that were directly relevant to the program that followed—playing with the percussionists, putting the rhythms of the music into their bodies. This changes the relationship between audience and music—it reduces the distance between "us" (the audience) and "them" (the musicians), and we feel we can successfully "get" the music. When Brian taught and rehearsed our vocal patterns, we got better, and we actively appreciated the difficulty of the musical challenge. Not only was this a hoot to do as an audience chorus, but we thrilled to perform with the ensemble. We realized more fully how hard it is to play that music well, even though all night we saw the musicians make it look easy. People had really learned those rhythms and responses, because "our" piece was the last on the program and everyone remembered their part—you could feel the energy go through the roof.

Multiple modes of engagement.   Tango and samba dancers performed with several pieces, and they accomplished a delicate balance. As showy as those dances are, watching the dancers took us further into the music rather than away from it. Music ensembles sometimes use visual elements in performance, and it can work if the other media serve, extend, or illuminate the music. But sometimes it actually distracts from the focus on listening. At this concert, they got it just right—the dancing drew the eye, but the choreography was so intimately attuned to the structure of the music that we could hear and understand more as a result of watching the gorgeous body expressions. I have seen this effort go awry—to include a clown onstage with an orchestra in a concert. The clown attempted to comment on the music wordlessly and interact with the musicians to make it more fun for the audience. All it did was make the audience of kids watch the clown all the time, waiting for more funny bits, and get bored when the clown sat and listened to the classical music, not doing anything fun to watch.

Sharing who you are: the law of 80%.   The musicians were having the time of their lives. They were listening, appreciating one another, responding *visibly* every minute. Sure, this was the first time they had tried this program (which makes that "first-time" feeling easier to find)—but every performance must have some edge of first-timeness. This creates an atmosphere of excitement and aliveness that draws us into the people onstage. The identity, personality, and "vibe" of performers are crucial information for an audience, who read performers more profoundly than most players realize (or like to think). If performers' bodies or energies are disengaged; if they are not bursting with enthusiasm for this very performance; if they do not share themselves with the audience, much potential engagement is squandered. This doesn't mean that the wind quartet announces what they had for dinner in a local restaurant the night before, but it does mean that the more the ensemble finds authentic ways to share themselves and their musical processes and passions with the audience, the more the audience members invest themselves in the music.

There were a few flaws in the program that the performers realized; it was a first try, of course, they would learn from it. But the cheers, the number of people dancing in the aisles, the universal tapping and thumping and dancing in chairs (and eventually in the aisles) were unmistakable signs of wholehearted involvement. The program ended with a samba line led by the musicians and dancers that drew in the entire audience, leading people out of the space and onto the sidewalk where a samba jam continued for a couple of hours. In the unanticipated street scene, audience members were clapping, stomping, grabbing plastic bottles to thump; one had a garbage can lid and a stick—it was a genuine Rio sidewalk experience. This concert lasted for more than a few hours inside the hall and a couple more hours on the sidewalk; for everyone at that event, the memory will last far longer.

25
Speak Up or Shut Up?
Using Words in a Performance

I am sitting in the audience. I have plunked down my forty bucks to hear the Midas Quartet play late Beethoven. Let's see... would I rather listen to the violist tell me about Walla Walla, where she grew up, or lose myself in the rich complexities of Opus 131? The answer seems obvious: I paid for a high-quality musical experience, and that player has a lot more skill and confidence in playing the opening chords than in using her vocal cords.

In this chapter, I am going to argue that the actual answer is not always so obvious. If that viola player can pull it off, then I, sitting there in row D, want her notes *and* her words, because together they can take me further into Opus 131—and I will go home the happier for the combination.

Why Talk at All?

When leading workshops with musicians on this topic, I often ask them to think of all the reasons they might talk in performance. After a few predictable smarty-pants answers, such as "To ask whether there's a doctor in the house" and "To explain how much to put in the hat that is being passed," we end up with a list that looks like this:

- To break the ice
- To make a personal connection with the audience
- To illuminate a crucial aspect of a piece to be performed
- To create an atmosphere
- To acknowledge something about the audience or occasion
- To reduce the gap between performer and audience
- To entertain
- To contextualize a piece, historically, socially, or musically
- To weave a thread of connection among the pieces
- To suggest a way to listen to the piece

- To cover a transition
- To fill time
- To address something that has just happened unexpectedly
- To thank people
- To promote future events
- To sell CDs

I then ask the ensembles to enumerate the risks, eliciting good reasons to avoid talking from the stage in performance. The following are typical responses:

- Talking can reduce the focus on the music.
- Some audience members want only music.
- If the talking isn't good, it drags down the whole event.
- Speaking makes many performers nervous.
- There is no time or inclination to rehearse the talking as well as the music.

The standard solutions to this dilemma are to talk a little (only as much as necessary); to let the best talker in the group do the talking; to aim to survive the talking, rather than using it to advance the program; and to address only the least risky material, such as historical information about the piece—that is, to create audio program notes.

You will never hear me recommend talking for the sake of talking. However, you will hear me urge musicians to focus on and develop the presenter's verbal skill. I do this because the potential upside hugely outweighs the downside risk—especially with audiences filled with less sophisticated listeners. If we can set aside the awkwardness, lack of familiarity, and nervousness often associated with talking in performance (all quite natural, and all able to be alleviated with practice), we can focus on if, when, and how to add the talking piece.

To Speak or Not to Speak, That Is the Question

Here is the beacon I use to guide decisions about if, when, and how to include speaking in an ensemble performance. You have read this credo before in different wording in these pages: *the goal of a concert is not to perform great music well but to cocreate personally relevant experiences together inside the music.* To accomplish this goal, of course, playing great music well is a crucial part. But it is not all you can do to achieve the goal. Otherwise why would we bother with written programs and other traditions in and around concerts? If we are to employ all the tools we have available to us to achieve this ultimate goal, then we have to admit that speaking from the stage can be one of them. It can be a way to help people connect to the music in ways that really matter to them. If your speaking helps audience members make personally relevant connections to the music you are going to perform, then speak right up. If not, zip it and play.

Let's assume you are going to play brilliantly—obviously that is an essential part of helping audiences make satisfying personal connections to the music. I have seen a hundred instances in which performers have used words effectively to boost the experience of the audience. Let's look back at some of those reasons musicians offer for speaking to see how they work in relation to this guideline.

To make a personal connection.   We know that if the people "out there" in the audience know something about the human beings "up here" playing the instruments, they will be more actively engaged as listeners. It's basic human nature—we instinctively try harder for people we feel for and like. The skillful presenter uses that impulse strategically. While you might be comfortable telling the audience where you were born, when you started playing an instrument, what your history with their city or town is, or what your favorite car is, those info-bits are hardly the *best* ways to get the audience's attention and link it productively to the music. Yes, share something personal; audiences love that. But focus on something personal that takes us into greater insight about the music, too. Perhaps there is something about this particular piece that is relevant to your life, or perhaps there is something personal about performing the piece that would open it up for me in the audience. I recall a story of a flute player talking about a tough twenty-two-note passage in a piece, and how intimidating it is, even for a professional. Before the performance, she played it for the audience, explained the nature of the difficulty, and why it has to be perfect, like a high dive in the Olympics. The audience was hanging on every note when she performed in that piece. So my advice is not to avoid pleasantries but to emphasize something that opens a shared personal window into the music.

To break the ice.   Same story. An anecdote or two about your travels, or about being tired, or a joke about viola players may break the ice socially, but it does not warm the audience to listen. How can you use words, creatively, theatrically, to get over the awkwardness of beginning and take them into hearing? Most ensembles choose to start programs with music as the icebreaker. That can be a good choice, but it doesn't have to be that way. Ask this question of every program: Is there anything we can say or do at the top that advances the audience's ability to really receive this first piece? The ensemble eighth blackbird sometimes composes a verbal introduction to a piece that is built upon a key musical aspect of that piece (imagine three musicians speaking quickly in a form that precisely matches a rondo in the piece they are about to perform). By following the structure of the introduction, we not only appreciate their playfulness but are cleverly prepared to take in this new piece more fully. Think specifically of ways into a particular piece, rather than looking for general icebreakers that might "work" for any piece. Such answers may not come quickly at first thinking; keep at it. If you can find an elegantly effective way to break the ice in a way that enriches the listening, you have just lifted the whole concert up a notch.

To create an atmosphere and to entertain.   Some ensembles have a lively joke teller who can crack up an audience. Nothing wrong with sharing a good laugh, but my challenge to that group would be to use the humor as an entryway to something about the music or the performing of it.

When you speak, we read your voice, your body language, your nervousness—and you tell us volumes about who you are. (We get uncomfortable if you seem very nervous, or if we sense that having to speak makes you suffer. Relax and remember: we don't require perfect sentences.) If you can share yourself with us in a natural, enthusiastic way, we will follow you further inside the music. If you can communicate that you are having fun, we have more fun. Use that energy to share something interesting or evocative about the music. I recall an ensemble telling the audience a story of how a screwup in the photocopying of a piece wrought havoc with rehearsal. The demonstration was full of intragroup dirty looks, rolling eyes, and very funny frustrations; but all the while they were helping us get a sense of the piece to follow. They showed us the notation and described some of the particular difficulties presented by the mixed-up pages.

Lightness and humor are not the only possible mode. You can also share something relevant about a heavy or mournful work. I recall being in the audience for a piece about grief, at which the performer delicately mentioned his feelings at his grandfather's death and explained how the piece mirrored several of the shades of grief he had experienced when he was just ten. Among these was a sense of dissociation, as if witnessing the sadness in others at a slight remove. The performer then played two short passages that conveyed that elusive, ambiguous experience, of a child facing the confusion of death. The illumination of that specific feeling, and other aspects of a young person's sense of grief, beautifully expanded my sense of the piece.

To provide information or context.   Certainly this is comfortable terrain for almost any ensemble. However, it is also a place where talking can turn us off—if it suggests that music requires a lot of knowledge to appreciate or that you think the audience members are more (or less) experienced than they are. (Given the fact that almost all audiences are quite diverse in their makeup, you are likely to miss the mark with a portion of the audience anytime you rely on information.) Your talking may even *weaken* my musical experience. If you tell me about the structure of the piece to follow, I will tend to listen for the structure of the piece—is that the best possible way for me to discover personally relevant connections to it? Don't just tell me the stuff off the CD liner notes. Select the information that opens up my hearing and caring. Imagine the differing responses of an audience member hearing these two little speeches:

> Next is Beethoven's quartet no. 14, op. 131. One of the late quartets, it has seven movements, and in the fourth movement, it displays a structure the composer also employs in the slow movement of his Ninth Symphony. It begins with a long passage that reappears with variations in alternating sections...

versus

> In rehearsing this late quartet by Beethoven, we were struck by the elusive story that the collage of movements seems to tell. Beethoven was old, deaf, lonely, and angry when he wrote this quartet, yet the piece seems to express spiritual wisdom and a measure of acceptance. Particularly in the long, slow movement, we were struck by the poignancy of this sublime wisdom, that is how it seems to us, that mixed in with other aspects of reflection on a long, hard life...

To weave a thread of connection among pieces.   Too often audiences think an evening's program is a handful of good pieces that have been put together because they fill about the right amount of time. (Fess up—that sometimes *is* the case.) Too often, the theatrical shape of an evening— the larger, more satisfying point—is not apparent to listeners who can't pick out a purely musical thread. Even an obvious theme, say, "American Music," conveys only the idea that these are a bunch of pieces composed by Americans—so what? I urge ensembles to go deeper, to find what it is about American music (or whatever the theme is) they wish to say; what is the arc of learning, the contour of the American experience, you want us to follow on this ninety-minute journey with you? The speaking component of the concert is crucial to making this larger point. While not a lecture, speaking can illuminate the thread that ties the program together, makes it build to more than the sum of its parts. And be sure to be as enthusiastic about opening up this larger theme as you hope the audience will be about following it. What you're doing is far more than imparting information. Instead, you are sharing your own thinking about why this evening's journey is worth taking with you, and what the reach of our evening could be.

Practical matters. It is very clear to audiences, and usually just fine with them, that speaking from the stage accomplishes some practical tasks: the stage setup needs to be changed; the instruments need retuning; the cellist is offstage having a coughing fit; you need to pause while a siren outside the hall is dealt with; people must be thanked; CD sales need to be mentioned; future events must get described. All are opportunities as much as necessities.

How can you turn the information delivery into something that takes people back into music? Think like this. During a change in stage setup, can you share some of the reasons that setups are they way they are—why are the seating arrangements of the players crucial? While retuning, can you include us, to see if we can hear the difference? If a musician has to leave the stage, can you share with us some of the real physical difficulties of performing at this high level: What parts of your bodies tire, what kinds of energy does performance demand? In thanking people, can you link that gratitude to the performance? For example, "Andrea Jones made this evening possible, and special thanks to her for remembering to provide us with bottles of water. The finale of the first half of the program leaves us panting, and we will need them."

Finally, selling tickets and CDs: don't be apologetic; these are opportunities for the audience members. Assume they love you and that they were hoping to learn about how to hear more. Why? It takes them further into your music. And because your speaking has been as elegant, thought through, and engaging as your music, they are eager for more.

26
Interactive Performances

An ensemble's educational impulses can find expression beyond the classroom workshop or lecture, the preconcert talk, or instrument "petting zoo." One extension of education practice reaches right inside a performance to create an interactive concert (IC). This chapter presents some IC basics. I wrote it with David Wallace, a former student of mine and now a well-established teaching artist, musician, and an innovator who has done groundbreaking IC work. David's name is becoming synonymous with interactive concerts; he has published a popular new book that is a bible in its own right on the topic, and I highly recommend it to readers of this book (*Reaching Out: A Musician's Guide to Interactive Performance*, 2007).

David and I agree that an interactive concert is one in which audience members actively perform, create, or reflect in ways that deepen their responses to the music on the program. A true IC means exploratory engagement *during* the concert, not activities before or afterward. (This is not to denigrate pre- and postconcert learning activities. They are also fine ways to expand the reach of a performance. The most common forms of these are the preconcert event that is participatory more than lecture-y, and the postperformance discussion.)

Active experiential learning, which forges immediate and personal connections with the music, is the key to ICs. Take, for example, a family concert that David hosted at the Bridgehampton Chamber Music Festival. The concert was to culminate in a performance of the *Rondo alla zingarese* from Johannes Brahms's Piano Quartet in G minor, op. 25. Engaging the listeners in the music from the outset, David helped them compose their own rondo episodes. One volunteer improvised a light, quick solo on a xylophone tuned to the G-minor scale; another paralleled the piano cadenza with a drum improvisation in the rondo's pervasive gypsy dance rhythm. Each participant-created episode—including an exuberant major-key "Happy Birthday" sung by the whole audience—paralleled a segment of Brahms's original and was performed in alternation with the theme, played by the ensemble.

When the interactive experiment ended, the musicians applauded the audience and segued into an uninterrupted performance of the Brahms rondo. The standing ovation they received afterward was testimony to a completely captivated audience.

Why Bother?

ICs demand extra preparation and rehearsal time, as well as group management and presentation skills—a challenging task for musicians who are not trained in this approach. So why not stick to traditional concert formats?

I would answer that we find ourselves living in a time that invites (almost demands) us to experiment and to think unconventionally, to draw young and new audiences into our beloved music in active ways, rather than just putting it out beautifully and hoping they "get it." David expands on this thought: "When performers take the time to craft potent activities that enable listeners to enter a piece with 100% of their concentration and emotions, the audience leaves with a profound and powerful aesthetic experience. If we do our jobs well, we do more than entertain; we equip people with the tools for being successful hearers. These skills in turn may be transferred to subsequent listening experiences."

David cites an IC he performed in with the Teaching Artist Ensemble of the New York Philharmonic. The concert was entertaining, he said, but it was also "extremely calculated in its pedagogical and perceptual intentions. As a result, children were not only saying, 'That was a great show!' as they were leaving; they also were saying, 'I want to learn more about timbre next year!' "

Because it is experience-based, you can use this high-impact method to engage audiences with nontraditional as well as familiar genres. Active preparation for an IC widens an audience's "comfort zone," creating receptivity to music that might have otherwise provoked resistance. As long as you prepare audiences well, you can perform just about anything. A case in point is provided by a Juilliard student ensemble that was preparing to give an interactive performance of George Crumb's *Black Angels: Thirteen Images from the Dark Land*—an intense, modern work for amplified string quartet. In the third movement, Crumb has the performers play their instruments with glass rods, thimbles, and paper clips.

At a dress rehearsal, the group meticulously demonstrated Crumb's "special effects." But then, when they actually played the movement, the audience knew what was coming and was no longer surprised and delighted by the unusual sounds. Realizing that it had to find a way to familiarize the audience with the objects and their timbres without robbing the performance of its "edge," the quartet changed its tactics and substituted an inquiry-based presentation, in which the audience could do some experimenting.

Each quartet member held up one of Crumb's objects, asking the audience to suggest how such an object—by itself or in combination with the player's instrument—might be used to make "sounds from a dark land." The audience now stepped into George Crumb's shoes. Now sound explorers and not mere passive recipients of information, listeners made suggestions—many of which proved humorous and challenging—and were fascinated as the performers tried them out. They were primed for the listening challenge: "Now let's see and hear how George Crumb did it!"

This time around, Crumb's novel effects revealed themselves in the moment. The audience was pleased to recognize not only many of its own techniques but also novel ideas it had not considered. The quartet's performance was just as good as it had been in the dress rehearsal run-through, but this audience was leaning forward and listening with the mind-set, "What happens next?!"

Oh, and two additional answers to the question "Why bother?" One is money. A dynamic, cohesive IC is a powerful and distinctive offering that stands out in a very competitive marketplace and probably will put money in your pocket. You can take exciting ideas of interactivity not only across the invisible stage boundary but also right to the bank. The other reason is that it is artistically enriching and rejuvenating for the musicians. Interactivity means music is going to be explored in ways you can't predict; new ideas and challenges will appear during this performance that will provoke a fresh and bolder attack on the playing of the piece. It is an intravenous shot of aliveness, channeling the power of improvisation for performers by adding the unexpected, but in appropriate and positive ways.

Key Ideas

David and I concluded that among the many considerations for creating such a concert are four key ideas:

1. *The music is the touchstone.* Everything you do or say should relate to the music or the audience's perception of it. (This is an affirmation of the earlier chapters about entry points and speaking from the stage—the goal has to come back to supporting audience capacity to connect personally with the music, directly or even indirectly, or it detracts.)

This keeps the focus where it belongs, and it maximizes your chances of enhancing people's sense of discovery. Be cautious about introducing activities that stray from the music. Performers are sometimes asked to connect their presentation to the school's curriculum. This can only work if the musical focus remains central; the program weakens when it is forced to make strained analogies with, say, molecular structure or the history of France.

2. The entry point should be specific.   Every choice of activity ought to derive from an aesthetic feature specific to the music. Invite the audience to enter that unique work of art through a gateway constructed of no more than one or two features. Rather than making a general point about rhythm, draw the audience in with a specific, particularly intriguing, rhythmic feature in the piece you are about to play. Selecting the entry point is crucial: it needs to be open to anyone with some simple musical participatory play; it must lie at the heart of what is exciting about the piece (so audiences will actually hear differently as a result of their experimentation); and it should tap one of your musical passions.

3. Engagement before information.   The warhorse guideline reappears. Let the *doing* open up the learning. In an IC, we are drawing people into musical inquiry, not demonstrating the key points. Certainly information may be perfect to add in response to a discovery, but the activities must not covertly seek right answers, and you must not deliver "right answers" after the joint exploration.

In a concert about heroic music, for example, let the audience members experiment with the components of "heroic sound" and use their suggestions to tease out those elements *before* you list the ones composers typically use. In fact, use the *audience's* list rather than fixing it up with your more sophisticated answers. (If the audience has missed something important—no mention of brass instruments for the heroic music, for example—you can elicit the answer by asking which instruments have the best qualities for such music and why.) Audiences that have suggested compositional tools will have much greater ownership of them in subsequent listening, and they will listen more actively.

In a family concert my students and I designed at Tanglewood, the theme was "What Makes Music Heroic?" One of the activities was to have the Tanglewood Orchestra play the world's most boring version of "Twinkle, Twinkle Little Star" and then ask for suggestions from the audience to turn it into a grand heroic statement. The kids and parents made suggestions, and the orchestra tried them out. The result was getting slightly more heroic. Finally one little boy at the back yelled out, "Brass!" The orchestra played it, and wow, that was the key idea the listeners discovered in a flash of recognition. They then made great suggestions to complete the stylistic transformation. They learned all the key elements of heroic orchestration, having the time of their lives doing it (audience *and* musicians found it to be great fun), and we never had to *tell* them anything. They were then able to follow their discoveries as used by composers throughout the rest of the pieces performed.

4. Elegance.   Activities must be fairly simple to execute. Minimize instructions and explanations, and let the musical action do most of the talking. I recall the very beginning of another interactive family concert my students and I designed for a different Tanglewood family concert on music inspired by nature. Four young conductors came to the edge of the stage and silently indicated a section of the audience that was to follow each of them. They then led the audience in a ninety-second sound improvisation of a thunderstorm, from light wind and gentle rain through its loudest torrent (moving the thunderclaps among the groups in patterns directly related to how they appear in the piece that followed) and back to quiet. Audience members began with finger tapping, then hand rubbing, then thigh patting, and so forth to create the sounds. The leaders shaped the improv to mirror as much as possible the choices demonstrated in the piece that followed. And then, without a word, the orchestra came in with the fourth movement of Beethoven's Sixth Symphony, the thunderstorm movement, and the entire audience was riveted all the way through. They could feel Beethoven's choices, in relation to their own, and even the youngsters could follow the movement without losing focus.

Structure

Does an interactive concert have a preferred structure? No. David and I have designed dozens of such concerts between us, and we feel that the format must be responsive to the music, the specific audience, and the setting. However, some ideas should be kept in mind.

• *Start with success*. Make sure the first activity is fast and fun and has an immediate experiential reward. This initial payoff builds audience confidence that the activities have a point and that effort will be rewarded. The interactive activity need not be the first thing on the concert program, although it often is. I recall another Tanglewood family concert we designed in which, without a word, a conductor got the audience members to clap responsively with him at the very top, building their pattern in complexity and speed. When they had the pattern just right, the orchestra surprised them by booming in with the theme from *Star Wars*, coinciding exactly with their clapped ostinato. It took less than a minute, was all in the language of music, and brought such a rush of success that the audience was primed and ready to try anything afterward.

• *Follow a line of inquiry.* The ideal IC builds activities, one on another, rather than linking unrelated investigations. A concert of the Teaching Artist Ensemble of the New York Philharmonic explored a composer's palette of tone colors. The listeners were first sensitized to the sounds of individual instruments and families and were then invited to blend and contrast those sounds in collaboration with the ensemble. Later, the audience had a chance to explore new instrumental timbres revealed by extended techniques such as key clicks by the woodwinds, *col legno* effects from the strings, and multiphonics from the horn. The concert culminated in a piece that featured individual instruments, various timbre combinations, extended techniques—and an audience sing-along in which the listeners got to create their own timbral variations!

• *Build to a payoff.* The best final activity is one that invites the audience to pull together *everything* it has learned. A Carnegie Hall Link-Up concert addressed theme and variations, demonstrating the many ways a composer might vary a theme: by adding rhythmic accompaniment, changing the dynamics, adding a countermelody, and so on. The concert culminated in the finale of Beethoven's Ninth Symphony, which contained every type of variation.

• *Design appropriately for the setting.* We had to work hard to break expectations and create clever kinds of interaction in Ozawa Hall at Tanglewood; in other situations, such as comedy clubs and informal venues like bars, where back-and-forth exchange is the nature of the setting, constant interaction is absolutely essential.

Pitfalls

• *Not knowing your audience.* Sure, an audience of Teamsters is unlikely to be thrilled by singing "Row, Row, Row Your Boat" to experience changes in tempo—but such mismatches may not always be so obvious. Design activities that are relevant, interesting, just a bit challenging, and inherently fun for the particular audience.

• *Too many words.* Musicians often get wordy and imprecise when they speak off-the-cuff. This dilutes the impact of the interactive exercise and the dynamic connection to the listening that follows. Get all instructions down to the fewest possible words.

• *Underrehearsing the interactive portions.* Deciding what the activity should be is not the same thing as preparing it. Lack of preparation leads to sloppy delivery and can undermine the whole point of what one is doing. Script and refine the instructions. Practice them aloud in rehearsals. Get friends to do the activities with you—it is amazing what you learn with practice. No matter how carefully musicians plan, I always see them learn something obvious and important in practicing the interactive parts with a test audience, which leads me to this advice: never try out an activity in concert unless you have already practiced it with a "volunteer" audience (however small).

- *Activities that don't relate to the music.* Just because the activity is cool and fun doesn't mean it improves the concert. What gives ICs their viability is that they catalyze musical satisfaction. David cites the example of a PBS broadcast in which an otherwise effective conductor made important musical observations and then introduced a comedic juggling troupe that performed while the orchestra played. Whatever the musical selection was (David couldn't even remember), it became mere wallpaper for a humorous shtick.

- *No variety in the activities.* Just as you wouldn't bore the audience by putting three very similar pieces on the same program, you need to include experiential variety in an IC. If you precede every piece with a clapping activity, don't expect your audience to remain enthralled. Remember to plan for surprise, contrast, and balance in the activities as well as in the musical selections.

- *Musical selections that are too long or too short.* No hard rules here, but you must be attuned to the audience. Variety helps. Too many short pieces do not provide a substantial, satisfying payoff for the participatory work. Pieces that are too long may lose the benefit of preparation. In our view, three minutes is short, and eight minutes is long.

- *Unengaged performers.* All onstage players must take part. You can't expect the audience to participate in an activity if some of the musicians look as though they're waiting for it to be over. This doesn't mean everyone must be equally vocal, but it does mean everyone must be actively engaged, interested, and attentive to the audience.

David Wallace and I and a growing number of bold experimenters believe that the time for interactive concerts has arrived. While you may find them a challenge to create and present, we urge you to experiment. The benefits of a good IC far exceed the effort. What benefits? Audiences that are more engaged are more satisfied, more excited by the mysteries inside the music you care about. Audiences that are having more fun are more likely to come back and bring friends. Musicians who are more alive and excited by what they learn and try in performance are musicians who courageously draw audiences further into their world.

27

The Very Open Rehearsal

Interactive performances succeed to the degree that teaching artistry moves onto the stage and into concert traditions. And probably the boldest kind of interactive performance is the very open rehearsal. Take a deep breath... you can do this.

"A regular live performance of classical music is powerful. A workshop exploration or a lesson about a piece of music can be powerful, too. But putting them together in this way makes it so alive for the listener. They join the extravagance of the musical experience. There is just nothing like having the real thing right there to experience together and have everyone dig into together." Those are the words of violinist Denise Dillenbeck, describing her experience of leading very open rehearsals (VORs) as part of an ensemble, and even all on her own.

We all know what an open rehearsal is: an audience is allowed to watch a rehearsal in progress, which is a way of inviting fortunate individuals to witness the workings of music-making. As an educational opportunity, the open rehearsal has one great strength—immediate access to some of the authentic inner workings of music-making. The weakness is that most people can't tap very deeply into the experience. Sometimes attendees can't even hear what is said onstage—a few brave orchestras are putting a microphone on the conductor. Often, the uninitiated miss the details that give life to the process, or they simply don't grasp what the heck is going on. An open rehearsal may even disappoint those with some musical background because it may or may not explore areas of particular interest or relevance to them. Usually handled by administration and orchestra with a combination of indifference and caution, the standard open rehearsal squanders its rich possibilities. (I am forever urging orchestras to make the *first* rehearsal of a week the open rehearsal, so the average audience member can see the mistakes, revisions, and immediate improvements, even tensions and disagreements—the real stuff of this complex art—rather than the third rehearsal, which is usually little more than a run-through. Alas, none has been bold enough yet to take up my challenge.)

A VOR is neither casual nor cautious; it is bold. As we saw in the last chapter, there are many types of interactive concerts, in which the range of interactivity can swing from the minimal—audiences are asked to clap or answer questions—all the way to Bobby McFerrin's getting the audience to sing all the parts of *Bolero* or Yo-Yo Ma's having the audience sing "Dona Nobis Pacem" as he plays to their accompaniment. Interactive concerts are not just for orchestras; they are becoming much more popular as successful ensembles increasingly perform in clubs, in community venues, in salons and private homes.

The VOR is probably the most extreme kind of interactive concert—anything more would have to be a BYOI concert, bring your own instrument. I have a hunch the VOR may become the most widely adopted kind of interactive concert—because it is so fundamentally simple and works so powerfully, sometimes almost magically. As far as I know, the concept was pioneered by Thomas Cabaniss when he was the New York Philharmonic's director of education, but I am sure imaginative ensembles and musicians have created events like it over the years. At the Phil, Tom had the enviable opportunity to experiment with his programs, and he was particularly interested in exploring how to engage high school students more actively in classical music. In 2003 he enlisted the support of a wind ensemble (made up of tenured musicians in the orchestra) to try out a new kind of education event for the Philharmonic's high school program. At the first of the three scheduled VORs, he recalls, both players and audience were nervous. ("These students are actually going to stop us and ask us questions?" "Are we really supposed to stop their playing by raising our hands?") Tom was the facilitator, and he encouraged everyone to give it a shot. He noticed something that day that turned out to be typical of VORs—the participants were hesitant to break the ice with that first question; even typical high school students knew that was taboo. But after that first tentative question and interesting openhearted answer, the event took off.

In that first VOR, the students got interested in the issues of tempo—who controlled it, the difference between a metronome's tempo and the performers' impulses. It came out that one of the players had been pushing the tempo because he felt the piece should move faster. The ensemble had to work through the disagreement (which had surfaced because of questions from the audience) and came to a solution with feedback from the audience. The students were fascinated. They did interrupt, but appropriately; they did respond and ask for demonstrations of some points. Though surprised and delighted by the students' insights, the musicians were not completely sold on VORs until their second outing—when they realized that nothing else they had tried could top the VOR at drawing a young audience inside the music.

Time has shown that the VOR works with audiences of all ages. I "borrowed" Tom's idea with his permission and have used it widely since 2004. When I am given free rein to shape an event, I usually seat the audience in a complete circle (with aisles), with the musicians facing one another in the center. Certainly VORs can work with traditional "theater" seating, but the circular arrangement reduces the expectations of "performance," eases the hesitancy to interrupt, and unsettles the musicians in a healthy way. Getting the audience pulled in as close as possible to the musicians is a help—the proximity boosts the intimacy, even with more than a hundred people present. If it feels a little crowded, that is probably just about right. A VOR is not an event for large numbers in the audience; it is essentially a personal, intimate exchange, so I try to limit audience size to under one hundred, although I have survived slightly larger gatherings.

In events I organize, I usually use a facilitator (myself or someone who is good with groups) to manage the event. This host kicks things off, calls on the people with hands raised, interrupts the questioning when it has gone on too long (to make sure the ensemble gets enough rehearsal time to accomplish what they need to get done), and prevents anyone from hogging the conversation or grandstanding. The facilitator also asks direct questions of *all* the musicians (to make sure the less verbal ones are heard from), rephrases questions that are stated unclearly, and sometimes asks a follow-up question when he or she intuits a juicy musical issue under the surface. The facilitator sets the tone (which should be playful but seriously curious) and rhythm of questions/answers/playing (which should be lively but have variety within it). With a mixed-age audience, the facilitator encourages the (usually more reticent) younger people to ask questions and calls on them often. When I led a VOR at the University of Michigan recently, a music department ensemble was working on a movement of a Hindemith woodwind quintet, and the six preteens in the audience asked the best questions of the night.

Some ensembles lead their own VORs with no facilitator. Often the musicians ask the audience to listen to a passage two ways and give them some feedback; the players describe (and disagree about) their feelings or thoughts about different sections. Some bold musicians, like Denise Dillenbeck, have dared to fly solo—rehearsing and handling the question-and-answer parts as well.

Audiences ask all kinds of questions; you never know what is coming next: "Why did you just replay that section?" "I couldn't tell why you guys felt the second time through was better—could you show me what was wrong and what you are trying to do?" In one VOR I led, a string quartet from the Chicago Civic Orchestra was working on a movement from a Shostakovich work, and the audience included both sophisticated listeners and first-time hearers of chamber music. Back-to-back questions were: "I have heard that last phrase in over twenty different recordings, and I can't understand its intent—what do you make of it?" and "Why do violin players all have hickeys on their necks?" The openness of the players in answering both questions, from opposite ends of the sophistication continuum, lessened the audience's inhibitions about asking things they'd always wondered. It also united the crowd and had them following every nuance of the rehearsal. A VOR is profoundly inclusive, and for an art form that has the reputation of being elitist, this is radically important.

I usually urge the musicians to think of the following when choosing the music for a VOR:

1. Select something that you really *do* need to rehearse (this is essential—don't fake it).

2. Keep the rehearsed segment short (say, six minutes maximum for an eighty-minute event; a single movement is fine).

3. Try to pick something that it is not entirely familiar to the audience. (A genuine rehearsal of a classic can work, but the event is weaker if your group doesn't really need to rehearse and is just polishing.) When the Chiara Quartet presented a VOR for sixty graduate students from top conservatories at a conference, they made a brave musical choice: part of the second movement of Jefferson Friedman's Third String Quartet, a work they were scheduled to record one week later. What's more, they had largely refrained from rehearsing the movement they used in the VOR so that there would be authentic pressure to solve complex problems with a lot at stake. This made for a thrilling VOR that revealed how decisions get made in an ensemble, as well as the deep implications—musical, personal, and professional—of the choices and decision-making processes.

4. Even if it is just part of one movement, the selection should stand alone theatrically, with a satisfying beginning, middle, and end.

A typical VOR format would include the following (please feel free to design your VOR entirely differently—this is the most basic skeleton, and other formats could would equally well or better for you):

1. The host takes a couple of minutes (not too much talking at the top) to introduce the event, along with the basic ground rules about raising hands, interrupting, making sure the players get enough rehearsal

time, seeing if people have questions about the logistics, and so on. The host also sets the tone and expectations—casual and fun. Include some laughs, a few words from the individual musicians (you can include introductions of musicians here, but I put usually put them off, to avoid too much talk before music).

2. The performers will often play a run-through of the music, or part of it, to orient everyone.

3. The performers may discuss among themselves what they noticed in the run-through—what they need to work on, and disagreements about interpretation or priorities and how they should organize the process. (I often ask for *really short* self-introductions at this point, or I'll ask each performer to say his or her name and then answer the same question, such as, "What is one thing about this piece that challenges you?" or "What's one thing you personally want to accomplish in this rehearsal?"

4. The musicians begin to rehearse in earnest, and the audience begins interrupting at some point. (I admit I have been known to plant a first question with a friend or colleague, and look at that person to raise her hand if the crowd feels scared to break the ice. On difficult occasions, I have asked the first question myself as facilitator if the crowd feels scared to break the taboo.)

5. The rehearsal continues, with frequent interruptions (these may be short, or up to 5 minutes even, but they shouldn't delay the ensemble for too long from digging back into the music); the event may run for 70 to 100 minutes. (VORs for school groups tend to run toward the shorter side.)

6. The event culminates with a performance of the whole segment. The players and audience members may offer some closing comments about what they enjoyed or learned. Typically, the VOR audience becomes so invested in myriad details of the music that the brief final performance has a disproportionately large impact on them; I have seen audiences jump to their feet to cheer a five-minute piece. Once, after the Chicago Civic Orchestra's string quartet performed the Shostakovich movement, an audience member told me he had found more satisfaction in those six minutes than in any full symphony he had ever heard. Score one for chamber music.

I asked Denise Dillenbeck for her advice for musicians who have the urge to try their hand at being both performer and facilitator. Denise focused on several VORs she led that explored *Suite Italienne*, the violin-and-piano reduction of *Pulcinella* that Stravinsky himself arranged.

When Denise was the lead teaching artist of the Philadelphia Orchestra's Education Department, she gave a VOR workshop for teachers who were preparing to bring their students to a performance of *Pulcinella*. This predetermined focus with a shared educational goal, along with the teachers' eagerness to dig into the parts that Denise and the pianist rehearsed, made the VOR particularly effective. When she conducted a similar event for the general public, she encountered a bit more caution and uncertainty in the audience before they got into it.

Denise recommends that in general-audience VORs, when you don't have the benefit of a shared goal, the performers should have a clear purpose and entry point in mind for the occasion: "Know what you want to accomplish in the rehearsal, and know how this particular VOR can help you get there. And tell the audience about it; enroll them in the entry point and the goal." Because audiences are usually hesitant to ask that first question, she recommends having a few key questions in mind that really interest you. If the audience seems shy, ask them yourself and get the audience involved in answering them.

"With *Suite Italienne*," says Denise, "the serenata movement has a place where the performers repeat one single motivic idea a whole bunch of times in a row, like a broken record." She goes on:

> That repetition always bothered me, so it was an easy place to jump in with "Why the heck did Stravinsky write this? Why are we having to say the same thing so many times in a row? Should we try to make some kind of shape out of it, or let it stand on its own?" That led very easily to "And what is the purpose of repetition in general in music? In conversation? In life?"
>
> It was fascinating and hilarious to me that the audience had already picked up on my annoyance with this section even before I said anything about it—just from hearing me play it. Admitting my qualms about it allowed some laughter and then a very rich conversation that delved into the topic.

Taking up some of the audience's suggestions, Denise played the section in various ways and asked the audience how they liked the different interpretations.

VORs work, says Denise, because participants are not passive watchers. "Audiences discover through you that what goes on inside a piece of music for a musician is a lot like what goes on in life in general—and they know about that. So they relate to the musician and the rehearsal process in a very active way. They get to experience from the inside why you love it so much. They are actively experiencing and noticing and thinking and questioning *inside* the piece. The energy in the room gets thrilling. It puts them on the spot—and they rise to it, it makes their listening much more active and honest and detailed."

She admits she still gets nervous just before doing a solo VOR but says she gets over it pretty quickly once she is into the exchange with the participants. When there is a facilitator with the performers, she says it is easier, but there's a special excitement when there's one less layer between her and the people around her.

"People are smart," she says. "For me as an artist it is fun to have other people's questions to consider and experiment around. They love it when they surprise me or give me a new idea. There is a lot of laughter and discovery in a good VOR. They get to feel what it's like to have their hands on this clay; and I get pushed to try things I never would have thought of."

A few other nuggets of advice from Denise to musicians who want to take on a VOR:

Bring your best, open, authentic learning self. Don't be afraid to be imperfect, to let things fall apart. Don't worry about making mistakes. Break the rules: walk around the space to be in different physical relationships with the audiences, ask questions of other players, ask the audience your genuine questions. Get out of your comfort zone. The more you try new things bravely and in the spirit of play, the more the audience will open up and try new things in their listening and entering the music.

Denise also cautions musicians to listen really hard when people talk, to make sure you grasp what is really being asked. "If you don't quite get it, ask for clarification. Try a lot of experiments, and use music as much as possible, rather than words, to try ideas out. Try not to talk too much—go to the music."

It does take courage to dare the openness of a VOR, but I have seen the format succeed in every setting I have tried, from bastions of music traditionalism to art museums to hotel conference rooms. The Chiara Quartet just wrote me that they are doing a whole series of them as part of a special grant during a University of Iowa residency. I have seen it work well with the most sophisticated audiences, with first-time audiences, and with mixed audiences. Violist Kelly Dylla has produced and facilitated several VORs and finds, "Ideally I like to work with players that have a sense of playfulness and curiosity about a layman's point of view. Also, a certain level of musical maturity is desired so musicians can make the most of participants' suggestions. With that in mind, really the straightforward process makes it perfect for adapting it to different situations, involving super young players or amateur musicians."

Just the other day, I got an e-mail from violinist Amy Schroeder, whom I knew when she was a student at Juilliard, and who is now thriving with the Attacca Quartet. The group had just tried its first very open rehearsal, as I had suggested to them, on their own. Here (with her permission) is the text of her unexpected and timely e-mail:

Hi Eric!
I hope this message finds you well. Just wanted to tell you that I am with my quartet on Hilton Head Island, SC, right now, and we are performing several concerts as well as doing a pretty good amount of outreach, as we did here last year. Do you remember telling us about the "very open rehearsal" idea? Tonight we tried it! We had to do a play-and-teach session to a youth orchestra, their parents, and random adult members of the community.... We first played a movement of a Beethoven quartet that we knew very well, so that they could just hear us play. Then we told them that we were going to play the exposition of another Beethoven quartet that was fairly new to us and that we would have a rehearsal on it. We told them that they were free to come up and look at our parts after we played it through and were actually working on it. We also said that they were free to ask questions about anything we were doing, or could ask us to try things at any point during the rehearsal. Also, when we came across a place where we couldn't necessarily tell which of two ideas which sounded better, we asked the audience what they thought, and they always had an opinion. It was extremely successful, and everyone said how interesting it was, how much they learned and how fun it was. Plus... we got some feedback from a live audience!! Then we let the kids play, and we gave them tips, and they sounded much better when they played their piece again after working with us. All in all... YOUR IDEA ROCKS!! Amy

Part VII Expanding the Roles of the Teaching Artist

28

The Essential Educational
Entrepreneur

Earlier (see chapter 9), I mentioned the first-time conference of leaders of major American conservatories and arts service organizations
(Chamber Music America, League of American Orchestras, Theatre
Communications Group, and others) in 2002. I facilitated and helped
design the conference, which was titled "Preparing 21st Century Artists."
I can tell you that with a topic that complex, the participants didn't
reach quick consensus or hammer out a tidy three-point plan. Rather,
they grappled with the messy realities of today's arts environment, considered many trends demanding change, and began to distill priorities for
the future.

The participants agreed that, overall, the technical preparation of
artists is being accomplished at a higher level in America today than
ever before in human history. There is increasing parity among musician training institutions, but, they agreed, fine technical training isn't
enough anymore. A new set of skills has become crucial to the success of
a twenty-first-century artist.

What are these skills? The participants couldn't identify these additional skills with the same certainty and specificity as the technical skills,
but they generally felt that education, entrepreneurship, advocacy, communication (verbal and written), and problem solving were the areas in
which musicians and other artists have to develop proficiency to build
fulfilling careers. They didn't agree on ways to incorporate these subjects
into training programs—do you require new courses and take time away
from studio practice, or do you make classes voluntary for those who can
squeeze them in? Participants argued about building a priority around
these additional skills. The League of American Orchestras representatives
claimed that musicians with education skills were solid gold, essential to
the future of orchestras—so why don't conservatories produce more of
them? The conservatory honchos snapped back, "Then why are those skills

completely ignored in all orchestral hiring? Consider those skills in hiring, and we will happily train them for that."

Such testy episodes aside, the understanding I took away from that conference was that the music field as a whole now acknowledges that the "extra" skills are no longer extra. So here it is, musicians: your supplementary skills—as educator, entrepreneur, advocate, communicator—are as important as your musical skills to creating a full, rewarding, and sustainable career. The following are some conclusions and quotations from the conference report, and their implications for musicians. Bottom line? Educational entrepreneurialism is an essential part of a twenty-first-century musician's success.

According to Henry Fogel, then president and CEO of the League of American Orchestras, symphonic repertoire is slowly becoming more diverse, while venues and audiences are growing—contrary to some media reports. Each of the performing arts disciplines is changing, which demands modifications in conservatory students' training. While the thinking in the "classical arts" is still firmly grounded in the traditional Western canon, audience interest continues to migrate toward other forms, and the arts institutions and training programs need to respond.

Musicians can leap into this gap. They not only can develop programs with musical variety and creative ambition but also can reach out to audiences looking for something other than the traditional canon. To succeed in this, ensembles and individuals must think expansively about how to engage new audiences, and they must listen to and communicate with new audiences with the mind and open heart of an educator.

The educational entrepreneur doesn't just offer a program of new music, say, a focus on Latin rhythms, and hope people come; he considers engaging and developing that audience, making connections to communities and organizations with Latin interests, such as Hispanic organizations, salsa and tango dance groups, and clubs, and tapping existing interest in audiences who love Latin rhythms. He doesn't just hand out and post flyers and hope people show up; he listens to potential audiences, holds conversations and workshops at community centers and social clubs, and builds the audience, shaping his offering in response to what he hears, not what he thinks he hears. His goal is to extend his musical strengths and loves to meet what that audience cares about—not to find a way to convince them to come hear what he likes to play. If that sounds charming but unrealistic to you, read up on the work of the Providence String Quartet and the Community MusicWorks, the quartet's neighborhood connection (http://www.communitymusicworks.org). They have gone beyond mere outreach, all the way to welcome, creating deep ties with the community in which they live and work, committed to having their high art make a difference to the lives of those in their community.

Even symphony orchestras are beginning to adopt the flexibility and approachability that chamber ensembles enjoy—the Philadelphia Orchestra is engaging with young adults and untapped audiences by sending players to college settings and ensembles to community centers to perform lively and diverse programs that reach as far beyond the traditional canon as the players can enjoy going. Musicians spent weeks composing music to accompany Camden senior citizens telling the stories of their lives to a celebratory packed house of half Camden residents and half orchestra family. In other words, to build their future, orchestras are borrowing from chamber music's arsenal of ideas—not planning for an immediate turnaround into ticket sales at Verizon Hall but in changing the understanding of the nature of the orchestra, that it listens, responds, is musically imaginative and *theirs*. The conference report states:

> As our society's demographics shift, so must audiences and potential audiences, who are becoming younger, more diverse and less aware of the arts through their schooling and youth. There is a need to reach these new communities and "illuminate" the art form, building new audiences and their appreciation for an arts experience. This need requires a new type of presenter who can communicate with audiences to educate and engage them in the various works they are performing. Graduating students must have skills that allow them to connect their art with various communities in various ways.

Outreach skills. Certainly symphonic musicians can develop and use outreach skills, but chamber musicians are positioned to thrive in this arena—becoming that new kind of presenter that engages old and new audiences and illuminates art forms. Although the number of music students who have education and community-connection skills in their training is slowly and steadily increasing, most current performers have to develop proficiency on their own. So if you didn't graduate with these skills, start learning. Take advantage of the occasional formal professional development opportunities and ways to learn through arts education institutions. Autodidacts—self-guided learners—that is what this generation of musicians is challenged to become. The challenge is to set an ambitious arc of lifelong learning; be confident that you are going to get better and better at engaging audiences through ongoing experimentation. (Note: the term "outreach" is falling into disfavor because of its connotations of condescension—reaching out from the mother ship to those "out there." "Community relations" and "engagement" are becoming the preferred terms to describe these skills of connecting with people who don't have a classical music concertgoing background.)

The educational entrepreneur not only creates the programs but also creates the opportunities to perform them. Are you in dialogue with religious, education, and community organizations, with businesses, to build a performance or performance-and-education series that speaks exactly to their members? The Atlanta Symphony was the first major orchestra to create a position titled community catalyst; Mariel Reynolds was the orginator. Can you be your own community catalyst? The education entrepreneur does not just take advantage of good offers that come along but actually goes out, stirs up possibilities, and creates the dialogue that spawns opportunities. The conference report cited earlier states:

> The arts sector is growing, yet there is less of a professional
> track for graduating students to make a living. While there
> are more than 700 volunteer-driven community symphony
> orchestras, there are only 200 professional orchestras. Upon
> graduating, most students will be working other jobs to support
> themselves while acting, singing, dancing or playing instruments,
> requiring that they understand resource management and career
> flexibility. Most will have to generate their own projects to
> sustain their creative edge. A career in the arts does not look like
> the traditional model for the vast majority of young artists who
> stay in the arts. There is a need for conservatories to teach their
> students about other opportunities available in the field, to help
> them develop the entrepreneurial mindsets to piece together
> a life in the arts, and inform them of other possible trajectories
> that tap the potential of their talents.

The conference report didn't include the sobering claim most conservatory leaders agreed with—that fewer than 10% of graduating music performance students will enjoy anything resembling a "traditional career" of musical employment. As readers of this book well know about the survival of the fittest in a music career, for more than 90% of new graduates—be entrepreneurial or die. That law of survival applies to education skills, too. The players who dedicate themselves to creating richer educational offerings, for schools and adults, for unusual repertoire and traditional concert settings, are the players who get to keep playing. Create several such offerings—programs that turn you on and that appeal to schools and presenters who book them.

A note of caution. I know there is pressure from schools to offer programs that overtly address nonmusical topics—"The Science of Strings," "Math and Melody," "Winds around the World." There is nothing inherently wrong with marketing to what your audience wants; however, keep music as the unmistakable priority. Why do that when most teachers and administrators would love to book music that improves student attitudes about math, or test scores in science or social studies? Because the opportunity for those young people to discover the richness of our live music is so rare and precious that it can't be subsumed into curricular convenience. Yes, attend to what schools and presenters want, but don't let me hear that you presented "Fiddling with Fractions."

Flexibility is a crucial part of educational entrepreneurialism. Can you create a new program for a special opportunity? I recall one ensemble that received a last-minute request to create a performance for a nursing home. Rather than expediently use an existing program with a few tweaks, they created a whole new offering, with new interactions targeted to the nursing home audience. They did their homework too—they went to the facility, talked with residents and caregivers about what might work. The program was such a success that it grew into a series used with other presenters. When new opportunities arise, flexible educators don't groan and wonder how to fit what they currently do into the new setting, but grab the chance to extend and expand what they do. The musicians mentioned earlier decided to take a single piece, familiar to the audience, and work with it for a full twenty minutes of the program—getting the audience to sing and clap and move with it, pulling apart its structure, and culminating in a very satisfying performance.

Education performances thrive with support materials—teacher's guides, preparatory workshops, classroom visits, in-concert speaking, post-performance events, e-mail exchanges with upcoming audiences—and the education entrepreneur prepares to deliver these with quality and flair. The finest guidebooks I know (and they are so rich that each could spark a full semester of intensive study) are the Windows on the Work series produced for every touring ensemble of the Lincoln Center Institute. I have seen independent ensembles' guidebooks get steadily more musically engaging, more aware of school reality, more thoughtful in giving the classroom teacher both preparatory and follow-up activities.

Guides enhance the appeal of an ensemble's program—if they are good. Take time preparing them because they can turn on the audience you will play for. Even if only part of what you offer gets used, that is better than having given the class or group no preparation at all. And if you don't know how to create strong guidebooks, find someone who does—and study her work so you can do the next one. Teacher's guides turn into money if they demonstrate that you really know the education audience and opportunity (they can work almost like an elaborate and impressive business card or credential), but they can be a turnoff if they miss the target. Invest time and money in getting them right—and right means that they represent what you care about musically, even as they speak to the realities of schools. Keep them short. It is usually better to offer three one-page activities with a photocopied cover than a glossy twenty-page booklet. Balance information about the program with activities that will prepare students. Remember the oft-repeated dictum—engagement before information. While facts about the composer and the piece can be good context, they don't engage young people. Instead, offer activities educators can lead that will spark a sense of musical discovery. Crossword puzzles and word games do not take learners into musical thinking, even if the right answers are about music and musicians. Instead of generic rhythm activities, create activities that illuminate the specific pieces in a particular program. And make sure the activities aren't daunting to the teacher who doesn't feel musically adept. Also, from the conference final report:

> Although the artists attending the conference expressed appreciation for the arts education they received and complimented the caliber of their particular conservatory faculty (if they attended a conservatory), most admitted that they were not prepared for the professional world upon graduation. They did not feel that they had the skills needed to create or sustain their own projects or to create a career in the realities they encountered. Service organization representatives underscored this lack by discussing how professional artists in the field need help with their writing skills and business plans, as well as how to create self-sustaining projects.

A good educational entrepreneur does her homework. She learns what schools want, and how to speak edu-language without sacrificing what the musicians involved really care about artistically. She speaks to presenters about what they want educational offerings to look like, and I bet the answers about preferred education offerings include the words "flexibility," "high energy," and "understanding" (and liking) educational opportunities. Presenters love ensembles that can take over and completely handle the educational outreach with competence and enthusiasm—this translates into annual bookings and extended stays.

An entrepreneur in any field gets work by demonstrating competence, flexibility, enthusiasm, and just the right product. The same applies to education entrepreneurs. If you love the work, show that by using language sensitive to audience age and school setting; show that you are keen to shape your work to the setting. Again, do this in a way that genuinely engages *your* musical interest, because doing education work just for the cash may be expedient, but it wears you down in the long run and devolves into cynical or perfunctory performance. The conference report states:

> Arts education is one way to help build future audiences for the arts, but K-12 school administrators are quick to eliminate art classes in schools when faced with budget restraints. There is pressure on performing artists to engage communities and begin to cultivate new audiences. Today, there are programs that place professional artists in residencies at presenting organizations. Conservatories need to better prepare students to learn how to work with diverse groups and help these audiences learn more and appreciate various art forms. To this end, conservatories are experimenting with the development of education and outreach skills with some remarkable successes.

In the year before completing this book, I led two conferences on these "extra" skills musicians need. One was hosted by the Shepherd School of Music at Rice University and was called the "Careers Forum." This convening was built around teams of graduate music students from twelve conservatories and training programs. We listened to them, challenged their thinking, and explored with them to learn about their needs and aspirations. A conclusion of that gathering was the need for project-based learning throughout a musician's training, the same conclusion that had arisen at the conservatory leaders conference. These graduate and just-graduated students believe that from their first college year, students should be required to produce and promote concerts; they should be required to create an education concert—from concept through partnership planning, to guidebooks and logistics, through performance, and interviews with students afterward. This conference acknowledged that it is all well and good to have "Business of Music" electives available, but young musicians really only learn about the nuts-and-bolts information and skills when challenged by the necessity of deadlined reality. Students concluded that projects in which they *had* to learn the entrepreneurial, organizational, and communication skills, in direct relation to their artistic learning, would work best for them. Research on how humans learn best would confirm this—people learn more, learn it faster, and retain their learning longer when it appears in meaningful hands-on contexts.

We challenged these students artistically too—they were randomly assigned into ensembles that made no musical sense, and given twenty-four hours to create a performance for the public in Houston that had bold creative communicative choices outside traditional performance norms. Perhaps it was the electricity of the conference environment, but those were some of the most dynamic, delightful, moving, and hilarious musical presentations I have ever seen. They had become artistically entrepreneurial—bold, smart, edgy, passionate, innovative, and fun.

Later in 2007, I led a two-day national workshop sponsored by Entrepreneurial Leadership in Music Schools and the Eastman School of Music held at the National Association of Schools of Music annual conference. This time the participants were music school administrators who were considering entrepreneurialism, but they came to virtually the same conclusions the students did—project-based learning was essential; school experiences need to more closely model the challenges students will face after formal schooling; and there is a direct, positive, essential link between the artistic and the entrepreneurial impulses. Artists want to bring compelling and beautiful things into the world. In the twenty-first century, this process includes more than making the music; it includes efforts to bring an audience to the work as well. I see this as merely an expansion of the artistic challenge, not a mix of tacky financial necessity muddying artistic purity. We all need to remember we thrive in the experience economy, and there is much more to creating a valuable experience than just being able to play well. Let me leave you with the etymology of the word *entrepreneur*: one who takes action, one who begins.

The report *Preparing Performing Artists for the 21st Century: A National Assembly Hosted by the Kenan Institute for the Arts and the North Carolina School of the Arts* is available for download under "Archives" at http://www.kenanarts.org/kenan-archives.asp. Print copies of the report can be requested by e-mail through the institute's Web site as well.

29
The Private Music Lesson

Teaching artists bring an additional set of tools and gifts to the private lesson—if they apply what they know from other settings to the one-on-one intensity of this partnership. The best private teachers I know are those who use all their teaching artistry in the closed room. In this chapter we will remind ourselves of the teaching artist basics that are sometimes overlooked in private lessons, and we will explore those learning foundations, like motivation, atmosphere, and self-assessment, that make the crucial difference to the private student's learning journey.

Did you ever notice this? A friend is telling you about a problem, and if you listen really hard with openhearted, full attention, your friend starts solving the problem on his or her own before you have said a single thing. It's the quality of the listening that works the miracle; it's also the safe atmosphere you created by accepting that person completely in the awkward, potentially embarrassing state she or he is in.

In discussing private music lessons—no matter what skill level or instrument is addressed, and whatever the ultimate goal—we must begin with the quality of listening. Listening is one of those essential capacities to which we all give lip service, but which in practice we too readily forget. To remind ourselves about the importance of listening in the isolating role of teacher, let's focus on fundamentals. Apart from making music, I'll bet the role of one-on-one music teacher is the one more musicians share than any other. The private lesson is an improvised teaching and learning duet, a work of art as much as of science, and it succeeds as much from the interpersonal as from the technical, just as ensemble performance does.

The quality of the teacher's listening is a reliable gauge for the quality of the lesson. All teachers—good, bad, or brilliant—agree that the capacity to grasp exactly where the student is, and meet her there, is basic. Most teachers assume they are pretty good at that. Some admit they get sloppy at times and mentally check out of the room while going through the motions. Several confess that because they have too many students, they attend really well to only a few of their favorites. A small group of teachers reduce their teaching load to only those students they can wholeheartedly attend to, without going on automatic pilot or draining energy from the joy of their own musical life.

What is your definition of success in a private lesson? When I ask musicians this question, I predictably get the answer that it "depends on what's being taught that day." Allow me to propose two ultimate goals for private lessons that *always* apply: nurturing motivation and developing musicality.

In my years of talking to private music teachers and students about goals, I find a gap between perception and reality. Teachers almost always believe they are good motivators, and that their priority on developing musicality is unequivocal and clear. They think they push students just hard enough, and that their technical instruction is always in the service of advancing their overriding goal—musicality.

Students, on the other hand, tend not to see it that way. Many report that their teacher is encouraging and happy only when they have practiced a lot, but they don't feel that the teacher cares about or fosters their love of music. Students feel a lot of "shoulds" and "ought to's" from parents and teachers and often grudgingly acknowledge that such an attitude is probably necessary. They report that technical issues are paramount—"My teacher is trying to get me to do this," or "I am learning how to do that." It usually takes some pushing for me to start getting sentences with, "I am dying to do this," or "I want to do more of that." Perhaps teachers take for granted that their underlying goal is always musicality; but when I ask students about the teacher's level of concern with their musical growth, they usually identify it as ranking low on the list of the teacher's priorities. Teachers: I urge you to clarify, perhaps even overemphasize, your focus on musicality, on expression. Learners like to master a technical challenge, but what they love is music—that's what keeps them pouring themselves into the science of those challenges.

This leads me to hoist a major banner: Teachers Are in the Motivation Business. With advanced students, the teacher can assume strong motivation; but all students—from those just beginning all the way to those at the top—need the teacher to keep focused on the learner's motivation. With the less experienced, we must—almost above all else—consider how to stimulate and nurture their natural curiosity and interest. With advanced students, we must develop the hunger for depth, the habits of healthy self-assessment and wide-ranging curiosity. To assess your teaching, ask yourself at the end of every lesson whether or not the student leaves more invested in music, hungrier to discover its mysteries and find its locations in himself. Do you prepare students to adopt the uncomfortable, unfamiliar, and very uncontemporary-American challenge of moving slowly, step by step, toward a seemingly unreachable goal? Do you help them learn how to find beauty in a lifetime on the path, though they will probably never reach the ultimate destination?

The other overriding goal in all lessons is to sustain the balance between the technical and the musical. Being musical is always the goal, and the technical serves to get you there in ever-more-satisfying ways. Does your teaching reflect that priority? I find that the best teachers routinely improve technique without the learner overtly knowing it, through wholehearted delving into the musical issues. For example, Misty Tolle (whom you have often met in these pages, now the director of school and family programs at Carnegie Hall's Weill Music Institute) asks her horn students, "What are you trying to say when you play this phrase? Where is your phrase going?" By putting the focus on the musical intent, she finds students naturally apply greater breath support; so without saying, "Use more air," she often elicits the desired result by asking the student to think first about phrasing. (Let's admit this often works the other way too—a teacher's insight into a technical problem can liberate a burst of musicality.)

There is a lovely way teachers motivate youngsters in the Venezuelan youth music network called El Sistema. (It is the most exciting program in the world of classical music today, in my view. More than a quarter of a million of the poorest kids in Venezuela participate in this national music program, more than in organized sports programs, with centers all over the country. Their top orchestras, like the Simon Bolivar Youth Orchestra, composed of fifteen- to twenty-seven-year-olds, are now among the best orchestras in the world.) With their youngest players, just learning recorder, they teach the notes of the national anthem. The students can barely play it. Then they evoke their students' feelings of national pride and love of their country and leave them alone to practice the piece. Full of national pride, the students learn to play the piece better, faster, and with far more ownership than if they were given direct instruction. The technical improvement emanates from the personal motivation, from their innate musicality, and speeds their growth faster than other kinds of instruction.

This goal of balance applies to the student's hearing capacity as well. A student needs to learn that playing a note this way not only is *right* but also *sounds* better in specific ways. Then she can grasp why the change needs to be made and what the artistic implications are. *Skill* is a central word of the private lesson—we want to develop musical skills as much as possible. But we do well to remember that the etymology of the word *skill* has nothing to do with the hands or overt demonstrations of capability; at its origin it meant "the capacity to make a distinction." Those moments when we help a student to make discriminations, up in his head and in his heart, are the beginning of the skill. All private teachers know this in the "Aha!" moment they treasure with their students, a breakthrough that arises in the head, heart, or hands, or all three.

A teacher can't *make* someone learn. As Rachel Shapiro, a violist, member of the groups Concertante and Mishmosh, and on the faculty of the New York Philharmonic told me, the good teacher "searches deeply to find the best way to stimulate each individual student's musical motivation." We can compel many kinds of behavior and action, but not the action of the heart and spirit that lead to curiosity, hunger, and dedication. There are many things teachers do to create an atmosphere that welcomes and encourages those inner commitments. They listen and witness accurately; they place specific learning in larger contexts; they love and believe in the students; they have a kit bag full of many teaching tools. Three things in particular underlie the development of motivation and commitment to learn in all subject areas:

1. *Pleasure*. It feels good to learn. If learning doesn't feel good, it slows or stops. The teacher designs challenges that have the player consistently succeeding, experiencing musical pleasure and satisfaction. Another way to support the pleasure of learning is by keeping the atmosphere playful and experimental. This environment takes the curse off "failure" that weighs so heavily on learning, particularly musical learning, which is so hard and slow. A number of good teachers tell me they develop games that play directly with failure—expecting it, going for whoppers, raising the bar too high on purpose. Failure must become just another part of the process. I believe most people quit playing because the product became more important than the process; the demands of endurance have not been balanced with adequate enjoyment along the way. The final straw of an injury, technical frustration, or emotional setback just becomes too much imbalance to sustain.

2. *Relevance and interest*. The learner commits more deeply if the work is relevant to her life. We can explore not only the ways in which the music is relevant to the learner but also the ways in which the particular musical challenge at hand, or the problem-solving process, can connect to life outside the arena of the lesson. The teacher guides the learner to discover why this music or musical effort might really matter to her as a person, and apply in other places in the learner's life. For example, every student will hit the wall of frustration at some point; that is an opportunity to explore what choices she has when she wants to give up—find out where else in her life she gets frustrated, and how she handles those situations, and how else she might.

3. Self-assessment. Developing the student's capacity to hear his own work, to recognize he is getting better, to question and experiment with his own processes is more important than the teacher's capacity to point out what's happening. Students tell me they have experienced private teachers using the following expedient ways that didn't work (except in the very short term) to build motivation or musicality: nagging, threatening, expressing disappointment or threatening to give up, making demeaning comments, being overdemanding, using parents as enforcers, imposing time pressure, lecturing, repeatedly pointing out the same things, cynicism.

If you refer back to Figure 22.1, you will find that little self-assessment grid we considered earlier. I encourage student teachers of mine to use this simple tool. First, I have them fill it out for themselves as beginning teachers, to speed their improvement; it develops their self-assessment skills about how they taught each class or lesson and how the student or class succeeded as learners. Second, I urge them to give the form to students in private lessons, so each student fills out a form on a regular basis, sometimes at the end of the lesson, sometimes during the practice week. The student-teacher and I go over the answers and follow the leads that students have supplied in the right-hand box. This practice builds both the capacity to assess oneself and, as a result, confidence.

Some teachers use an informal version of this written tool by asking students, "Okay, what am I going to say about how that run-through went?" or "What are three ways we could address that issue? And have one of them be totally off-the-wall!"

To teach an artist, the environment is more important in the long run than the specific teaching tools. In a dynamic, healthy, one-on-one environment, a student can work around and forgive a number of the teacher's limitations or even flubs. I am humbly grateful at the number of times I have seen my students learn beautifully even when I wasn't teaching very well, because they had learned how to learn and were thriving because of the environment more than my moment-to-moment insights or ideas.

Pedagogy

In the education biz, the term *pedagogy* means "how we teach," and the key pedagogical term for the private lesson is *differentiated instruction*. This means the teacher shapes the teaching to the particulars of each student—customizing what each student needs to learn next, tapping strengths and inclinations, remaining aware of weaknesses, improvising within the flow of the process. Even good teachers who rely on a particular method adjust their approach to the level, character, and interests of the learner. The best teachers have a variety of tools in their kit bag. They can work with a learner technically, of course, but can also shape emotional challenges, engage through the body, work visually or with multiple senses, use games and experiments, use singing or speaking, invoke the imagination and make powerful metaphors, explain with intellectual clarity, improvise, demonstrate, and invent games.

As every musician knows, it takes incredible energy to improvise as a soloist, and an improvised duet takes even more; there is no letup. A private lesson is a relaxed version of that, with the teacher striving to find co-learning connections, looking for the specific edges where learning is ready to happen. Variety and consistency must remain balanced—enough newness of approach to refresh and provide new ways in, with enough consistency so the learner feels the through line and is clear and confident about the goals you share.

Homework

What to do about homework? Practice is the acid test—how well, how much, how effectively a student is able to keep developing on his own determines his growth as a musician. That is why motivation and musical expression must be the focus, because they drive the quality and quantity of practice as much as expectations and demands. Certainly parents have a lot to do with the practice time of younger musicians, so the good private teacher works a balance according to the parent-child particulars, often becoming a balancing third angle in a tense triangle. Many private teachers tell me that their greatest challenges come more from parents than students. Interestingly, the teachers in Venezuela's El Sistema, mentioned earlier, hold in-depth workshops for the parents of their students on ways to help by giving effective feedback themselves. It is common for the families to sit around and listen to the student practice at home because they feel involved in and important to the process.

Two things that musicians know from their own practice that they must not forget as teachers: practice quality is more important than quantity (although quantity does have its advantages), and, as you know from your own experience, practice varies (sometimes you just can't hack it, and other times it flows).

Just as variety is crucial in lesson teaching, so is variety in practice dynamics. A week of "practice that the way we just did it" is far less motivating than "create a little cadenza that uses what we just did in three different ways and play it for me next week." Don't just teach a great lesson; send the playfulness, the attention to process, the musical expressiveness home with the student. For example, ask the student to record those six measures every day this week, and after each playing to record her comments on how it went and how it is developing. Ask the student to put a surprise in one of the recordings. It simply takes practice to master many musical skills, just as sports require practice. But sports have friends and teams and socializing play; since much music practice doesn't, we need to support our students to find "play" on their own.

Don't make assumptions about practice. Experiment with it. It's interesting to note that almost all of us assume school homework helps learning, although there is no evidence to support that assumption (except scant data that some high school science homework may improve grades, and projects done at home do boost school learning). Researchers report that students would be better off, would do better in school, if they spent the time required by homework in socializing play. If such a universal belief, such as homework's being valuable, is dubious, let's not make assumptions about student practice. Let's not let practice become like homework— tedious and probably not helpful if undertaken in a mindless way. Let's shape it, play with it; let's experiment with the student as colleague to observe the results and together shape an individualized learning tool. Cultivating in students a joyful feel about practicing is a great gift, because the time will come for the most dedicated when they have no teacher but themselves, and at that point their practice skills will make or break them.

I was once part of a think tank that focused on issues of teaching young artists. We identified eight crucial roles the teacher assumes at various times and finally identified the most important one: the witness. We felt that the capacity to recognize what is going on inside the learner (both on the surface and underneath), and mirror it back to her clearly, is the single most important thing we do.

The private lesson is sacred ground for this most essential act of an artist's development. We get to be present when the breakthrough moment comes; we are the ones to say yes. Yes, that's it—that is you as an artist. Yes, this process is hard, and you are doing just fine. Yes, that was beautiful to my ears and heart, too. The private lesson is the circle of earth where we plant and care for the future we wish to see. It is also the ancient testing ground of the spirit, where we are challenged to authentically be the artist we would like to bring into the world, even when the situation feels tedious, lonely, pointless, nonmusical, and downright annoying. Listen hard for the future you want to create; some part of it sounds in every student.

30

The Everyday Advocate

I'll make a deal with you—a deal that will change the future of music. You get to complain about the way things are, but only in direct proportion to contributions that you make toward changing the status quo. For every action of advocacy, you get one complaint. Deal?

Sounds like a bad bargain? Maybe you feel that way because complaining can feel so good, but it could also be that you share a popular, but somewhat distorted, view of advocacy. So let's dispel some myths, clarifying your advocacy game and getting us all rolling toward a future with no need to complain. In this chapter, we will look at some of advocacy's truths and tools; the next chapter will detail some of the strongest arguments out there. I believe teaching artists have a powerful role to play in advocacy. When I have had the opportunity to spend just a couple of days with teaching artists clarifying the challenges and opportunities, helping them take ownership of their individual way of advocating, they have invariably become among the most effective advocates I know. This chapter seeks to give you the framework you need to become a more effective agent of change.

First, the myths:

- We should leave advocacy to the professionals, whose job it is to promote music and music education.
- If musicians must be advocates, leave it to the good talkers with outgoing personalities.
- Advocacy is about delivering prepared presentations on specific, often formal, occasions.
- Advocacy is like debate, in which research is wielded to convince the dubious.

Perhaps the most common misunderstanding about advocacy is that its core action is *convincing*—that it involves *making a pitch for something*.

It's interesting, then, to notice that the word *advocacy* derives from the Latin verb *advocare*, which means "to call someone in." This suggests a couple of truths we sometimes forget: first, that advocacy usually happens in a one-to-one or small-group situation, not as a harangue to a crowd; and second, that good advocacy is more about *invitation* than *presentation*. It's about bringing people inside a world, not about selling them on how great that world is.

The myths insist that advocacy tries to change what people think. In truth, advocacy seeks to change what people *do*. But people's behavior is shaped by what they *believe*—and beliefs are only partly logical. Did you ever try to logically convince someone that he or she should love you? How well did that go? Other kinds of convincing may not go so well, either. As teenagers we have knock-down-drag-outs with grown-ups over issues vital to our very identity. As young adults, we argue passionately with friends and family, trying to convince them of the rightness of a passionately held political position or a whole worldview. Not an easy thing to do, to change what someone else believes, is it?

You can argue people into a pulp, win every factual and intellectual point about the benefits of classical music, and they're still not going to buy tickets. People buy tickets when they feel they are going to have a personally valuable experience—when they believe that the experiential payoff will be worth the investment of time and money, or at least worth taking a chance on. In our effort to make convincing arguments, sometimes the best we can do is to unsettle others' entrenched thinking on any given occasion, while we commit to change over the long term.

Here, as I see it, are some of the realities of advocacy:

Advocacy unfolds over time, not on a single occasion.   Prepare your mind and heart for building relationships, not for miraculous conversion. We change beliefs by building trust, taking small, successful steps into the new beliefs, which may lead to changes in action.

Remember that in the best advocacy, invitation trumps argument. My brother instinctively understood this when he turned me on to classical music when I was twelve. He asked me to listen to one short cut on a record album—one "picture" from *Pictures at an Exhibition*. He set me up, gave me the title of the canvas being musically depicted, seeded my imagination with a few images to build on, and listened *with* me. The music evoked intriguing, bizarre images, and I wanted more. Over time, he did share more with me until I was hungry to listen with him regularly. Part of the appeal was the music, part was the chance to spend time with my cool older brother. After a while, I developed a personal relationship with the music through the relationship with my brother.

Imagine someone trying to convince you of the importance of making hula dancing a major part of your life. You would certainly need to experience hula, as well as learn something about it. But even with a good first experience, you would probably need to feel its cultural (and therefore emotional) pull to really get involved. You would need to trust that the trade-offs you would have to make to find the time for committed hula studies were going to be worth it. This is what happened in Hawaii, where hula has reemerged as a popular art form for people of all ages. Advocacy worked to revive its relevance and popularity—and even teenagers think of it as hip.

Now imagine someone trying to get you to vote for a school budget that included significant increases for geography courses, compensated for by a cut in funds for music. What would it take to gain your enthusiasm for that idea? No matter how good the arguments, it would take time, credible advocates, and repeated experiences in which you got a gut feel for the importance of geography, for you to even begin to engage seriously with the arguments. For many Americans, particularly those entrusted with education policy authority, that geography example is pretty much how they now feel about the case for the arts.

Advocacy requires superb listening. The advocate needs to hear not just what is said but what's *underneath* what is said, where the real beliefs live and motivate choices. For example, if you had a new friend who liked symphonic music but had little taste for chamber music, you would have to listen to that friend's history with music before you just started telling him why he was wrong; ask why he finds chamber music less interesting than symphonic; hear his embedded interests and prejudices. Then begin the dialogue around those specifics.

As with any kind of teaching and learning, advocacy draws out what people know and understand and then builds on that. If you do not grasp a person's interests, concerns, and beliefs, you will miss your target. If, for example, you have an occasion to promote the merits of chamber music to a software salesman, don't assume he is a musical naïf or that he hates new music. Better to start with the question, "What music do you love?" than with "What classical music do you love?" Ask and listen. Find points of agreement and build on them. If he mentions a social function that had a string quartet in the corner the other night, build on that. Was the music just pleasant background, or did he focus on some of it? What did he think or notice?

There are one-shot advocacy occasions to prepare for. Allow me to contradict myself. Sometimes we do get onetime opportunities to advance the cause. Perhaps it's a twenty-minute lunchtime speech to the Rotary Club to encourage its support for a music series in town. (Have you ever asked if you can address local business organizations in your hometown, or in towns where you perform? You can and should.) Or perhaps you encounter the ultimate challenge—*the elevator speech*. This is the one- or two-minute pitch you would deliver if you stepped into an elevator with *the* person in charge, and it contains what you would say on the ride to the twenty-third floor, where she gets off.

Practicing the elevator speech is good discipline. Many musicians think they are excellent advocates, able to talk passionately for twenty-five or even fifty-five minutes—but can they be effective in three minutes, or one? Probably not. The good elevator speech distills all the elements a one-shot presentation should contain: a key idea expressed in a succinct, memorable way; an image of why it is so important; a clarifying example; research data to support the claim (preferably local research); perhaps a success story, especially one with an emotional hook; a great question; an offer to support further exploration; a specific request for action. Yes, of course, that is too much for a minute. But those are the pieces to have prepared, so the one-minute improvisation can be drawn from them and targeted to your particular listener. The twenty-minute Rotary Club speech might contain all those elements—seeking to speak to the head, the heart, the imagination, and the gut.

Advocacy's greatest weapon may be information. The more you know about the person you are addressing, the more you know about the cause you're advocating, the more effective the advocacy becomes. Professional arts advocates are dedicated information gatherers. For example, the North Carolina Arts Council has gathered deep data on all elected officials—not just their voting record and public statements, but right down to arts classes they took in college and lessons their children may have taken. This enables them to customize their communications, say, to a state senator who played in a jazz ensemble in high school with, "After-school jazz programs can make a real difference to at-risk kids who might otherwise play video games alone for hours or hang out on the street."

You need to find out about the person or group you are talking to. Do your homework. Ask questions. Find out where they are coming from, rather than making assumptions. Assumptions are almost always off target, and people pull back if they sense you are assuming things about what they know or believe. Do you assume that large, three-piece-suited insurance executive doesn't love classical music? Don't be so sure—and the merest hint that you are stereotyping someone kills your opportunity. Incidentally, Wallace Stevens, arguably the greatest American poet of the twentieth century, was a large, formal insurance executive who loved classical music. Ask. And listen carefully to the answer.

Advocacy must be filled with authentic passion and enthusiasm.   You have to live, breathe, and embody the value of your subject—but curb your enthusiasm! Your passion must drive the occasion, but the more you express it, the more the occasion centers on *you*. Instead, advocacy seeks to tap the passions and enthusiasms of the person you're addressing. It's sometimes effective to use examples from your own life, but it weakens advocacy to use too many (or only) such examples. The law of 80% applies here—be filled with enthusiasm, but don't let it spill over. Advocacy is not about you.

The advocate sometimes respectfully attacks specific, crucial aspects of another's beliefs.   But the advocate never attacks those beliefs wholesale. If someone holds a dramatically different view, don't give up, and don't contradict her views in general ("You are just *so* wrong"). Rather, listen and find one specific part of her belief system that you can influence. Someone says, "Arts education is a nice extra if there's time. But we have kids who can't read or add. And until every kid can do that, we can't afford to spend the time on performing in musicals or teaching the recorder." I might respond with, "I agree with your sense of priorities, for sure. But you might be interested to know that research on the impact of theater activities shows that they boost achievement in the language arts, significantly and reliably. So those theater classes actually *advance* the skills of reading and writing, especially for kids who are struggling the hardest in other methods of instruction." Using advocacy judo, I have acknowledged her areas of concern, addressed a mistake in her logic, and got us working together to solve her problem with my solution. If I had said, "You don't know what you are talking about—there is a wealth of research on the value of arts education," our dialogue would have gone nowhere.

Advocacy often reframes issues.   If you allow a discussion about arts education to be framed in terms of *arts versus sports*, you've just lost—no matter how good your points are. Start an advocacy discussion with the question, "Do you think all students deserve the most enriching, engaging, relevant school day possible?" rather than "Do you think all students should have more arts education?" The frame of that former question means the dialogue is about the ways in which schooling can dampen the natural urge to learn, and what we can do about it—and arts education becomes a good solution to a shared problem, rather than the problem itself. The right frame can change the usual dead end of discussions. A discussion about chamber music with a symphony fan might start with, "Isn't it great sometimes to be so physically close to the music that you can feel how the musicians are creating it?" If the person agrees enthusiastically, you just made a strong advocacy link for chamber music.

Include active engagement.   I never deliver an advocacy speech without including at least one activity to ground the heady points in immediate experience. For example, I might deliver a Shakespearean soliloquy—and then, after a four-minute preparation, speak it again. The audience members, because they can feel how much more they got from the second hearing, grasp the power of teaching preparation. And because they got something from that second hearing, that makes them curious about Shakespeare—they might even reopen their copy of *Hamlet*. Now they better understand my point that the arts spark learners' motivation and boost language learning. And yes, I would do an activity like that with a Rotary Club or a Chamber of Commerce, even though they don't expect it and might be uncomfortable participating in an arts activity if they were forewarned. That is my advocacy challenge—find a way to introduce active experiential learning, in an appropriate and engaging way. Then use the experiential results to drive home my point.

I encourage you to use a musical demonstration to make a point whenever you can. Might you play a little segment to uncover the way music excites the mind and imagination? Perhaps you can demonstrate the way music awakens delight or curiosity. Try out, polish, and keep a kit bag of efficient, effective demonstrations you can use to make a point, experiences that speak more eloquently and powerfully than words.

Advocacy is not an activity; it is an attitude, a way of life.   Like it or not, we live in a time when it is the responsibility of every artist to be an advocate. Given Americans' overall lack of interest in the arts, including classical music—and with our economic viability looking less than bright—we do not have the luxury of assuming others will be our advocates. We all must advocate, all the time. We must resonate with the benefits of a life inside music and engage people in the best of what we have to share. Call everyone you meet into the power of your art—the stranger on a train, the family member you usually don't talk music with, the social or business club in your hometown. Get active, practice your skills, and change the status quo, one listener at a time.

31
The Telling Facts of Advocacy

In the overview of advocacy in the last chapter, I challenged all music teaching artists to take on the role of active advocate by aiming to change not just people's thoughts but also their *beliefs*, because beliefs underlie thoughts and actions. I admitted that logic alone doesn't prevail in the court of belief, so I detailed the kinds of communication and preparation needed when we slip into the role of advocate. That role is one all of us need to assume as often as possible, with people in authority, with family, with strangers in grocery store lines, and especially within our own ranks of musicians and fellow teaching artists—where we don't speak with a united voice.

Most musicians aren't aware of recent research on the value of the arts to learning, so either they're not equipped to make a strong case for the inclusion of the arts in schools, or—the opposite extreme—they may make overblown claims that undermine their credibility. It may be tempting to assert, "Learning an instrument changes a kid's life forever"; or "When music is brought into the classroom, the students learn better." Yes, these statements *may* be true, but if you are challenged about your claims (as I often am), you will babble and damage the very case you were trying to make.

I found myself in a jam like that some ten years ago. Local advocates in a midsize city had proposed that business leaders make a major investment in arts education. The businesspeople were prudent and flew me in from New York as a consultant to review the proposed plan. They showed me the "research-based" claims the advocates had made and asked me to affirm their validity. The claims cited in the proposal were the kind of overstatements I often hear, and I was pinned into the awful position of having to support the advocates' intent without affirming the specific claims. The business leaders pressed me hard and were so irate at the loose play with facts that they turned down the plan, which had taken years to prepare. In a warning borne of hindsight, let me say that those advocates have never had another opportunity to change the status quo; a decade later, that city's arts learning has remained stuck in mediocrity because they blew their chance.

Let's face it: the "Mozart Makes You Smarter" research played out in a way that hurt our field. Two fine university researchers (Gordon Shaw and Francine Rauscher) did excellent work and reported their findings appropriately, but the media grabbed the headlines and ran. A number of arts education advocates tried to ride the wave of public attention by making overblown claims based on the "Mozart-effect" research. The researchers had found that listening to Mozart or a few other complex composers temporarily boosts spatial intelligence scores; what the public heard was that listening to classical music would raise their kids' grades or make their SAT results go up. After that bubble burst, some people came to see arts learning advocates as snake-oil merchants. It is interesting to note that the next wave of studies from these same researchers reported far more dramatic cognitive advantages for early childhood music education, yet these findings were not widely reported.

As we saw in chapter 20 about arts integration, researchers at Harvard Project Zero became concerned about hyped and unfounded claims for arts-integrated education and undertook a review of existing research. The resulting REAP report, published in 2000, found the data supported few of the claims our field was making. This did not mean that the arts had little effect on learning, the REAP authors clearly stated, but that the research did not *prove* that it did, if test scores were used as the basis. (Exception: the REAP report did find a solid case for the positive impact of classroom drama on language arts learning, even with test scores as the only evidence.) The report was a shock to the field, sparking heated controversy and leading, I believe, to more responsible thinking among arts education advocates. Many researchers in the field refuted the REAP report, principally on four grounds: by using such a limited basis as test scores to judge impact, it seriously misled most Americans except research wonks about the powerful benefits of arts learning; its basis in test scores all but guaranteed sporadic evidence of impact because that is not where arts learning appears, and it ignored the back-and-forth learning that happens in good arts integration practice; it completely ignored the strong circumstantial case that a large body of good correlational research makes; the research took no account of quality in the arts learning, only statistical participation, and we would not expect weak music instruction to have demonstrable improvement on understanding of math. This is not the book for a technical debate about research matters, but it is important to know that the REAP report presented an accurate slice of the truth, that many objected to because they felt its narrowness obscured a larger truth of the strong benefits of arts learning. Through the REAP findings and reaction, the field did come to realize that we do ourselves no favors when we make sweeping claims or cite unsubstantiated facts.

One oft-cited claim, for example, is that arts classes improve SAT scores. The basis for this idea is the interesting research finding in a national study by the College Board (*2005 College-Bound Seniors: Total Group Profile Report*) that students who took four years of arts coursework outperformed—by an average of 58 points on the verbal portion and 38 points on the math portion of the SAT—peers with a half year or less of arts coursework. Unfortunately, we can't assert the arts classes *caused* the increase in scores—because certain factors weren't taken into account. What if smarter kids were the ones who took more arts classes, or what if the kids who take more arts classes live in wealthier, higher-performing districts with more arts offerings? Still, that piece of research, while not conclusive, is provocative and valuable, and along with many others like it, strongly suggests that the arts have a significant positive impact on learning generally. "Scientific research," which is the standard the government sets, must rule out other variables before the test-score claim can be made in any absolute or causal way. It is extremely difficult, of course—perhaps impossible—to scientifically prove *any* causality in an environment as complex and fluid as schooling. Indeed, we *want* many factors to contribute to learning in a school; to isolate one factor is unnatural, even anti-educational. You can prove Suzuki classes improve violin skills because you can control the variables, but you will never *prove* Suzuki instruction causes students to feel better about themselves as learners or be more interested in math. That learning connection may be true, and you may be able to build a strong case that leads to that conclusion; but "scientific" truth?—never.

Nonetheless, many important studies have appeared since REAP, and several compendiums of research provide strong new foundation stones upon which to build a case that the arts provide a wide array of intellectual, social, and school-cultural benefits. The case may not be perfect, but arts learning shouldn't be held to a more absolute standard of proof than other parts of education—there isn't even a *weak* research case to affirm that homework makes a positive difference to learning, and look at how widely homework is used.

The list of resources at the end of this chapter guides you to research that will help you support the case for arts education, but I must single out for praise the work of the Arts Education Partnership (http://www.aep-arts.org), because the AEP has taken the lead in sponsoring and publishing research we all can use. Now let's get to the nitty-gritty: What arguments can you use to bolster your case in the logical part of changing beliefs?

Claims You Can Make with Confidence

My overview of the research that's out there as of this writing (and there are new reports appearing several times every year) tells me that you can make this general statement: a school that invests in a strong, consistent, and well-planned arts learning program is highly likely to see a medley of benefits, which may include better attendance, improved attitudes toward school, higher student educational aspirations, a more engaged faculty with better morale, more active parents, better student social skills and cooperation, more active learning, improved academic achievement, and even improvements in standardized test scores. (Test scores are currently the predominant measure of success in education—and although the strongest case for the arts isn't based upon test results, the benefits of arts programs are so widespread that we frequently see, among other results, significant improvements in standardized test scores.)

You can affirm that UCLA researchers—as well as a number of other studies—have found that students who are very involved in the arts perform better on standardized achievement tests than students who aren't very involved. (Caution: You cannot claim that arts education *caused* the test scores to rise. This difference between *cause* and *correlation* may seem like an academic nuance, but it is important enough that we all master it.) Moreover, the UCLA study "Involvement in the Arts and Success in Secondary School," by James S. Catterall (published in Richard Deasy, ed., *Critical Links: Learning in the Arts and Student Academic and Social Development* [2002]), found that students who were very involved in the arts also watched fewer hours of TV, participated in more community service, and reported less boredom in school.

You can make the general claim that arts education seems to have the greatest impact on students who are struggling the hardest, either because they have specific individual learning challenges or because they live in low-income neighborhoods, where conventional measures of academic achievement are broadly lower. Indeed, arts education has largely been spared in the "across-the-board" budget cuts in the Los Angeles Unified School District in recent years because the school board believes arts learning is an "equity" issue—that students in areas with below-average schools get such a strong learning boost from the arts that it is unfair to reduce their chance to succeed. This argument, based on local hard facts about student achievement, has redirected the flow of millions of dollars in the district—and local research is always more powerful than national data.

Richard Deasy, founding director of the Arts Education Partnership, has summarized the facts coming out of dozens of very specific studies;

individually, these may not be compelling, but when braided together, they make a strong rope. Deasy claims the arts have demonstrated reliable, measurable impact in the following six areas, beyond mere test scores, in fundamental cognitive capacities. As you examine these arts learning benefits that many researchers affirm, don't you feel most Americans would say, "Those are exactly the kinds of skills I want every child in this country to have"? I find even the most rigid back-to-basics traditionalists stop dead when they recognize what the arts really deliver; they see, if only for a moment, that hammering away at reading and math skills with relentless testing is just too puny an aspiration.

- *Symbolic understanding:* The capacity to decode and communicate in multiple modes of representation, such as text, image, sound, motion—essential for mastering our multimedia world.
- *Spatiotemporal reasoning:* The ability to organize and sequence ideas and concepts in multiple modes—essential for making sense of complex information.
- *Conditional reasoning:* Developing and testing theories, which is how we learn and navigate our way to understanding.
- *Self-identity/self-efficacy:* Realistically valuing and assessing oneself; making productive use of one's own capacities.
- *Self-directed and motivated learning:* Learning how to learn, and enjoying the process of learning.
- *Cooperative learning:* Embracing multiple points of view and contributing to a group's effectiveness.

The Public Mood: Up and Down

Advocates should know about the climate they find themselves in. Report after report, public opinion survey after survey announces that officials and Americans generally feel arts education should be an integral part of education. We have a public ready to believe that arts education provides an answer to the better schools we all seek. And yet, school arts instruction is decreasing. More than half the states have reduced the number of arts teachers and/or arts education time since the passage of the No Child Left Behind (NCLB) legislation. Only a handful of states report an increase in arts instruction in the past five years, and even those few seem to have lost ground since the research was completed in 2006. (The law boosted the arts to equal status as a subject with math and language arts for the first time but has—ironically—squelched the presence of the arts in schools.) Studies show children from low-income families are less likely to be consistently involved in arts activities or instruction than children from high-income families. However, the general public attitude is arts-receptive. A 2005 Harris survey of American adults found the following:

- 93% agreed that the arts are vital to providing a well-rounded education for children, a 2% increase over 2001.
- 86% agreed that an arts education encourages and assists in the improvement of a child's attitudes toward school.
- 83% said they believe that arts education helps teach children to communicate effectively with adults and peers.
- 79% agreed that incorporating the arts into education is the first step in adding back what's missing in public education today.
- 54% rated the importance of arts education a 10 on a scale of 1 to 10.
- 79% said they believe it's important enough for them to get personally involved in increasing the amount and quality of arts education.

I am no Pollyanna. It is easy to tell a researcher you value arts learning, but those percentages do not translate into active support. However, I believe the time is right for us to redouble our advocacy efforts. I sense that the public recognizes and is concerned about the damage that No Child Left Behind has left behind in the creative vitality of school life; parents are becoming impatient with their children reporting disengagement with learning and distaste for school. The pendulum is about to swing away from sole reliance on test scores, and the arts can respond with the strong case we continue to assemble.

The AEP helped affirm this case strongly with the release in early 2008 of the findings of a new study of American attitudes toward creativity and schooling, which claimed, "A significant number of voters believe that today's educational approaches are outdated, impair critical capacities of the imagination, and stifle teachers and students alike, blocking potential for innovation. These data show a large population we call the 'imagine nation' are hungry for imagination in education and are going to take action accordingly—both in their local schools and at the voting booth, so that children are prepared for the world in which they will live." The following four bullet points from the study provide important substantiation for opinions that can begin to change actions and beliefs with verifiable data. The AEP researchers cleverly coined a term they hope will stick as shorthand for a big idea—"the imagine nation." They also polled voters, rather than random Americans, to give the results a political spin in a presidential election year. Detailed findings included the following:

- Almost nine in ten voters (89%) say that using the imagination is important to innovation and one's success in a global knowledge-based economy and essential to success in the twenty-first century.
- 69% of American voters believe that, when compared with other nations, America devotes less attention to developing the imagination and innovation.
- 88% of respondents indicated that an education in and through the arts is essential to cultivating the imagination.
- 63% of voters strongly believe that building capacities of the imagination that lead to innovation is just as important as the so-called basics for all students in the classroom and that an education in and through the arts helps to substantiate imaginative learning (91%) and should be considered a part of the basics.

The case for arts learning is so strong now that, in my opinion, it would take a hardened opponent to deny its validity, to withhold the benefits to students. Yes, we have some hardened opponents, which is why we need to press our advocacy as often as we can. Advocacy may be most potent with individuals who aren't quite sure what they think (a majority of Americans), rather than with die-hard opponents, who might change only if an arts learning miracle happened to one of their kids. Which does happen…I recently had a conversation with a politically conservative businessman who said he believed arts in schools were a waste of time until his son, a school dropout who had no direction in life, discovered spoken word poetry, got actively involved, and within months was back in school; he has completed college and now is serving in VISTA.

The public is getting ready to change beliefs if we become active, effective advocates. Now is the time to contact your local school board and parent association; show up and speak directly to them in public—this makes a huge difference. Now is the time to write your local paper and talk to your neighbors; praise the work that is being done and invite people to come see it. Now is the time to change our advocacy practices to change beliefs.

Research Resources

- *Journal for Music-in-Education,* from the Music-in-Education National Consortium (MIENC) based at New England Conservatory. There are now several volumes of this journal, which constitute the most comprehensive and provocative collection of

research on music and learning that I know. These are available
through the organization's Web site: http://www.music-in-
education.org/journal, and some articles are available for download
at http://www.music-in-education.org/articlelist.php. I also
recommend you cruise the Center for Music-in-Education's Web
site, which has a lively presence with articles and blogs from
inspiring colleagues doing important new work: http://mieatnec.org.

- *Gaining the Arts Advantage.* A 1999 report featuring case studies
  and profiles of ninety-one school districts throughout the United
  States that are recognized for offering arts education throughout
  their schools. It identifies the critical factors that must be in
  place to implement and sustain comprehensive arts education.
  Also, a companion publication, *Gaining the Arts Advantage: More
  Lessons from School Districts That Value Arts Education* (2000),
  reports the findings from a 2000 conference on the report.
  http://www.aep-arts.org/Publications.htm.

- *Champions of Change: The Impact of the Arts on Learning* (1999).
  A report that compiles seven major studies to provide new
  evidence of enhanced learning and achievement when students
  are involved in a variety of arts experiences. http://www.aep-arts.
  org/Publications.htm.

- *Critical Links: Learning in the Arts and Student Academic and
  Social Development* (2002). This compendium summarizes and
  discusses sixty-two research studies that examine the effects of
  arts learning on students' social and academic skills; summary
  articles with each section are very helpful to advocates. http://
  www.aep-arts.org/Publications.htm.

- *Critical Evidence: How the Arts Benefit Student Achievement* (2006).
  From the National Assembly of State Arts Agencies and the Arts
  Education Partnership. This booklet connects the arts to academic
  achievement and student success. http://www.nasaa-arts.org.

- *Third Space: When Learning Matters* (2005). This research-based
  book tells the stories of the profound changes in the lives of kids,
  teachers, parents, and schools in ten economically disadvantaged
  communities across the country that place their bets on the
  arts as a way to create great schools. http://www.aep-arts.org/
  Publications.htm.

- *ECS, Education Commission of the States, Governor's Commission on
  the Arts and Education, Findings and Recommendations, July 2006.*
  This summary of the two-year Chairman's Initiative, instituted by
  Arkansas governor Mike Huckabee, provides a handy advocate's
  compendium of valid arguments. http://www.ecs.org/html.

Part VIII Beyond the Borders

32
They Take the High Road

How is this possible?" I asked myself. Nine high school students from a rural Scottish town—average kids learning about music, not hardcore music geeks—were having their compositions performed by a quartet from the BBC Scottish Symphony Orchestra, live on national BBC radio. The students had worked with composer-educator Alasdair Nicolson and four instrumentalists (flute, violin, viola, bass) for just three days. The short pieces, including one called "Ode to Procrastination," were all better than the best student compositions I have heard in ambitious school compositions programs in the United States. The professional performers took the kids' pieces seriously; twice they asked to play a work again because they felt they hadn't done it justice. And this was just the first hour of the "Music and the New Musicians" conference in Glasgow, Scotland, in November 2006—three days that, to my mind, firmly planted Scotland as a world leader in connecting professional musicians and learners; three days that expanded my sense of the possible.

The mostly European conference of people connected with large and small orchestras and music ensembles (with representatives from all the other continents, but only me from North America), funded by the Scottish Arts Council, put performance foremost—most of the events with talking heads responded to and expanded upon the work with government school students we were seeing. And we saw very significant work. My role was to kick off the conference with a speech that set the tone, and to wrap it up with a keynote that distilled what we'd learned and challenged the participants to consider what the next steps might be. My detailed impressions of the events follow, but first, some background for American musicians.

Scottish orchestras and ensembles (and to some degree English ones, too) truly serve the community. What musicians described to me as "a revolution" occurred in Scotland in the 1980s, as the Margaret Thatcher government sought to eliminate government support for orchestras. British orchestras receive a significant percentage of their funding from the government, so the threat of a cutoff provoked a crisis. The result was a deep commitment to serving the community, which led to a change of purpose—from the traditional one (producing great music, and only that) to a socially informed one (both producing great music *and* serving as a major public resource). Almost all British orchestras now have some version of the words "be a resource to the community" carved into their institutional mission statements. This conference showcased what such a change in mission can look like in just one generation if followed wholeheartedly.

From what I could observe, and glean from interviews, these musicians don't just like their work with youth, they love it. In one of the conference's three major concerts, for instance, the Scottish Royal National Orchestra performed for an audience of three- to five-year-old kids. Before and after the concert itself, instrumentalists were out in the aisles, doing one-on-one demonstrations; some even had to be shooed out of the hall at the end so the teachers could get the children back to school. These musicians have not been specially trained to do education work—an issue dealt with at the conference—but they nonetheless see it as an essential part of their job, the right way for their time to be spent, part of the reason an ensemble or orchestra exists.

Classical music holds a far more visible and honored place in Scotland's culture and education than it does in ours—and educators are successfully pushing for more. Of course, it must be said that the significant government funding fosters musicians' sense of the necessity of service to the larger society. While our music institutions in the United States do not have anything like this degree of public support, the lessons of Scotland still stand as inspiring, replicable models.

The quality and sophistication of the musicians' work that I observed at the conference are directly related to the excellent foundation in music offered by the schools. At the conference's closing concert, the Culture Ministry formally announced—with the modest Scottish version of hoopla—the launch of the new National Youth Music Strategy. This initiative aspires to raise the nation's already high standards—as well as music's visibility in the community—by providing every schoolchild in Scotland with (1) the chance to learn an instrument, and to develop that music-making to as high a level as the student aspires to; (2) instruction that supports individual musical preferences—that is, electric guitar is as respected as violin; and (3) equal access to good instruments and well-trained teachers. Both music-making and composing are essential learning components for every student.

The culture and government administrators walked their government talk. The ceremony that followed this announcement included student performances by a brass band, a jazz band, a bagpipe ensemble, and an almost-all-white gospel choir. At the culminating moment, another group was introduced by culture minister Patricia Ferguson herself. A somewhat prim, soft-spoken older woman, she cheerfully called forth—not the brass ensemble or classical orchestra I expected but a punk rock band of four boys, who went full out with screaming and shouting, gyrating, dressed in grunge splendor. The culture minister tapped her foot happily through the raucous five minutes, and the rockers received enthusiastic applause.

Here, I saw, all musics are equal. All music-making is honored. All musicians and music teachers aspire to contribute to the national goal. Music-making is considered both a civic and a learning contribution.

The stars of the conference were the *animateurs*. This is a term first launched at the London Symphony Orchestra in the 1990s, although the idea seems to have emerged from the Guildhall School in London, and it is used in the community cultural development movement there to describe community artists. (America has had one musical Animateur, at the Philadelphia Orchestra, who is composer Tom Cabaniss.) The term may seem odd or pretentious, but the role will be familiar to teaching artists—an animateur is basically a teaching artist placed in a position of musical leadership. For the British, animateurs are usually project-based freelancers hired by ensembles for various projects or series, although some large orchestras have an animateur on staff. Their animateurs design (and often lead) youth concerts; they lead teachers in classroom work and in professional development seminars; they compose for and with students; they create programs that connect musical ensembles with schools. They take the teaching artist's skills to their fullest flower. One animateur, Paul Rissman, designed and presented three radically different events at the conference (I will describe them later): a dynamic lecture-demonstration concert for high schoolers, a community performance by a hundred ten-year-olds, and the previously mentioned symphony concert for three- to five-year-olds. The thrill for me was to see musicians with highly developed educational skills not working quietly in isolated classrooms or with unprepared groups in cafeterias, as so often happens in the United States, but instead celebrated and elevated to national prominence—creating, leading, conducting on the main stage; designing compositional and performance programs in schools; designing active-engagement programs for adults; guiding student compositions that are performed on BBC Scotland. For so many years, I have talked about teaching artists as a hugely underutilized resource here in the United States; there, I witnessed that resource used powerfully and naturally.

Here are some examples of the performances put on display at the conference. *Radio Café*, the BBC Scotland broadcast that opened the conference, combined two projects. In an initiative called Soundtown, the network places a radio studio in a different small-town high school each year. The studio is used for a variety of purposes—from focus groups for political response to young people creating programming and getting excited about mastering the technology. Soundtown aired the performance by nine students from the small town of Kelso and four BBC Scottish Symphony players—emanating from City Halls in Glasgow—as a small group of students and faculty back at the radio studio in Kelso High School listened and offered responses. The live national broadcast went smoothly, including the moment when two students in the high school studio requested the microphone and did a spontaneous mouth percussion and verbal rap performance about the presence of Soundtown in their school. (I immediately pictured how tense American teachers would be about a student asking to perform an unscheduled, unpreviewed rap on national radio. It was beautiful to see how relaxed the teachers in the studio were with this playful bit of musical commentary. The rap was cheerfully supportive of their student composer peers.)

The students whose works were performed that day had not composed seriously before. They had worked with animateur Nicolson for a mere three days, using a well-tried approach he has developed for beginners. (I recommend you check out his Web site, which includes materials he has published as *Composition Kit 1* and *Composition Kit 2*; see http://www.soundinventorprojects.com.) The four symphony musicians were part of the process throughout, helping the students try out their ideas. The resulting two- to four-minute compositions were stunningly successful. Imagine—excellent, relatively sophisticated composing within the three-day reach of a large percentage of Scottish high schoolers!

That first night we saw the world premiere of *Thrie Heids* (Three Heads), three short pieces based on famous heads in history, composed and conducted by animateur Stephen Deasley—a musically thrilling half hour performed by the new music ensemble the Brewhouse and four guest musicians. It was written for eleven instruments and four electronic instruments that manipulate the sounds with feedback loops and distortions, and the electronic elements of the piece were designed by tech guru Martin Parker. The sheer force of the sound, enriched by the beauty of the electronic elements, would have been thrilling enough. However, the four guest musicians playing the electronic instruments were teenagers with severe physical disabilities. I had never witnessed the like of it—the musicians and kids working as well-rehearsed and relaxed partners. The electronic instruments (operated by joysticks or light boxes or some means through which the students' extremely limited movement could manage) allowed the teenagers to make informed musical choices, to improvise within the structure, to make excellent music. I found myself nodding in appreciation as much for the musical ideas introduced by the boy frozen in a wheelchair as by the dashing Brewhouse percussionist behind him. It was breathtaking to see them work so well within the ensemble and to see their musicality freed through the technology. Deasley told me he purposely did not compose obvious solos for the electronic instruments that would have enabled audiences to aesthetically isolate an individual musician from the fabric of the piece—he kept them as a part of the ensemble, in the collaborative spirit.

After the performance, we heard from Professor Nigel Hawthorne of Edinburgh University, who dedicates himself to creating new instruments for people immobilized by disabilities; he is currently making instruments that can be played by eye movements alone.

That evening we also saw *The Four Seasons*, the joint creation of a hundred nine- and ten-year-olds from two schools, performed before an audience that, in addition to conference attendees, included families, supporters, and members of the general public. The event was the culmination of work led by animateur Paul Rissman and twelve musicians from the Scottish Ensemble. Half of the children had choreographed a thirty-minute dance to selections from Vivaldi's *Four Seasons* and Piazzolla's *Four Seasons in Buenos Aires* as performed by members of the excellent professional ensemble. The work expressed the kids' feelings and thoughts about the global environmental crisis. Dancer and teaching artist Rosina Bonsu coached, but the choreography was obviously the children's own—chaotic, yet rich with the students' ideas and filled with their exuberant metaphoric responses to the music and to the environmental concept. One girl who clearly takes ballet lessons did impressive splits and arabesques, as kids all around her were sliding into base and doing kid-friendly smashing into one another in the "Spring" section of the Vivaldi.

The other half of the program featured instrumental pieces composed by students who were coached by several members of the Scottish Ensemble. These composer-performers were far more controlled than their dancer peers, and they also based their creations on the environmental theme and included musical references to the Piazzolla and Vivaldi works. Clear in their musical ideas and performed with focus and flair, these pieces were written by general music elementary school students rather than music-focused students (no traditional orchestral instruments here, just instruments anyone could play).

The support and "buy-in" from the schools for *The Four Seasons* were extraordinary. For example, two days before the performance, one teaching artist told her principal that her students weren't going to be adequately prepared and asked for an entire day off from school, with all the kids, to rehearse. The request was granted on the spot.

The next morning, we saw "Monster Music," a Royal Scottish Symphony Orchestra concert for three- to five-year-olds that was cleverly shaped by Paul Rissman to keep the little ones focused throughout. He included a composition-with-story of his own, and the other musical selections were fun, short, and engaging. The program was not much different than one might see for such an audience in the United States, but the feel was different: the orchestra musicians were laughing, enjoying the kids, going out into the audience whenever they could. I talked to some of the players, who told me this performance was typical, that they do a lot of youth concerts, and that the musicians consider them a delight—they said they wished they could do more. Let's just say that is rarely the view of highest level American orchestras and ensembles.

One morning I participated in a forty-five-minute workshop that prepares teachers as partners for the Masterworks series of the Royal Scottish National Orchestra. The workshop was very like one in the United States but more sophisticated because this was designed specifically for music teachers. Animateur Stephen Deasley, the leader, had us composing and performing for one another in ensemble, solving complex rhythmic challenges that would feature prominently in the one-hour concert we were to see later that afternoon. The concert, attended by 500 high school music students, had two pieces on the program: James MacMillan's *The Exorcism of Rio Sumpul* and John Adams's *The Chairman Dances*. That's right, those subtle, complex modern works, with deep political themes, made up the entire repertoire.

Paul Rissmann created a speedy and cool lecture format, very music-analytic, occasionally participatory, filled with useful and lively visual elements that he had designed. For me, it worked well, and I am a bit over high school age, opening up the pieces so I could grasp them more fully. Picture 500 high schoolers in rapt attention following the structural quirks and subtle rhythmic patterns in MacMillan and Adams. As if that image were not mind-boggling enough—this concert was a kickoff for the students who were about to start a composing project using those two works as inspiration. Again, remember, these are not music-track students pursuing an elective, but mainstream high schoolers, excited to create their own politically themed compositions in the style of John Adams.

Late that night, at the open-bar conference bash, we were treated to music created by the kids who have participated in the Fusion Project of the Glasgow City Halls. This is a small-group program for the kids at the bottom of the city's economic ladder, the kids Americans call "at-risk" youth. This project takes great care to create an environment at this upscale, downtown performance hall that is youth-friendly, driven entirely by the interests of the students, with technology at the center. Students work on projects of their own invention, some involved in mixing, others in DJ-ing, some create electronic music, with animateur Pete Dowling guiding but not teaching. They rely on peer mentors, who basically run all the work with the students, creating a tight group that becomes committed to their projects and the process (and that recruits its own future participants). Picture the culminating cocktail party of the conference, the key social event of an international orchestral gathering. The conference entrusted the responsibility for the music at that event to the toughest kids in town to shape appropriately, while we schmoozed as conference-goers do. The teenagers handled it beautifully, creating a lively, appropriate, and energized party that was far richer for their contribution. And they knew it. They didn't pick safe "old folks" music, or impose their tastes to teach us a lesson; they created a mix that did what great DJs can do—tweak, surprise, delight, vary the pace, and support the event—but with a real sense of their teenage aesthetic.

As if the current state of musical learning and engagement with professionals weren't enough, Scotland is poised to make a historic advance. A national dialogue is now under way, led by the government, focusing on the concept of "cultural entitlement." The nation is trying to determine what every Scottish resident should be able to expect in terms of arts and culture. This debate is not received cynically or as a political tool, as it might be in the United States, but rather is prompting government officials and members of the public to come to agreement about long-term spending, priorities, and goals for the cultural life of the nation, institutionalizing universal access and greater equity, and shaping policies to provide what every resident is entitled to.

Concurrently the government was preparing to launch the nation's Creativity Agenda, to identify ways that governmental, corporate, social, and educational institutions can boost the presence and priority of creativity. Unlike in the United States, where nonarts institutions do not immediately see arts creativity as a resource, in Scotland they do see the arts as having essential elements to provide.

A new national educational curriculum, called the Curriculum for Excellence, was under construction at the time of the conference. Remarkably, it does not emphasize quantifiable measures of success as its goals but instead prides itself on being learner-centric, with these four essential capacities as its goals: confident individuals, successful learners, responsible citizens, and effective contributors. Arts education supporters there were only beginning to realize that these goals place them in a central position within schooling, more than ever before, with an emerging mandate for creativity across the curriculum.

Finally, the new National Youth Music Strategy, mentioned earlier, aspires to make both music-making and composing essential learning components for every student, and to support every student to learn whatever instrument to whatever level of expertise her interest drives her.

The modest Scots were at pains to point out the ways in which they are less than ideal, the ways in which they have much to accomplish: the partnering between orchestras and schools is not strong; their education training for musicians is no stronger than in the United States; their preservice training for emerging schoolteachers does not include much use of the arts; and their understanding of arts integration is not advanced. Nonetheless, they are doing world-leadership-quality work in many areas and are committed to significant new achievement in the years just ahead.

I left with two main impressions: first, the mind-bending and heart-expanding experience of actually witnessing the kind of education work by musicians and teaching artists that I have spent decades describing as possible to the often-doubting fields of education and the arts in America; second, a determination to find out what happened in that "revolution" in the 1980s in England and Scotland that could lead to a nation of professional musicians and ensembles dedicated to becoming a vibrant, relevant, effective, and creative community resource.

33

The Planet Gets It Together
for the First Time

The many separate worlds of arts education began to grow into one community during four days in Lisbon in March 2006. Twelve hundred arts education leaders from ninety-seven countries were invited to Portugal to attend the first-ever worldwide arts education conference, sponsored by the United Nations Education, Scientific and Cultural Organization (UNESCO). The United States had about forty people in attendance. Because the sole representative from the African country of Niger could get no funding support from his government, he sold his car to attend and to learn what the world knew about the present and future of arts education.

I got a cold shower of perspective right away. In talking with the UNESCO organizers, I learned that they had initially forgotten to invite the United States. This is partly a result, no doubt, of America's tepid participation in UNESCO in recent years. But also, the United States has not been seen as a major innovator or contributor to international arts education thinking.

In some ways, the conference bore all the hallmarks of most "first" conferences: too many speeches read from podiums, too much formal politeness (UN protocol), endless talking with little doing and little artistic experiencing, too many points of view. People wanted to get somewhere, to accomplish something tangible, to leave with an action agenda, and it just wasn't possible at a first gathering. Did any revolution ever take place without a lot of speechifying?

Yet the sheer force of so many people—most of whom have dedicated their lives to arts education—spending four long days in dialogue, with a lot of translators and little sleep, ended up creating spiritual and aspirational bonds. I was slated to deliver the closing keynote speech, so I listened hard all week to try to draw together the material filling our overstuffed days into conclusions we could all take home and put to use.

I interviewed everyone who got within my reach and attended every session I could. I learned a tremendous amount from eavesdropping. (I was so focused listening in on one fascinating trio of women that I accidentally followed them into the ladies bathroom without realizing it—and didn't want to leave because they were right at the most interesting part. Yes, I did bolt in embarrassment when they looked at me.)

In reality, there were three concurrent conferences. One consisted of the printed program and formal presentations onstage, mostly mind-numbingly dull. (The model was the scientific conference, during which "papers" are read to an audience that takes turns napping.) The speakers were simultaneously translated through headsets everyone wore and were also projected onto a large video screen, all cut off at the neck where the podium edge appeared. The schedule also offered a few dozen "panels," or smaller meetings, where UNESCO-selected programs and practices were presented by those who do the actual work. Specific and practical, the panels grounded all the metatalk. They described arts advocacy strategies, teaching methods, and the ways in which arts learning plays out around the world. I must say the Americans on the panels shone brightly as passionate and expert contributors.

The second conference happened in the hallways, over meals and on breaks, in bathrooms. This was where the real nitty-gritty of asking and answering, comparing and challenging took place. This was the most productive conference for most attendees.

The third conference happened at night, in the restaurants and bars of Lisbon. There—over the excellent, inexpensive wine—international networks began to be built. There, ideas sprouted, and promising friendships and plans for future exchanges were born.

To be fair to the formal conference, the opening keynote speeches challenged us effectively. The first was delivered by Antonio M. Damasio, the Portuguese neurologist (now in America at USC) who wrote *The Feeling of What Happens* (2000) and *Looking for Spinoza: Joy, Sorrow, and the Feeling Brain* (2003). Damasio spoke of the dual way the brain processes experience—*fast processing* (information exchange, multitasking, etc.) and *slow processing* (emotional, reflective, metaphoric). His research shows that fast processing is actually getting faster, keeping pace with our technological gains. The downside, he says, is that fast processing is starting to dominate, or even subjugate, slow processing—and slow processing, he maintains, is essential to mental health and ethical and moral behavior. He describes a coming crisis of citizenship, as people become more information-driven, with less emotional and ethical balance. He predicated increasing numbers of cases of highly effective leaders making choices without ethical foundation. Damasio's take-home message was that the arts show young people how to balance these aspects of their inner lives, and arts education is essential to creating the citizens we need to make a better world.

The second keynote speaker was Sir Ken Robinson, an authority on creativity in education and business. Arts learning, said Robinson, builds the creativity-associated skills—and he emphasizes that these are indeed *skills*—needed to solve the crush of problems we face around the world.

Creativity was the rallying cry for school-based arts, with many speakers, especially government ministers, urging its primacy in every child's learning. By the time I spoke at the end of the conference, I got to be the one to say the culminating words that marked the historic significance of the occasion: all the world's arts educators are marching behind the same education reform banner, which bears three words: "Literacy, Numeracy, Creativity." Certainly all arts educators believe young people must be effective with words and numbers, but we believe creativity is the third element that brings the other subjects, schooling, and students' lives to life. Creativity complements, catalyzes, and reinforces the other two skill categories, and all three should be taught across the curriculum.

But I also cautioned that "teaching" creativity ain't so easy. Just because a teacher and student are working in an artistic medium doesn't mean creativity is being developed. A student can spend a year playing a clarinet and not develop creative capacities. Does your own teaching always emphasize, illuminate, and assess the creative skills? Do you know how to support the creative development of your students? Probably not. As a field—locally, nationally, and internationally—we all need significant professional development in this area. We need to focus on the specific elements that develop creative capacity and prioritize them in our teaching. In fact, music learning was cited by the conferees as the artistic discipline in which creativity was conspicuously given lowest priority. In music, technical accomplishment *always* ranks higher. Nothing is wrong with fine technique, of course; but our colleagues from around the world said we must make creativity a much higher priority in all our teaching—and that we must do it now. Again and again, they turned to artists as the providers of the expertise and commitment to lead this exploration. They didn't exactly say it, but they were turning to teaching artists to lead the way.

During the conference, every social crisis—from an explosion of mental health problems in youth, to global warming, AIDS, and worldwide economic disparity—was laid at the feet of arts education to help resolve. These were presidents, economic and cultural ministers, and other leaders looking to arts education as the resource to turn the dire future around. Poignantly, most presenters acknowledged how weak a tool arts education is right now—how little school time there is, how little funding, how little teacher preparation to accomplish such critical goals.

Still, that we have begun to form a global network, a coordinated vision, raised the possibility that arts education's day may be coming—perhaps not in our lifetimes, but before it is too late. One speaker claimed that the state of worldwide education is so rotten that one day, possibly soon, it will just implode overnight, as the Soviet Union did after its seventy-year run. If we in the arts have done our best in the interim to focus on creativity and active engagement, and if we have learned how to effectively assess the learning that happens in the arts, we may—when the dust settles—be standing at the center of a whole new era of holistic, student-centered, worldwide public education.

To address our task in the near term, the conference produced a "road map," a gathering of key points around major topic areas. (This document, still being refined, is available at http://www.unesco.org/culture/lea/roadmap.) From these, I have distilled emerging highways that our worldwide arts education community can travel to get to common destinations faster.

The training of teachers and artists. This was cited as a universal need and priority. In the United States and in many other countries, preservice teacher training is intractably stuck. The arts are not emphasized, the value of artistic engagement to the rest of the curriculum is not understood, and the essential elements of arts learning (creativity, development of individual voice, empathic capacities) are rarely stressed, even in the pedagogy of arts teachers themselves. I would add that as much as teachers need to be exposed to the ideas and promising practices of experts, what they need even more is time to reflect, explore, clarify what they already know, and experiment collaboratively. Change comes as much from working and reflecting together as from fancy new ideas. There are no magic bullets, just top-down and ground-level-and-up energy dedicated to improvement.

Assessment. This was widely cited as the current hell and as the future hope. The testing culture in schools exists worldwide, and it squelches the arts, indeed the aliveness, of schools everywhere. As Annie Cornbleet from England's Daniel House put it, "The arts are the antibiotic injection in the bum of the diseased body of twenty-first-century education."

A few examples of effective assessment were put forward (particularly from the International Baccalaureate and the College Board's studio art Advanced Placement program), but the global cry is for alternative and authentic assessment tools. We need to create new tools that both support the learner and provide reliable information to those who are not present to witness the learning.

We also need to develop *fair* ways to assess the work of teachers and teaching artists. No, you probably don't want to be assessed on your teaching—but without ways to determine the quality of arts teaching, it won't get better. How *would* you like to learn about your strengths and weaknesses as an educator? Start thinking from there, and don't stop until you begin doing it.

Technology. This was cited as both enemy and opportunity. Around the world, young people are breaking new ground (but not much of it in traditional arts) with their active, creative interest in Internet and electronic media. They share the music they love and play with sampling across national boundaries and language barriers. In France, for example, young people have created a new filmmaking art with cell phone video films, which they edit, share, and submit for awards. Will arts educators be able to ride such waves of energy and use them authentically in music and other learning—or will we be left in their wake? Are teaching artists taking fullest advantage of what technology can provide to deepen our creative engagement with students? Are we taking *any* advantage?

Balancing paradoxes. One challenge is finding common ground. The range of arts education practice is dauntingly wide, and apparent opposites coexist under the same umbrella. In some parts of the world, students are instructed only in traditional art forms, with no attention to individual expression. Other countries aim to engage all their young people in some artistic universals but emphasize technical capacity above all else in the training of professional artists. Still other cultures (notably, in Africa and Asia) do not honor virtuosity and seek instead the communal energies the arts provide. In most countries, production (performances and artworks) is favored over the creative process, but in England and New Zealand, educators have begun to stress creativity over the product. In some places, religious and traditional cultural values are paramount. In Iran, for instance, arts education is administered by the same governmental ministry that monitors conformity with Islamic tradition.

Standardization (through tests and codified curricula) was cited as creativity's enemy; yet creative artists themselves live by standards of excellence. And as we have noted in this book, arts learning is both an intrinsic value and an instrument for other purposes. The arts exist for the satisfaction and internal benefits they create in individuals, as well as for their long-term academic and social utility, but these latter benefits do not accrue unless the inherent benefits are prioritized.

Arts education and science education were often cited as opposites, yet the two require many of the same processes of head and heart. Education would do well to remember that much scientific work is aesthetic and intuitive, and much artistic work is cognitive and analytic. We do not help the arts by opposing them to science or sports. Great science, great athletics, great carpentry, great anything is creative. In my lifetime, I have heard reference to "the art of bricklaying" and the "medical arts." It was believed, just decades ago, that any endeavor raised to its highest level of quality and expression becomes an art form.

Art is always full of paradox, as is life. The arts invite us to hold concurrent, contradictory views of our complex world. Reductive ideas may be more comfortable and institutionally convenient, but a reductive view is simply a lesser truth. This is our way forward, still holding our paradoxes, as a worldwide arts community.

Networks.   Networks hold our future. Some of our arts education networks are formal—people who have similar job titles, for example. Some are focused around interests—committees, or action groups, listservs, or personal contact groups. Some are emerging; in the United States, groups of teaching artists have sprung up like mushrooms around the country to advance the quality of their work. Arnold Aprill, of Chicago Arts Partners in Education (CAPE), sees the future in our learning to manage a network of networks. The UNESCO conference sparked new, international networks as participants, seeing ways they needed to stay in touch, exchanged cards. But it also linked up individuals with colleagues in their home countries. The latter phenomenon struck me as particularly poignant because it highlighted the solitary, isolated aspect of arts education work as we practice it—teaching artists working on their own, arts teachers alone in classrooms. The sight of networks forming spontaneously—networks that will, over time, connect artists and teachers across borders—struck everyone as a powerful image of a healthier field.

In wrapping up the conference, I felt the need to challenge some assumptions that I had noticed in the flow of the days. An unspoken assumption in international relations has it that "developing" nations (also called "underdeveloped" and "third world") should aspire to be like the "developed" nations. Perhaps this applies to governance and economies, but it does not hold true in arts education. We must, without any implicit bias, adhere to the healthy community-building practice of identifying the individual strengths each nation and culture brings to arts learning. The arts are not better in the "developed" countries, or in larger industrial nations, and certainly arts education is not better. African and Asian countries that struggle economically are among the most arts-infused cultures on earth. Indeed, in the landscape presented in the UNESCO study of worldwide arts education (*The WOW Factor: Global Research Compendium on the Impact of the Arts in Education*, by Anne Bamford), we can see the variety of the international scene—students in tiny Finland seem to have the most advanced in-school arts commitment in the world, spending about 80% of their class time in the arts because their whole curriculum is taught through the arts. The international average is about 170 arts education hours per year for students, and the U.S. average is about 45 hours per year, with many U.S. schools providing little or no time per week in the arts. And Venezuela has the most remarkable music learning program in the world (see chapter 29).

We in the United States do indeed have expertise to offer the world. I noted two areas where we are world leaders—teaching artists (probably the world's best) and in-depth partnership experiments—but we don't have much to brag about when it comes to the typical arts learning of our average child. Every country and region has its greatness that we should study; every country has experiments we all can learn from. I must say that Great Britain's experiments seemed to exceed, in depth and quality, everyone else's.

1. Advocacy. Arts educators assume that strong advocacy means strong research—producing studies that back up our arguments about the value and impact of arts education. Indeed, while we were in Lisbon, an international conference on the best research practices and methodologies was announced—and then took place in Paris in January 2007—to advance the quality of arts learning research methodology around the world.

American Nick Rabkin, of the Chicago Center for Arts Policy at Columbia College Chicago, reminded the group that research is not the whole answer. Arts advocates need to think strategically, he said, about the other ways we can influence people's gut feelings about the value of music education. We need effective presentations, including strong local research, but also stories that touch the heart, examples that make clear sense, and more. Advocacy does not merely mean hiring ad agencies to get out the message. We advocates need to get smarter about how we present the case for music and arts education.

2. Partnerships. Partnerships were frequently cited as a way to advance the arts learning agenda—ministries of culture and education working together, arts organizations partnering with schools, right down to classroom partnerships. But, as I have emphasized repeatedly in this book, getting organizations and individuals to cooperate and work congenially together is one thing, but building effective partnerships takes long, hard, patient work—and unless it is viewed that way, and supported in that way, partnerships will be shallow and ineffective.

The conference had an understandable tendency to address arts learning as a classroom activity. Certainly we must focus energy on students in schools and in after-school programs, but we also need to include the far wider arena in which the arts play out. We need to engage new parents, and families, not to mention reaching out to community and senior centers. If we focus on creativity rather than just arts media, we then belong in businesses and hospitals, in government, and wherever young people come to do things they care about.

We must remember that a classroom doesn't look the same the world over. A Kenyan representative reminded us that her image of a classroom is an open-air structure, covered by a tin roof, with one teacher and more than a hundred students, a third of whom are falling asleep because of internal infections and a number of whom are AIDS orphans. What does a high-quality arts education look like in that setting? She said it was the children learning songs that would teach them how not to contract HIV. She said she didn't have much patience with American music educators who whine about getting an extra half hour of school time to teach music principles.

I concluded my own speech with an argument I raised early in this book. We tend to define art by the nouns—as the paintings or performances, as the "special events" that happen in special buildings. This is one valid way of talking about art, but it underscores art as a separate, elitist activity—irrelevant to most people's daily lives. The verbs of art—what it takes to *create* an artwork and what it takes to be able to *enter* the world another has made—must be included in our definition and prioritized in our instruction. The learning power is in the verbs; I believe our future growth lies in those verbs. Nouns separate us, and verbs unite us—and this is true for an emerging worldwide arts education community.

The future of the international movement is unclear. New networks were formed in Lisbon; new research emerged. The Korean delegation announced its willingness to host the next worldwide conference in Seoul in 2008, which came off as planned. Significantly, three international nongovernmental organizations—the International Society for Music Education (ISME), the International Drama/Theatre and Education Association (IDEA), and the International Society for Education through Art (InSEA)—introduced a joint declaration (available at http://www.insea.org). What struck me about their declaration is that for the first time ever, the various disciplines did the hard work of finding common language to state their beliefs and values. Imagine, representatives of the teaching artists and arts teachers around the world coming to an agreement over what is important, to focus our message and work, to intensify our impact! We have not accomplished anything close to this within the United States—even within our separate disciplines—and now there is a first statement for the world to study and work with.

If you think about it, asking me, a teaching artist, to present the conference closing address made quite a statement. We had heard from many academics and researchers, from government officials and administrators. Yet the opportunity was given to a teaching artist to bring it all together. This is a recognition of the emergence of our profession, and a reliance on the gift that teaching artists have—to connect. We bring people together, and we bring people inside the power and potential of the arts.

34
The Guiding Spirit

A closing note for our journey together. I am guessing you didn't read this book straight through. You sampled, skimmed, found pertinent sections, set it aside for a time, and came back. I trust you took away ideas that work for you. That's just as it should be with a book that hopes to serve as a resource for a lifelong journey. Like a bible, it also contributes even when it spends time on the shelf, reminding you that there are others who share your beliefs and aspirations, others who care that you care. For better or worse, we belong to a field that is creating itself as it goes along. This book contains the early chapters of our bible; it is my deep hope that you will write the next chapters and verses yourself.

I have left one essential element of teaching artistry until last. This concluding fact of life is one we usually don't talk about in our work because it borders on a taboo. Teaching artistry is spiritual work every bit as much as it is artistic and educational.

The taboo about mentioning the spiritual component of this work comes largely from the constitutional separation of religion and public schooling. The law of the land and the passions around some flash point issues of the debate make it a dicey topic to get near, so we give it wide berth in a country that readily conflates issues of the spirit with institutions of religion. The education world avoids, or at least approaches with extreme caution, anything that could be seen as in any way connected to religion.

Though this prohibition is driven by well-grounded concerns of governance, good educators know that young people have questions and curiosities about topics in their studies that naturally connect to religious and spiritual matters. Good educators would love to follow teachable moments to address active concerns in the young spirits they care so much about. It's unnatural to proscribe dialogue about the meaning of life that arises when dissecting a frog. It is a crime against learning to blunt questions about God when we ask young people to consider the horrors of twentieth-century history. No, I don't think public schooling should be teaching doctrinaire ways of answering such unanswerable questions, but I do think we must nurture the skills of inquiry, affirm the importance of curiosity, especially in areas at the heart of learners' lives. Our foremost job as teachers is supposedly to teach people how to become lifelong learners, and we abdicate our responsibility when we skirt exploration of matters of spirit.

From the rest of the world's view of America, we are seen as the most religious nation on earth. In my view this is true, and we are concurrently among the least spiritual. The learning that happens within good teaching artistry provides essential support of the spirit without touching the religious. Teaching artist work provides spiritual encouragement, enrichment, advancement, and growth.

Teaching artists are given a unique privilege and opportunity. The arts are the secular common ground, the agora, where people can meet to address the most important issues in life. Because the arts are so clearly not a religion, teaching artists are invited to give our best and engage students as deeply as we can. The educational system *wants us* to feed students' spirits, wants us to draw out students' authentic voices, wants us to tap their deep concerns and aspirations, because that is what artists do. We provide one of few sanctuaries in young people's public lives wherein we invite their spirits to come out and play. Of course schools don't provide anywhere near the resources we need to fulfill this responsibility well. Still, in spite of the grossly inadequate amount of time and dicey support, we undertake the mission anyway.

This, to me, is a sacred trust. It is largely, and probably wisely, unspoken. It's an agreement between us (teaching artists and those who make it possible for teaching artists to work with learners), the educators who bring us into schools and other settings, and the learners themselves. The agreement is unfamiliar and possibly strange, even risky, to all, especially to the young. It is that we will bring our spirits to the fore in this artistic work; we will yearn together, bravely, creatively while taking care of one another.

Yearning is the human urge for more of that which we most care about. Is it yearning that fuels our listening to the music so fully that we can make meaningful connections. It is yearning that drives the student to bother grappling to find the elusive words that describe what she hears in the timbre of your violin. Yearning is the energy of the individual's spirit pouring into life.

The spiritual invitation underneath good teaching artist work is antithetical to all the norms and rules young people have learned in our institutions. It is hard for them to trust that we really mean what we say—they have heard grown-ups say all kinds of things for all their years that are not backed up by action or real intent. It is an act of courage and faith for young people to believe that the yearning they feel in us, strangers dropped into their known system, can safely be answered with that yearning they feel but keep carefully hidden in school.

They hear us say we offer questions that don't have single right answers because we care about their own ways of seeing and their own new ideas. We say we want them to create things they personally care about. We say we want them to create their own personally relevant connections to the musical and artistic worlds we explore together, and that there are many truths, not just one, in making meaning. We say music speaks beyond what words can say, and we all bravely honor that spiritual veracity for one another and try to scratch some words together anyway; we do this to share some approximate sense of our individual truths with one another.

Young people have good reason to doubt what we say, to be distrustful of teachers and adults in school. Given the years of rigid compartmentalization of self that schools demand, given schooling's reward and punishment systems that teach control and compliance, students' spirits are wise to lay low in school. Enter the teaching artist, who says "come with me" to that spirit. We are often given so little time with a group that those spirits may not come out at all, or if they do, not far. But even under such constraint and caution, it is our sacred duty to our art to try our best, to begin with a wholehearted spiritual generosity in ourselves, and to craft learning invitations that are irresistibly appealing and deeply true. Fortunately, our art includes joy, pleasure, fun, idiosyncrasy, and creative challenge in its genetic code. We must come from art. In saying that, I use my preferred meanings of the word: the etymological sense of putting things together that matter to you, and my sense of art being the action of making personally relevant connections outside of what you already know.

I have set high goals in these pages. I'm sure that at times they have seemed unrealistic, quixotic, perhaps even annoying. I have asked that you never ask a question with a single correct answer because to do so even once violates the respectful inquiring world we seek to invite learners' spirits inside. I have urged you to do homework, to spend time with ten-year-olds if you don't have a gut feel for their minds and hearts. I have urged you to plan thoroughly for each opportunity in order to have every aspect of it authentically embody the best of what we love about the arts. I have even asked that you dedicate time to add reflection, and to structure in self-assessment and documentation, because they help affirm, help realize and give place in the heart to the feel of the arts. I have urged your vigilance as witness with learners because only you can recognize that wordless moment when the artist awakes in someone's spirit, when a person feels that surge of power, that spiritual blip of potential to make a world arise. Only you can confirm its truth and importance, perhaps just with a nod that says yes, perhaps with just a few words that say, "You are on the right track. Keep going." And let your subtext say, "Keep going. For the rest of your life. As I have done."

Of course this is impossible to accomplish. But that is what artists do. We yearn to change the world with what we can do, and teaching artists yearn to change the world through learning. We yearn to make the world more beautiful—and the etymological meaning of *beauty* is "the good."

You knew I was going to return to the law of 80% at the end, didn't you? That's what it comes down to in this artistic discipline—our capacity to live the larger truth that contains both art and learning. And that is yearning. We have yearnings that are particular to us as individuals, and there is yearning that is universal. These shared yearnings are the meeting place of art. Teaching artists must come from, teach within, and invite others into this spiritual clearing in the very confusing woods of our world.

Above all else, we are in the yearning business. Our job is to awaken the culturally suppressed yearnings of young and not so young learners. Once we awaken this aliveness, we must guide it into artistic engagements. Given the power of art, we can trust in creative engagement—well guided, it reliably produces enough excitement and satisfaction to reward the courage and effort it takes to fully attend and create. We seek to give each learner a feel for the value and pleasure of yearning their way into worlds made by others, and of making their own worlds, so they will pour themselves into such experiences on their own, and often. Our goal is to create lifelong yearners. So that is what we must embody every day of our artistic lives. So that is what we must be every day of our teaching artist lives.

Although we are not well supported in this goal by the institutions or circumstances of our employment, we are well supported in this high aspiration by art. Not just works of art, which are powerful and magnificent objects, but the universality of the *verbs* of art, which everyone knows and uses in bits and pieces throughout their days. We can tap and focus those natural capacities and reward them well with exploration of the nouns of art, with the exploration of worlds of music, which can deliver such experiential reward.

Artworks brim with symbols that allow audiences to tap their power. The arc of a musical phrase makes the audience weep. The crash of a culminating chord makes the heart explode in joy. The poetic image of lovers frozen in time almost kissing on a Grecian urn evokes an understanding beyond words. The word *symbol* derives from a tradition in ancient Greece. When a host had a particularly wonderful social occasion, a weekend with guests, or a memorable dinner party, he would take a coin or ring and break it, giving a piece to each departing guest. The piece, called the *symbollon*, was the tangible, specific part that connected people to a meaningful, absent whole. Symbols are powerful only when we share an experiential understanding of the positive whole and can make the connection. This is why symbols from unfamiliar cultures do not speak to us until we can share the understanding of that culture in some way—another miracle of empathy the arts can deliver. Teaching artists empower learners to create symbols that hold the great truths in their lives, and to connect with the spirits of others through them. Teaching artists provide access to the greatest truths of the human spirit through the symbols artists have made for them.

This is the responsibility and opportunity of teaching artistry. May we find joy in this lifetime of chances to let what we love as lifelong yearners be what we do.

Index

Page numbers in bold indicate figures or tables.